AN AFFIRMATION OF FAITH
The Autobiography of Chaplain Thomas David Parham Jr.

Thomas David Parham Jr., Ph.D.

Copyright © 2010 by Thomas David Parham Jr., Ph.D.

An Affirmation of Faith
The Autobiography of Chaplain Thomas David Parham Jr.
by Thomas David Parham Jr., Ph.D.

Printed in the United States of America

ISBN 9781612154466

All rights reserved solely by the author. The author guarantees all contents are original and do not infringe upon the legal rights of any other person or work. No part of this book may be reproduced in any form without the permission of the author. The views expressed in this book are not necessarily those of the publisher.

Unless otherwise indicated, Bible quotations are taken from The King James Bible.

www.xulonpress.com

For my wife, Marion, and our three children, Evangeline, Mae, and David III

Acknowledgments

H. L. Bergsma, Commander, Chaplain Corps, United States Navy, who compiled *THE PIONEERS*, a monograph on the first two Black chaplains in the Chaplains Corps of the United States Navy, compiled from materials taken from Chaplain Corps files and from personal interviews – Nav Pers 15503 S/N 0500-LP-277-8140*US GOVERNMENT PRINTING OFFICE: 1981 O – 334-343.

Commander H. Lawrence Martin, H. L. Bergsma's successor, who edited *THE PIONEERS*, which was published in December 1980. In the Foreword of this monograph Ross H. Trower, Rear Admiral, Chaplain Corps, U. S. Navy Chief of Chaplains, states, "It seems quite appropriate that the first Black officer to attain the rank of Captain in the U. S. Navy, T. D. Parham, Jr., should be a member of the Chaplain Corps."

CDR. Moses L. Stith, CHC., USN, who interviewed Chaplain Parham for the Oral History Transcript *CAPTAIN THOMAS DAVID PARHAM*, as part of the Oral History Program of the Chaplain Corps, United States Navy, recorded interviews of 24 Chaplains, published in 1993. All existing rights in copyrights have been assigned to the Chaplain Corps of the Department of the Navy, acting on behalf of Chaplain T. D. Parham, Jr. One of this series of biographical skits gave the impetus for this writing.

An Affirmation of Faith

The Honorable Barry Black, Rear Admiral, Chief of Chaplains, U.S.N., Ret., and currently Chaplain of the U. S. Senate, several years ago urged that this book be written.

SCPO David Greene, USN (Retired), who worked tirelessly to get this book written. Unfortunately, he was called to rest before the book was published. From his death bed he pleaded, "This story must be told; get it published."

My special gratitude to Daniel Armstrong and Cheryl Woolridge, who waded through David's longhand notes and got his manuscript in legible form, and especially to Cheryl, who blessed his life story with its title.

My unending appreciation to Captain George Langhorne for editing this manuscript.

Finally, particular thanks to Rev. Addie Peterson, our minister at Messiah Presbyterian Church, who observed our dilemma as the deadline approached, put aside her obligations and spent several days inspecting our efforts to see that all was "decent and in order" and facilitated our submitting this manuscript.

Sincerely,
Eulalee Marion Parham

Chaplain Thomas David Parham Jr.,
Captain (Ret.), U. S. Navy

Foreword 1

Dr. Thomas David Parham devoted his life to ministry and for more than three decades served his God and country in the United States Navy Chaplain Corps. With his words of courage, comfort, and counsel, he blessed my life and the lives of thousands of others. He instilled hope, renewal, and confidence in God's grace through his prayers, presence, and professionalism, clearly embodying what Samuel Adams would have called "a gentleman of piety and virtue" and "a friend to his country."

As the first African-American to break the glass ceiling of O-6 (Captain) rank, Chaplain Parham's pioneering legacy is an inspiration to all who delight in humanity's triumph over adversity. He prayed for those who persecuted and marginalized him, often transforming them into friends. He eradicated negative stereotypes with exemplary excellence, earning his Master's and Doctoral degrees from American University with distinction. He forgave his enemies and catapulted obstacles by trusting in God and persevering in spite of great opposition.

The poet Henry Longfellow wrote about great people leaving exemplary footprints on the sands of time, thereby providing inspiration for those who follow them. Thomas David Parham, my mentor and friend, has done exactly that, and his wonderful book will delight you for years to come.

Foreword 2

Captain Thomas David Parham, CHC, USN (Ret.) is a maker of naval history. As the first African American to achieve the rank of Captain while serving on active duty in the Navy, he was a harbinger for fellow chaplains and other officers of his heritage credited with numerous significant milestones. His arduous career was marked from its very beginning by examples of tenacity and graciousness. His harmonization of these seemingly irreconcilable traits allowed him to unite elements within the Navy family which were never intended to be segregated from one another. His life was a testimony to the folly of the Navy's previous discriminatory policies: restricting the service of a Dave Parham, merely because of race, would have been a disservice to all.

Born in Newport News, Virginia, in 1920, Chaplain Parham was commissioned as a naval chaplain 1 September 1944. He had received his seminary education at Pittsburgh Theological Seminary, Pittsburgh, Pennsylvania, and was ordained as a minister in the United Presbyterian Church in May 1944. His career in the Navy spanned over four decades during which our country fought in three major conflicts, and a new consciousness of race relations was born. As the second African American chaplain in the Navy, he was often received with surprise and amazement, as people had never before seen a Black chaplain. He was a frequent victim of intentional discrimination, being forced to eat in the first class mess as his fellow officers prohibited him from joining the wardroom. In the face of unfair treatment, Chaplain Parham persisted in his calling to minister to sea service personnel.

Chaplain Parham's assignments spanned a broad spectrum of Navy duty. He served at both Navy and Marine Corps Recruit Training Depots, at sea as both ship and squadron chaplain, with the Fleet Marine Force, and on the staff of the Chief of Chaplains. While in Washington he pioneered innovative programs to combat the growing drug dominance in the Navy. His developmental work resulted in his being a member of the team which instituted the drug-free policy Navy wide. Among Chaplain Parham's many personal accomplishments are his earned Doctor of Philosophy degree from American University and his Legion of Merit, along with many other distinguished awards.

Despite the abundance of ignorance and hatred he encountered throughout his career, Chaplain Parham was patient and long-suffering. He reflected the image and likeness of God to his foes and persisted in ministry, even to those reluctant to receive it at first. One should not call Chaplain Parham a bridge-builder; he showed that the precipice to be traversed merely existed in peoples' unfounded fears! Once fears based on racial difference were overcome, the real fears of those engaged in the business of fighting wars could be confronted.

His service to others did not end with retirement. He continued to provide ministry to a congregation of his denomination and has served as visiting professor on a number of university faculties. He also continued to grace the Navy with his presence and interest at Chaplain Corps functions where he stood as a giant to be emulated by younger Navy chaplains.

This book preserves for us a portion of the remarkable insights and contributions made by a legendary figure of our Corps. Dave Parham's sense of calling and extraordinary gift of care should be embodied by us all. I personally count it an honor to write this foreword to preserve a portion of the contributions made by a man I have learned from and respected throughout my Navy career.

David E. White, Rear Admiral (Ret.), CHC, U. S. Navy

Foreword 3

On April 1, 1982 the United States Navy's first African American Captain to serve actively retired from active duty. One may assume that after 36 years of Navy service he would be ready to retire; one would be wrong! Chaplain Parham loved serving in the Navy because he loved helping people, serving people and making a difference in the quality of life for other people. He had served in the Navy all of his adult life. Why would he wish to start over at 62? He never said why, however, he did struggle to remain on active duty until he was 65. And he was quite upset that they were "putting him out."

He loved his U.S. Navy! He loved the uniform and wore it with great dignity! He was extremely loyal and patriotic, even when the Navy was not loyal to him. Like all pioneers, his experience had been difficult, at times bewildering and often painful, but it was difficult to let go.

The first time I saw Thomas David Parham was in the fall of 1969. He was a Captain and had been for almost three years. We were not peers or fellow officers. I was an enlisted Chief Petty Officer who had heard of "Captain Parham" and was impressed just to be close enough to see him. My first opportunity to actually speak to him was in 1974, during UPWARD (Understanding Personal Worth and Racial Dignity) workshops for upper management.

I retired from the Navy in 1977, lived in Norfolk and was very active in the Messiah Presbyterian Church and the Southern Virginia Presbytery. Chaplain Parham called me from his office at the Naval Hospital to ask me about the pulpit vacancy in our church. I visited him in his office shortly after that, and I liked him, much to my surprise. My church eventually hired Chaplain Simon Scott, Colonel, U.S. Air Force, retired, and through Simon, David became a friend. Unfortunately, Simon died in December 1984. David became our interim pastor for the next eight years, and during that time became a dear friend.

An Affirmation of Faith chronicles the life of an American hero and a gentle man of God.

SCPO David Greene, U.S.N., Retired

Table of Contents

Part I. Yielded to God: Inspired to Right Action

1 Prologue 21
2 Early Years 23
3 College Years 52
4 Seminary 69
5 Pastor, Butler Memorial (Youngstown, OH) 80

Part II. Moving Mountains

1 Chaplain School (Hampton Institute) 99
2 Great Lakes, IL (Camp Robert Smalls) 102
3 Transit to Hawaii 109
4 Pearl Harbor (Manana Barracks) 113
5 Guam (Serving Stewards and Longshoremen) 122
6 Charleston, SC (Questionable Acceptance) 130
7 Youngstown, OH (Separation from Navy) 133
8 University of Chicago 141

Part III. At Peace with God: Stepping Out in Faith

1 Great Lakes, IL 2 (Navy Requests Return) 157
2 Japan (Sasebo & Iwakuni, Serving the Fleet in Port) 172
3 Topeka, KA (Menninger, Post Graduate Studies) 196

4	First Marine Division, Camp Pendleton, CA	201
5	COMPHIBRON 1, San Diego, CA	216
6	MCRD, San Diego, CA	229
7	USS VALLEY FORGE (LPH-8)	242

Part IV. Walking Confidently into New Experiences

1	Quonset Point, RI (Navy Family Service)	259
2	Bureau of Naval Personnel, Washington DC	275
3	Bainbridge, MD (Navy Family Service)	299
4	Portsmouth, VA (Naval Hospital Service)	314
5	Retirement (Civilian & Retired Service)	336

Part I.

Yielded to God: Inspired to Right Action

Prologue

From the very beginning and throughout my life there were experiences, persons and events that validated my call to ministry. I was born and ordained by God to be in ministry. I did not know what my ministry was to be; but God revealed it to me when it was time to begin each phase. Therefore my life is an affirmation of my faith and its development.

Early Years

The announcement of my parent's wedding informs friends that the couple will reside at 1238 29th Street, Newport News, VA after May 1, 1919. I still use that announcement as a bookmark in my Bible. Ten months later, on a sunny Sunday afternoon, March 21, 1920, I was born at that address. My mother's former roommate from Scotia had come from Charlotte to be with "her Edith" during the birth of her first child.

My father had already left his position as cashier of the Crown Savings Bank to take a job at Newport News Shipbuilding. About a year later, in 1921, he received an offer of the cashier's position at the Fraternal Bank and Trust Company of Durham, NC; so the three of us moved to Durham. We lived temporarily with Dr. and Mrs. S.L. Warren across the street from the Duke Memorial Methodist Church on Chapel Hill Street. Their daughter Selena taught me to walk. Although they were not blood kin, Mrs. Warren was "Sister Julia" to my mother. Sister Julia called my mother "Sister" and my uncle Ward "Brother." My maternal grandmother, Mrs. L.S. Seabrook, was a teacher at the little Presbyterian school next to my grandfather's church in South Carolina. She insisted on being called "Mother Seabrook", the name by which she was called until she left us at 102 years of age.

We moved from Chapel Hill Street to a remodeled two story, five-bedroom house, complete with a well and a two-seated outhouse, at 1804 Swift Avenue. It was an unpaved street with no sidewalk. Like everyone else, we had kerosene lamps and a wood-burning kitchen stove, and only some of the floors were covered with linoleum. However, we had the only garage, the only car, and the only telephone on the block.

Our neighbors in the house on the left shared our well. Dr. Warren owned the house on the right which had been a school for Whites. It was occupied by a White family who not only rented the house from Dr. Warren, but a farm as well

I was still wearing diapers when my sister Edith Amy was born. She was named "Edith" after my mother and "Amy" after my father's only sister. My mother's parents were available to help out this time. At the time of my birth Grandmother Seabrook was preoccupied with my grandfather's physical condition. He had had a disabling accident, which left him on crutches for the rest of his life.

My grandfather was a minister. At each church he served, my grandfather had a farm as well as a school. On one occasion, he borrowed a neighbor's horse to operate a two-horse plow, but the neighbor's horse was not pulling its share of the load. As my grandfather moved to hit the horse with his cane, he stepped over the haymow and severed the tendon in his left leg. The leg never completely healed. My grandfather retired from the ministry and moved to Charlotte, where his son, Uncle Ward, was teaching at Johnson C. Smith University. Johnson C. Smith was alma mater for both of them.

Back in Durham I was elated over the arrival of Uncle Tommy, Grandmother's brother, who came to live with us while serving as pastor of Emmanuel A.M.E. Church in Durham. He spent weekends and occasionally a few other days with us, and traveled the 25 miles to Raleigh to be with his family the rest of the week. Uncle Tommy spent many hours with my sister and me while my father was at work and Mother was busy with the household duties. I remember one day my sister Edith rolled down the entire flight of stairs. Uncle Tommy dashed down, picked her up, comforted her and asked, "Did Uncle Tommy's baby get hurt?" That impressed me so much. I used to pretend I was a preacher because I wanted to be like Uncle Tommy.

Eleven months after my sister Edith was born, my brother Ward, named after my grandfather's brother Ward, was born in Fayetteville, NC. At the time of his birth, Uncle Ward was Dean

An Affirmation of Faith

at Fayetteville State University. Dr. Melchior and Nurse Broadfoot attended Mother. Dr. Melchior also built radios. He made more visits to Grandmother's house to work on the radio than to treat the ill. We had to walk very softly through the living room for fear of jarring the radio. We could get three stations: WPTF in Raleigh, KDKA in Pittsburgh, and WJZ in New York.

Not long after Uncle Tommy was transferred to another church, my other grandparents moved from Petersburg, VA to live with us. Grandpapa and Grandmamma Parham were quite different from Grandfather and Grandmother Seabrook. Grandfather Seabrook had finished college and seminary; Grandmother Seabrook completed two years at Claflin College before she dropped out to marry Grandfather. I doubt Grandpapa or Grandmamma Parham ever attended school anywhere. Grandpapa told me he wrote so poorly that he could hardly read the names of the men who were working for him making brick. He could read only the Bible. My father, whom we called "Papa", got to go to college because Grandpapa Parham was hired to make brick for Kitrell College, near Raleigh, and took Papa with him. My parents met there. Uncle Tommy was on the faculty at Kitrell, so Grandfather Seabrook thought it was safe for Mother to attend Kitrell.

Grandpapa liked to garden. In addition to our plot, he planted another large plot behind the wooden fence on the other side of our house. I used to bring him a half-gallon jar of water from the icebox. He would drink it all down, put me on the crossbar of his hand pushed plow and carry me down the rows as he plowed. Back at the house, I listened with rapt attention to his accounts of burning brick in the kiln by stoking and feeding the fire for what seemed to me endless days and nights. Sometimes a whole kiln of brick would be ruined by inattention. Often on Saturdays, Grandpapa and I would take vegetables Grandpapa had raised to Kroger and exchange them for meat and groceries.

On March 31, 1925, Sister Ella Lucy, named for both grandmothers, was born in Durham. Both grandmothers were on hand. Grandmamma Parham was busy cooking, feeding and entertaining Dr. Thompson. Grandmother Seabrook was complaining that Dr. Thompson should not be distracted while attending Mother. A few weeks later Uncle Tommy brought Grandfather Seabrook to Durham to baptize Sister Ella Lucy in our parlor. I remember wondering what it was all about and being impressed by the importance that everyone attached to the visit and the ceremony. It was the first baptism I remember.

The first wedding I remember also took place in our parlor. My Aunt Amy married Holloway, a barber in Norfolk. I was the ring bearer. Someone put the ring around the stem of a day lily picked from the front yard. Somehow, I got the impression that the ring was mine, so when it was taken from me I cried.

Our house was only two blocks from the Training School, later the Normal School. Two of the members of the faculty, Rev. and Mrs. Harry Albert Smith, lived with us and had the front bedroom downstairs. They were from Boston, with Harvard accents. Rev. Smith would practice his sermons in front of a mirror while Mrs. Smith listened and offered suggestions. He had two sets of boxing gloves and was forever trying to get someone to spar with him. He would tie the gloves on me and then emit peals of laughter as I tried to hit him with my wild swings. He then peppered me with his open gloves. One day I asked him what he would like for me to draw for him with my crayons. His answer was, "A big church." Every time I asked that question, I got the same answer.

Cousin Clarence came to live with us when the Normal School became a college. The Smiths and my grandparents were still in the house. One day when Cousin Clarence and Rev. Smith were sparring, Rev. Smith slipped and gave Cousin Clarence a fat lip. Although Rev. Smith apologized profusely, Cousin Clarence was angry because he had a date that night.

Cousin Clarence eventually moved to the dormitory, but he always came back on Wednesdays, the day Mother baked rolls and molasses bread. He had worked as a steward on a cruise ship, and his pass key fit our front door. We could always tell when he had been in the house because the ring would be missing from the bathtub.

We got a bathroom added to the back porch in time for Aunt Amy's wedding. The septic tank was near where the outhouse had been. The City of Durham annexed Swift Avenue, changed the name to Concord Street, sent someone to nail the house number above the

An Affirmation of Faith

door, and ordered that the well be filled. I watched the house number go on and the men dropping logs into the well. It had been my job to empty the pots in our rooms into the slop bucket in my parent's room and take the contents to the outdoor toilet. So the wedding marked the end of an era.

Three girls in college in succession lived with us room-and-board-free to help Mother with us and the house. The first was Lorena Suit, who in addition to some cleaning and cooking, combed my sisters' hair and gave all four of us our Saturday night bath in the bathtub. I don't remember when the boys were separated from the girls or when assistance was no longer needed, but the second student, Etta Spaulding, did not have this duty, nor did Vera Bruner, the third student. Lorena died; Etta married; Vera became a high school principal in Danville, VA.

We later had two male students in succession living in the house and helping with heavier work: Christopher Columbus Franks and Carson Beckwith. Chris became a principal; Carson became a beauty shop owner and bank director in Charlotte, NC.

All of these were, to some extent, role models for me. I listened attentively to their advice, responded gratefully to their concern, and felt that I always had a friend in my court when called on the carpet about anything.

Each one of us children had some reason to feel like a special person. We were born in boy-girl, boy-girl order as my mother wanted. I was the first and named for my father, a new departure in our family with no precedent among the Parhams or the Seabrooks. Sister Edith Amy was special because she was chocolate brown with glossy black curls and was named for Mother and our only aunt. Brother Ward was special because he was named for Uncle and his middle name was Seabrook. A great, great, great grandfather was Governor Whitemarsh Seabrook of South Carolina. Sister Ella Lucy was special because she was the baby and of fair complexion, a definite asset in those days, and she was named for the two grandmothers, the true matriarchs.

Because my birthday is in March and I would be six by the end of the year anyway, my parents wanted me to start school at the age of five. Miss Ora Sneed, a favorite first grade teacher at Hillside

An Affirmation of Faith

High School, agreed. The principal, Mr. W.G. Pearson, organizer of the Fraternal Bank and Trust Company, told Miss Sneed, "You can have your baby." With all the college professors and students living in the house, I had a built-in tutorial staff. School was never a problem for me until I reached the Ph.D. level.

The year 1925 was significant for another reason. Dr. J.W.V. Cordice moved to Durham, NC from Aurora, NC to get better school opportunities for his four children, the oldest of which, and his namesake, was also assigned to Miss Sneed's class. We were classmates through the eleven years to high school graduation. Dr. Cordice replaced Dr. Thompson as our family doctor. Our parents held up the four Cordice children as role models for us, and their parents did likewise. In 1951, the number one Parham married the number two Cordice.

The matriarchal tone in our family was unmistakable. When Grandmother spoke, the last word had been said. Every summer Mother, my sisters and brother, and I went to Fayetteville to spend the vacation months with her parents. One summer we took Lorena with us. Grandmother Seabrook was head of the house since Grandfather Seabrook was crippled. She called him "Husband" in a tone that to me, communicated at least, subordination, at most, contempt. She considered the Parhams ignorant and poor.

Grandfather's pension from the Civil War and the Presbyterian Church was twice as much as my father's salary as a bank cashier in a small bank. My father's real estate corporation, T.D. Parham and Associates, was also small. The reason we went to Fayetteville annually was to let Papa catch up with the winter's grocery bill.

The Parham female dominance was just as pronounced. I often heard Grandmamma say, "The hand that rocks the cradle is the hand that rules the world." She also said that the Parhams were no good because they were not slaves, so they never learned to work. Grandpapa never objected to either statement. He did, however, explain how the Parhams escaped slavery.

His grandfather had been a slave. One day while plowing, he struck a box that turned out to contain gold coins. He bought his and his wife's freedom, a block of property in the Blandford section of Petersburg, and retired for life. The owner of the land where he found the gold, sued to recover it. The judge, in what must be the most unusual ruling ever made in Virginia, said that if the landowner had known the gold was there he would not have had anyone plowing at the spot. Later the house burned down and melted the gold in its basement tunnel. When the gold was re-minted, income tax had to be paid.

The next generation of Parhams found no reason to work either. When Great Grandfather died, the only one of the ten children with him was Aunt Mary, who thereupon appropriated whatever fortune was left. So, Grandpapa began making brick; Aunt Sarah opened a boarding house; Uncle Bob got himself elected secretary-treasurer of enough organizations to keep him going. Uncle Willie became a Baptist pastor (Cousin Clarence's father), and Aunt Eliza married well.

When Aunt Mary died, Cousin Ruby got the residue, and Grandpapa always resented Aunt Mary's good fortune. Cousin Ruby drove down to Durham from Richmond one day to bring Grandpapa a fruit basket with a bottle of wine. I remember her Cadillac pulling away in a cloud of dust.

The roaring 20s brought us a measure of prosperity. The Fraternal Bank and Trust Company merged with the Mechanics and Farmers Bank. The latter bank was larger, so they retained its cashier, whose father-in-law was a chairman of the board. Papa became trust officer. His real estate sales increased, and a 1924 Dodge replaced the Model T Ford. The house was remodeled again, while we were in Fayetteville, to give us an electric stove, a furnace with steam heat, a living room, and a parlor like the Cordices.

Mother got her first and only fur coat, black sealskin. Papa's pledge of three dollars weekly to Pine Street Presbyterian Church was the largest in the sixty-member congregation and twenty-five percent of the pastor's salary, excluding his mission board supplement.

The 1920s also introduced me to grief. One day Mrs. Smith went to the hospital for an appendectomy but never returned from the operating room. Rev. Smith wore her rings while he grieved, and talked about how she and mother never had an argument while using the same kitchen. I never saw a man cry until the day I saw Rev.

An Affirmation of Faith

Smith in the attic. He removed a top sheet from one of his trunks, ran his hand over it, and said, "My wife ironed this," as he broke into tears and sobbed.

I next experienced grief when Mr. Decatur Pratt, who worked in the Mortgage Company of Durham alongside Papa, became our neighborhood's first suicide. He and Papa were studying law together through LaSalle Extension. One could take the bar after finishing the course in those days. Mrs. Pratt gave papa her husband's law books.

On another occasion, someone cut the screen and entered a neighbor's house in the next block, scalped the husband and wounded the wife with a hatchet. Blood showed on the sidewalk for days. I began screaming in the night and had to stay out of school and rest for a few weeks. The assailant was executed in the electric chair.

Then, in 1930, Grandfather Seabrook died of bronchial pneumonia. I was particularly hurt because my parents would not let me go to the funeral. I felt that I identified with him in his suffering at Grandmother's hands, though he never complained; in fact, he never responded.

Everything he ever told me about the Civil War was in answer to specific questions. He began as a drummer boy, and became an infantryman when he got older. Yes, he did eat horsemeat but did not know if he ever shot anyone. In my questioning, it never occurred to me to question God's allowing the series of tragic events.

I continued my interest in the church and held to my ambition to be a preacher. In 1928, I was the only non-adult attending the Wednesday night prayer meetings at the church. At one such session, the leader was Dr. I.H. Russell, who had once been pastor of the church and had later become the evangelist for the Presbytery. In a departure from the customary format, he extended an invitation for anyone who desired to accept Jesus as savior to walk up and take his hand. I asked my mother's permission and she gave it. Fifty-eight years later, it is still thrilling to recapture the moment I became a committed Christian.

Durham in the 1920s was practically two cities: one White, the other Black, with the railroad dividing the two. Facing the railroad on the south side of the tracks was Pettigrew Street with its ninety-odd Black businesses. Fayetteville Street, on which the Blacks of importance lived and on which the prominent churches were located, intersected the east end of Pettigrew Street. The business district was called Hayti.

Of the 25,000 Blacks in a total population of 52,037, 5,000 worked in the tobacco factories. It was thought that the tobacco dust would be harmful to Whites. These workers provided the economic base for the Black businesses, which they patronized because they were not allowed in some of the White establishments, such as hotels and restaurants, and segregated in others, such as theatres. There were a few exceptions to this geographical segregation: the Warrens lived on Chapel Hill Street; the N.C. Mutual Life Insurance Company, Mechanics and Farmers Bank, and Mutual Savings and Loan Company were on Parrish Street; the Warren-Strudwick office building was on Chapel Hill Street.

Mr. C.C. Spaulding was president of the North Carolina Mutual, the largest Black-owned insurance company, the Mechanics and Farmers Bank, the Southern Fidelity Insurance Company, and the Bankers Fire Insurance Company. He had worked with the founders of the N.C. Mutual, Mr. John Merrick, who owned a barbershop for Whites, and Dr. A.H. Moore, a physician. Mr. Merrick's son John married Miss Lyda Moore, the doctor's daughter, and became treasurer of North Carolina Mutual. Mr. R.L. McDougald married the other Moore daughter, Mattie Louise, and he became cashier of the bank. I remember the day Mrs. McDougald died and my mother's sorrow when she received the telephone call. The Moore daughters, my mother, and Aunt Fannie had all attended Scotia Seminary (now Barber-Scotia College) at the same time.

Mr. Spaulding was Durham's most prominent Black citizen. He hosted a forum for N.C. Mutual employees on Saturday mornings to which nationally prominent Blacks were invited as speakers. After the forum, many locals congregated inside of and in front of the bank, (which was on the first floor of the building), the Mutual Savings and Loan Company (of which Mr. Spaulding was president also), or Mr. Gilmer's tailor shop, all contiguous on Parrish Street. There the colorful figure was Mr. Louis Austin, editor and publisher of The Carolina Times, the local weekly Black newspaper.

My first effort to earn money was as a salesman for the five cent weekly with a two-cent commission. Mr. Austin taught an adult Sunday school class at St. Joseph's A.M.E., the first Black church in Durham. When called to testify in court he carried his own Bible to swear on and kiss, rather than use the Bible designated for Blacks. He, of course, could not use the one reserved for Whites. This newspaper was quite important in the Black community because ordinarily only crimes by Blacks were reported in the White dailies in those days. Mr. Austin was a true crusader. His logo showed an unbridled horse with the caption, "The Truth Unbridled."

Professor W.G. Pearson, principal of Hillside High School, was very prominent, particularly in the early twenties. It was his Fraternal Bank and Trust Company that brought my dad to Durham. He was Supreme Grand Scribe of the Royal Knights of King David, a fraternal order with a death benefit and owners of two office buildings on Fayetteville Street. Professor Pearson had grown up on the lower end of Fayetteville Street which was called Pearsontown. In our first grade class, when Miss Sneed asked, "What kind of car does Professor Pearson have?" everybody replied in unison, "A Pierce-Arrow."

Unfortunately, for the Pearson family, the fraternal orders were placed under the state insurance laws, which required cash reserves to be held for the payment of claims, among other provisions that most fraternal orders were not able to meet. The Royal Knights went into decline. The Fraternal Bank was combined with the Mechanics and Farmers, which already had a cashier, Mr. Willie Wilson, son-in-law of Captain Smith, who had served in the Civil War. I was one of the onlookers at Captain Smith's burial in a $1,000 casket, the price of a home or a Cadillac in those days.

Dr. James E. Shepard completed the Black big three of the era. He founded the National Religious Training School and Chautauqua, which became the Normal School and later, N.C. College for Negroes. Dr. Shepard was trained as a pharmacist, worked as a Sunday school missionary, and was awarded a Doctor of Divinity degree by Muskingum College. His cow was the source of our milk supply.

An Affirmation of Faith

Chapel attendance was mandatory for students at North Carolina College, and local residents were invited to the Sunday afternoon Vespers at which the school choir sang and to which nationally known leaders were invited. It was at Vespers that I first heard Drs. Mordecai Johnson and Howard Thurman. It was there also that I heard Edwin Markham recite his own poetry, "The Man with a Hoe," and the lines that are probably my most treasured non-biblical phrases, which I never forgot:

> *"He drew a circle that shut me out,*
> *A heretic, rebel, and thing to flout*
> *But I and love had the wit to win,*
> *We drew a circle that took him in."*

The pastor of St. Joseph, Dr. Hodges, Dr. McDowell of White Rock, and Dr. Miles Mark Fisher were also very influential in the community. It was the Brotherhood of St. Joseph that brought Congressman Oscar DePriest of Chicago to Durham for a speech in the Hillside High School auditorium. At the time, Congressman DePriest was opposing the appointment of a Judge Johnson to a federal court position. The judge had produced a letter of commendation from Dr. Shepard, whom Congressman DePriest called a "handkerchief head," whereupon Mr. Charlie Amey left the auditorium to report the incident to Dr. Shepard.

Because of the plentiful supply of prominent role models, life was exciting and education was pictured as the road to success. I thoroughly enjoyed school because of the genuine concern of the teachers and because of my success in the process. I think I was in the tenth grade before I received my first "B+." It was in algebra, and I have disliked math ever since.

In the second grade, Miss Lucy Royster was concerned about my weight. She would let me know when the school nurse was coming to weigh us so that I could bring two lunches that day. It didn't help. She had me demonstrate to the class how I could read silently without moving my lips.

In the third grade, I was preoccupied with Miss Edith Wilson's beauty and an opal ring she wore. It was a large blue stone surrounded by diamonds. She lived in one of the two teachers' homes owned by Professor Pearson and was a native of Richmond, which seemed so far away. While in her class, I began to read adventure stories, the *Tom Swift* and *Rover Boys* series. I would stop by the library before going home, read the book that night, and exchange it the next day for another. I also read the Horatio Alger stories and some of the Charles Dickens I found at home. I tried O. Henry but didn't appreciate him. My room at home had built-in bookcases containing the family library.

The first three grades were at Hillside. The third grade was in a temporary building on the boys' recess ground. In fourth grade, we moved to the new W.G. Pearson Elementary School, with Mr. E.D. Mickle as principal. My teacher was Miss McKelvey, who later married Attorney C.O. Pearson.

Mr. Mickle was a fearsome character. He kept a push-broom handle hanging from a nail in his outer office, and its sole purpose was for corporal punishment of boys.

The real love of my life that year was Miss Everett, the writing teacher. I had never before heard anyone speak in a voice with an aspirate quality; so soothing I thought. I was crushed when Mr. McDougald married her and took her from us.

This was the year that we were introduced to profanity, vulgarity, dirty jokes and jingles, all of which prompted Miss McKelvey to ask one morning, "And how are my little cursers today?" This was a great embarrassment to me, in light of my career goal as a preacher, so I stopped participating in such activities openly. On the other hand, I found a certain fascination in listening to others so engaged, even if only to congratulate myself on my own self-righteousness.

The fifth grade found me in Mrs. Whitehurst's class. She was the daughter of Rev. Woodard, pastor of White Rock many years ago, long since deceased. Her mother ran a small grocery store from which I bought kerosene for our cook stove and portable heaters for ten cents per gallon. Mrs. Whitehurst played the piano for the hymns we sang, led us in spirituals, and preached short sermons on accepting Christ and believer's baptism. I began to feel odd for not being a Baptist.

An Affirmation of Faith

Some of my classmates were sexually active and talked about it when Mrs. Whitehurst would leave the room. Two of the boys exhibited themselves and were commended by the most precocious girl, whose favorite expression of surprise was, "I almost had a baby right there in the street."

Mrs. Whitehurst had given birth to a son just before school began. She would not tell us the child's given name; all she would say was, "Junior Whitehurst." When she went out of the room one of the exhibitionists wrote "Goliath" on the Blackboard. When she returned and asked him if he did it, he denied it, saying that he thought the name was Eli. This same fellow worked part-time in Kroger's meat department where he had lost four fingers in the meat grinder. He took great pleasure in startling you by thrusting the nub toward your face.

Already feeling inadequate because I was not a Baptist, I began to feel inadequate for not being sexually active. I was somewhat comforted by one of the older boys who assured me that I would be when I got older. I was nine at the time; he was fifteen. It was also reassuring for me to talk to Mrs. Woodward when I went for the weekly gallon of kerosene. I felt that she accepted me because I wanted to be, as she put it, "a consecrated worker for the Lord."

My fifth grade year was also the year I was introduced to marital conflict. My Aunt Amy told me that Mr. Whitehurst, whom she had known in Norfolk, was no good and she could not understand why Mrs. Whitehurst had married him. Mrs. Whitehurst told me that Mr. Holloway was no good and she could not understand why Aunt Amy had married him. We made a vacation trip to Norfolk and spent some time with the Holloways. My only negative impression of him was his frugality. The washcloths were cut-up towels. It seems that towels and washcloths were the same price so he would not buy washcloths. When he died soon afterward his grown children overcompensated by spending most of his estate on the funeral. They even hired the Excelsior Band to march in the procession to the cemetery.

Mrs. Whitehurst was my last teacher until college who could "pass" for White. Except for Miss Sneed, a very pale blond, whose son appeared to be an albino, they had all been of fair complexion.

An Affirmation of Faith

The jingle "White is right, Brown can stick around, but Black must get back" was still current, but it was the expected standard of acceptance by Whites rather than the prevailing value of the Black community. Our one classmate who could have passed for White refused to tell us why he did not want to attend a White school. We heard that his father had been the pastor of a White Baptist church in South Carolina, but when the members learned he was Black, they wanted to lynch him. Of course, we never asked our classmate to confirm this hearsay.

My fifth grade year also brought my first experience with a movie camera. I was eating an orange when someone taking pictures on the recess ground one day came over and told me to take my cap off and take a big bite of the orange, which I did. After all, he was White and congenial. When the film was shown at the Regal Theatre (owned by a classmate's father) my classmates were unanimous in the opinion that the cameraman had made a fool of me. They told me if I saw it, I would want to scratch it out. I didn't go to the theatre, said nothing about it at home, and felt much better after that week was over.

Thirty-seven years later in Rhode Island I was being interviewed by the Associated Press on becoming the first Black to be promoted to the rank of Navy Captain on active duty. When asked to smile for the camera, I replied, "I do not ham it up for photographers." The reporter printed, "The Captain said he never smiles." Those who knew me were puzzled by this remark.

Miss Robinson was our sixth grade teacher. She did not play the piano and was accused of punching out one of the students. The high point of our experience with her was the day she rushed into the noisy room, slipped and fell in a sitting position. That incident was a conversation piece for the rest of the year. In some kind of dispute with a classmate, I angrily said I would see him after school. He was overjoyed because he had a pair of cowboy gloves. He spread the word that we were going to fight, put on his gloves and began clenching his fists in anticipation. Then, as Senator Dirksen used to say, "I reconsidered my position." When he and the rest of the class came toward me after school I told him I was not going to fight and turned and walked rapidly away. Strangely, he did not pursue. I was called a coward, but I was happy to be an unscarred one. This same classmate was taken to the principal's office the next year for trying to use brass knuckles in a recess fight.

This was the year that I had to share the spotlight with two of my classmates who received commendations from Miss Robinson. One of the girls wrote a paper telling of the relief work of Mr. Hoover before he became president. One of the boys wrote a paper on neatness. I was as impressed as I was jealous. I would have to try harder to stand out from the rest of the students.

The seventh grade happily brought us back to Hillside. My class (7-1) had Miss Lucille Johnson for homeroom. We went to other teachers for the various subjects. This was called "changing classes." The most exciting teacher was Mrs. Gertrude Winslow. We called her "Big Chief" behind her back because of her large hooked nose. She would drill us in arithmetic by calling out a number, then telling us to mentally add, subtract, divide, or multiply by other numbers she would suggest. When she saw that most of us had gotten lost, she would point to various students and demand an answer until somebody gave her the correct one. As I remember it, I never missed.

Mrs. Winslow also directed a musical play in which most of us participated. I sang soprano in the chorus. The words of the theme ran, "School is over, school is over, our vacation has begun. Through the laughing months of summer, won't we have a lot of fun?" Professor Buchannan, my violin teacher, was hired to play his cello as the piano accompanied us. The auditorium was packed.

I later substituted my violin lessons for piano lessons with Mrs. Shearin, daughter of Mr. C.C. Spaulding. I was fascinated by her grand piano and the sparkle of her diamond as she played. My uncle and mother played piano. Our upright was my mother's wedding present from her father. It was the only item, except possibly property, that he ever bought on credit. My father thought piano lessons were for girls. Violin lessons were $1.25 per month, and it was the only bill I remember my father paying promptly. In 1941 in Youngstown, Ohio, I resumed piano lessons and in San Diego in 1960 I bought a grand piano.

It was the custom at Hillside for the entering seventh grade class to be hazed, usually at recess the first day. One of my classmates

An Affirmation of Faith

had brought a pistol to protect himself. When he aimed the pistol at the leader of the hazing group, the recess ground became quiet. He lowered the pistol; the group moved toward him. He aimed it again. Thus, the hazing never took place, for which I was much relieved.

Hillside was rough in those days. Some fellows brought bootleg whiskey, "White Lightning," to school in small Vaseline jars. I had two switchblade knives. Many of the boys had at least one. The walls of the auditorium had burn spots the size of golf balls from firecrackers being exploded on them. It was great fun for those who could afford the torpedoes to throw them during a play or some other night performance.

Fights at recess were always exciting. One day one of the larger fellows, acting as my protector, told another boy not to pick up the mulberries where I was picking them up. When the intruder did not desist, he was hit in the head with a brick. We all had to go to the office where I gave the facts. The situation was so bad that Mrs. Lyda Merrick came to our assembly one morning, asked the students to behave properly, and promised to give an apple or orange to anyone who would come by her house and promise to behave. I never heard if she got any takers.

Although we heard that Professor Pearson lost a lot of money in the stock market, Durham weathered the depression remarkably. The tobacco factories remained open. Many people had to resort to buying cigarettes one at a time for a penny each, but the tobacco factory never closed. One could buy a bag of Bull Durham tobacco for five cents and roll his own.

Fortunately, I did not smoke or drink. My allowance was only ten cents per week, but after a penny tithe in Sunday school, I was still affluent. I could buy Baby Ruth and licorice sticks for a penny each. I agreed with the theatre owner's son who said, "I hate to break a nickel because it goes so fast.

We were proud that our bank did not close. The only Black business I remember failing was The Mortgage Company of Durham. My father paid only the interest on our mortgage for years, since he was selling very few houses. We never got another new car. There was a soup line, and some of my classmates ate clay. If it snowed, schools closed because some students did not have shoes. If it snowed on

Sunday, we went to the Episcopal Church. It was understood that the Presbyterian janitor would not come out to make a fire. He didn't think it was worth it, since so few would attend anyway.

The eighth grade was the first year of high school at Hillside. Four members of 7-1 the year ahead of us, including the principal's niece, had skipped the eighth grade. There was some discussion of whether the same privilege would be extended to members of my class, but it didn't happen. Excitement at school came through my introduction to Latin, which I found to be as interesting as it was easy. Although my uncle had finished Johnson C. Smith in 1909, he still remembered his declensions and conjugations. He could say them faster than I could.

I reached a real milestone at the age of twelve. I was eligible to join Boy Scout Troop 55. The fee to join was fifty cents. Whether or not Troop 55 could wear their uniforms on the White side of the railroad tracks was an issue because of a decision that had been made earlier concerning Black policemen. We could not have Black policemen because they could not be allowed to pursue fugitives across the tracks. Nevertheless, Troop 55 was granted permission to cross the tracks. We bought our uniforms from the Goodall store, and the owners were on our side.

I still marvel at the dedication of our scout leaders, particularly Mr. F.C. Pendarvis, chairman of the troop committee, and Dr. Harry McDonald Evans, a local chiropractor. Dr. Evans was from British Guyana, educated in Canada, and unmarried. Mr. Pendarvis was a bellhop at the Washington Duke Hotel. Strangely, we referred to him as "Pendarvis" without any title. On one occasion, he was in the outhouse on the Pearson School grounds when somebody got the idea of pelting the place with rocks. When we finally stopped, he came out, got into his car and drove away without saying a word. Dr Evans wondered if he would ever return, but he was at the next meeting.

On another occasion, we were very gleeful when a White man in a passing automobile almost slapped Mr. Pendarvis as we were returning from Raleigh on our bicycles, a 50 mile round trip. It was annoying to us when Mr. Pendarvis had to get off his bicycle and walk up the steeper hills.

An Affirmation of Faith

Our Scoutmaster, Bill Powell, and his assistant, Bill Pearson, were college students. Bill Pearson became a judge before he died a few years ago. They were with us at the Friday meetings. Dr. Evans and Mr. Pendarvis were with us for the morning hikes to Pearson School at 6 a.m., the bicycle rides to Raleigh and Roxboro, 30 miles away, and the football games where we appeared in uniform and were admitted without charge in Durham and Greensboro. They took us to the Moravian sunrise service on Easter in Winston-Salem. Dr. Evans volunteered to take five of us to the World's Fair in Chicago for $15 each, but only four boys could afford the $15. I would have been the fifth but my father said he could not afford it. He complained that the other four dads made more in a week than he did in a month. I vowed that no son of mine would ever be disappointed over $15. Grandmother was right; he definitely was inferior to the other dads.

In some respects, he had an inferior son as well. One day during recess, a truck loaded with baskets of oranges came through the playground gate en-route to the back door of the lunchroom. I remarked to one of my scout buddies that it would really be funny if somebody shut the gate so the truck could not leave. He closed the gate and put a brick in place to hold it shut. Sure enough, the truck returned at a fast clip, hoping to get out of the gate without losing any oranges. When the truck had to stop, the boys liberated all of the oranges. We threw them around like baseballs before we ate them with relish. The two White men on the truck left in great haste, and I suspect some thankfulness, as peals of laughter followed them. I felt that the oppressors got their just desserts. Then I turned to my buddy and said, "Charles, when we go to scout meeting Friday I am going to tell them how you blocked the gate and caused those guys to lose their oranges." He replied, "And I am going to tell how T.D. Parham cooked up the whole plot." The incident was never mentioned again and we never saw the truck again either. I suspect the school paid for the oranges and the salesmen returned when we were not having recess. Many years later, I felt guilty about the whole thing.

I was picked as patrol leader of the beaver patrol and was promised the post of senior patrol leader. We would give demonstrations in knot-tying and semaphore signaling, our leaders would give short talks on scouting and we might sing taps or the bugler might play. In those days, there was no TV and many groups were eager to sponsor us. One night we gave a program at Lyon Elementary School. On this night a deacon was called on to pray. His English was unusually poor and I led the giggling. The program ended with no mention of the senior patrol leader appointment. When I asked Mr. Pendarvis about it, he reminded me of my giggling during prayer, and then said with considerable feeling, "You will never get it." He was absolutely correct; I never did get it. This may be the most valuable lesson I learned from the scouting movement. "A scout is reverent" is the twelfth law.

We also played baseball and football. Because the football belonged to me, I got to play the position I wanted. I chose to play center because my father had played center on his college team. Ordinarily I was shortstop in baseball. One day we were playing a team in East Durham and Willie was getting knocked out of the box. Dr. Evans said, "T.D., go in for Willie." I told Doc I could not do as well as Willie was already doing. So the game continued to be a rout. The next week, around the campfire on a 6 a.m. hike, Doc was talking to the rest of the scouts while I was in the outhouse. As I returned from the outhouse, I noticed that several of the scouts smiling at me. When I got close enough to hear what was being said, I heard Dr. Evans say, "If T.D. had taken the mound we might even have won the game." Then it hit me: "A scout is obedient." Years later I came to understand the psychology behind the change in pitchers during a rout.

Mr. G.W. Cox, a vice president of North Carolina Mutual, spent more time with us than any other parent. He had real talent in baseball. He attended many meetings, activities, was full of good advice on many subjects, and was even better as a public speaker. He always used unforgettable illustrations. I attribute the phenomenal success of several members of that troop to the role models we had. G.W. Cox. Jr. became vice president of North Carolina Mutual. E.G. Spaulding, Jr. became chief accountant of the four Rockefeller family accountants. Clinton Mills became an ace pilot in the Army Air Corps. J.W.V. Cordice, Jr. has been chief of thoracic surgery at two New York hospitals; Jim Gillis is a scout executive in Washington and had frequent conferences with Vice President Hubert Humphrey.

I learned to drive our 1928 Chrysler in 1932. A local dealer had sponsored a contest in which the winner would receive a $50 discount on a car. Contest entrants were to send in as many words as one could make from the letters in the word Chrysler. The cost of the car my father chose was $240, which was $190 with my discount. Therefore, I felt like a part owner of the car and also of the next one for which it was traded several years later.

When I was twelve I could easily pass for sixteen. Only Willie was taller than I. My first long trip was to Petersburg, Virginia for my grandmother's funeral. Grandmamma died in Central State Hospital where she was taken when Grandpapa could no longer take care of her. She would wander off, not knowing where she was. She would burn objects like the deed to Auntie's house and both of my switchblade knives. She said I didn't need them. It did not seem strange that only my father and I made the trip. After all, His parents were second-class citizens in our family, as was he. I remember nothing about the funeral except driving both ways. The speed limit in North Carolina then was 45 mph, in Virginia 35 mph. At that time North Carolina did not require a driver's license.

Through the years I had been assigned duties around the house for my ten cent per week allowance. Until we got the indoor toilet it was my job to empty the potties from the girls' and boys' rooms into the slop bucket in my parents' room, carry the contents to the outhouse, rinse all receptacles, and return them to their proper places. By the age of six, I was bringing in coal for the cook stove in the kitchen and the circulator in the dining room. When the kitchen stove became a kerosene type, I made the trips to Woodard's store with a gallon glass jug to buy kerosene for ten cents a gallon. Also, I took out the ashes from the circulator.

When Papa bought a steam heating unit, I took out the ashes from the newly dug basement, shoveled coal, banked the fire at night and broke it up at 6:30 a.m. to warm the house. Then I cooked a big double boiler of oatmeal as the first course of breakfast.

We ate big breakfasts. The oatmeal was followed by bacon or ham and eggs, sometimes lamb chops, creamed beef and sometimes

An Affirmation of Faith

leftovers from dinner such as beef stew, biscuits or hot rolls, fruit or juice. We also used grits, big hominy, and packaged cereal. Mother used to dry orange peels in the warmer of the cook stove to put in cocoa. Grandpapa drank coffee every day. Papa drank one cup on Sunday morning to help him stay awake in church; it didn't work.

We children took lunches to school. Often it was peanut butter, jelly, and maybe some fruit. Dinner was about 3:30 p.m. We could count on fish roe and codfish cakes at least once each week; beef stew, liver, fried or baked fish, lamb and chicken also appeared. Fish was on Friday, chicken on Sunday, unless we had lamb chops for breakfast and a roast for dinner. Our dinner at 3:30 p.m. was for Papa's convenience. Banks closed early in those days so Papa spent late afternoons and early evenings collecting rent and hopefully selling houses. Mother would often cook bacon and eggs for him when he came in, and my hungriest moments were when the aroma drifted upstairs. We were not permitted to eat at night.

I still have a large scar in the middle of my back from standing up too soon as I crawled under the stovepipe of the circulator in the dining room. My other duties included cutting the lawn with a push-type mower, washing the car, splitting wood for kindling, scrubbing the kitchen floor, sweeping the downstairs rooms and porches. It seemed to me that I did more work than anyone else, a penalty for being the oldest. It also seemed to me that as I grew older and gained more privileges, they were given to the rest with a much shorter waiting period.

We had only one long-term pet, a cat named Marion. Although it was a female, the cat was named after my best friend, Marion Fleming of Fayetteville. He had skipped from the fourth grade to the sixth, then from the sixth to the eighth grade. I was one day older than he. His grandfather ran a White barbershop and wore a wing collar just like Dr. Shepard. His grandmother was the first woman I ever saw driving a car. Marion had three older brothers. The oldest one was beaten to death by White policemen one night as he was returning home after playing bass violin in a dance band. I decided I would have four sons when I got married.

The Fleming boys had a tree house in their front yard. They told stories of stealing watermelons from passing wagons and taking them up to the tree house. It is likely not a coincidence that my wife's name is Marion. On many occasions, I felt that the cat was the only one in this household who loved me.

My feelings toward my father were ambivalent. He told me how he had carried me all over the neighborhood to show me off when I was a newborn. I was delighted when he bought me a new bicycle, which cost $32.50, ten days pay for him in 1932. On the other hand, I saw him as wearing a perpetual frown. He seemed to be extremely critical. On the tennis court, he asked me why I would knock the ball into the net. I liked to hear people say I could beat him. Once he scrubbed my neck and face, remarking that he hoped I would not catch cold now that so much dirt had been cleaned off. He said it was a good thing that I wanted to be a preacher because I would only have to preach one sermon on Sunday and could do nothing the rest of the week. I asked him to read a theme I had written, which I thought showed some originality. He called attention to the fact that I had used a word, "rubbage," which was not a word at all.

My Aunt Amy, his only sibling, told me he finished third in his college class, which had a total of three members. She said he had been spoiled by his parents because his complexion was lighter than hers. She also said he cheated her when he was told to share anything with her. The day that he told me a mouse would grow up to be a rat I decided that he was dumb. Mother complained that he did not believe that she knew anything, so he paid no attention to anything she said. She told me with some bitterness that when she finished high school her father did not think it fitting for a woman to go to college but agreed that she could go to Scotia Seminary, a Presbyterian finishing school for females. She took the placement examination, which was to decide which high school grade would be appropriate. She failed the examination by one point and had to take all four years over. I decided she was dumb also, in contrast to my uncle, her only sibling, whom I considered a sheer genius. He still remembered his Latin conjugations and declensions.

My relationship with my mother was also what one might expect of a son when there is a negative father relationship. In the first place, I was as much larger than she as I was smaller than my father. He weighed over 200 pounds. She weighed 98 pounds when they got married and never exceeded 135. He was six feet; she was about five. She and I commiserated with each other over his treatment of us.

There were uncomfortable sexual overtones in my relationships with both parents. In the first place, I felt terribly inferior to my father because of the great difference in penis sizes. I never overcame this, but rather reinforced it by further comparisons with my peers. One day Lonnie followed me to the bathroom and inspected me while I was urinating. He expressed surprise that I did not "have as much" as the smallest fellow in the scout troop. In fact, one of our scouts, the same one I had refused to fight in the fifth grade, used to carry a ruler in his pocket and coax people into betting a dollar that his penis was not 11½ inches "on the soft." I was somewhat comforted by the fact that the ministry did not require macho characteristics. In fact, it began to appear to me that the ministry was a creditable refuge for all kinds of puritan values.

It had also disturbed me that my mother told me that during my third grade panic experience when the neighbor was scalped, I would wake up screaming in the night and she would take me in her bed to sleep. I had not remembered this at all. Years earlier she had customarily taken me to the outhouse with her. Here I noticed that she had what appeared to me a small penis, comparable to mine. I wondered if I were deformed. At the age of eleven, my father had me circumcised at Lincoln Hospital by my father-in-law to be. Strangely, I had no conscious feeling of castration anxiety, but was tearful as well as fearful while being prepped. I remember asking my mother to kiss me before I died. The nurse laughed. On the operating table I asked to urinate. "As clear as a crystal," was the remark I heard twice about the specimen. While taking the ether I had the feeling of falling down a steel-lined well but never reaching the bottom. This memory became the content of many subsequent nightmares.

When the bandage was finally taken off of the surgical area, my mother demanded an inspection, which seemed to me to take too long. She added to my insecurity by commenting, "He certainly doesn't know how to cut meat." It appeared to me that my father had not been circumcised, yet there was no foreskin covering the glands. I asked, "Papa, you did not have to be circumcised, did you?" He said, "No." Therefore, I had been born with a disadvantage. I had been told that the operation was an aid to cleanliness and disease prevention. Yet, in one of the sex manuals my mother gave me to read, the doctor had written of the additional delight a man would experience in sexual intercourse if he could keep the glands covered by the foreskin until the moment of orgasm. This was a delight I would never know. So far as I could tell by casual observation, I was the only one in the troop who was circumcised.

My father did not talk to me about sex although he did speak of such things around older boys. One of my classmates told me my father told him one could get all he wanted for fifty cents at the warehouse in Petersburg when he was growing up. One day my mother, on the brink of tears, gave me several sex manuals written by doctors. She said her mother had told her nothing at all before she got married. She had painful memories of her enlightenment, both emotionally and physically. Until her wedding night, she thought the stork brought babies. My mother was small in stature; she weighed 98 pounds when she married and 75 pounds when she died.

There were many times during scout activities that we were not under close supervision. During those periods the older boys dominated the discussions with tales of sexual exploits. It seemed that three of them had been initiated into this kind of lifestyle by the same girl. Another of the scouts used to hide in the shrubbery near her porch to watch. Their standard remark about me was, "A piece of pussy and a glass of cold water would kill him."

I began to identify sexual activity with strength, aggressiveness, social acceptance and maturity, with sex as the key to it all. On the other hand I found much gratification in making better grades than they did, excelling in tennis and finding positive reinforcement in the small Pine Street Presbyterian congregation. It was also gratifying to make better grades than my sisters and brother. I was the family intellectual until we went to Fayetteville and were in the presence of my uncle.

There seemed to be little significance in becoming a teenager. It was not comparable to becoming twelve. Possibly the story of Jesus in the temple at the age of twelve had something to do with it. We had the picture at home. At that time, I thought the lawyers and doctors Jesus was answering questions for were LL.Bs and M.Ds. It is also strange that the representations of Jesus and the other biblical figures as White didn't seem to be a problem with anybody that I knew. It may have been my acceptance of the "White is right" philosophy. It may have been because we were told of the demonstrated concern by northern Presbyterians like Abraham Lincoln and Mrs. Johnson C. Smith (Although Lincoln was not really a card-carrying Presbyterian, we thought of him as such because of his attendance at New York Avenue Presbyterian Church when he was president).

The ninth grade found me even more enamored of Latin. The teacher, Miss Bass, was my mother's size, a genuine doll. She wore bangs and dresses with wide collars and pleated or puffed shoulders. Most of all I enjoyed the tests she gave. She would write a Latin passage from Caesar on the blackboard for us to translate. I remember once, when she began writing from "Post Mortem Orgetorix" (After the Death of Orgetorix), I finished my translation before she finished writing the passage on the blackboard.

A treasured memory of the ninth grade was my English class with Miss Long. She read us Henry Van Dykes' *The Other Wise Man*. It became then and continues to be my favorite Christmas story. I was a little resentful when she began the reading process. But she was so enamored of the story that we caught the feeling also. In later years, I appreciated the story even more when I found that Van Dyke was a Presbyterian and a Navy chaplain.

The only vexation I remember from this year was the algebra class with Miss Lanier. At the end of the first semester I received my only grade less than A that I had ever received. It was a B+. I thought that since our family had known the Laniers for a long time I would have been better treated. At the end of the second semester, there was another B+. I do not remember if I checked with my classmates to compare grades. My only negative thought about Miss Lanier was that she regularly wore open necked blouses, which to me looked like men's shirts. I preferred frills and lace for teachers. In any event, I began to feel negatively about algebra, a handicap that continues to this day.

This was the year that Mother decided that I should learn to dance. This interest seemed strange to me but I did not question it.

An Affirmation of Faith

I found one of the girls in church who would be willing to teach me and so began weekly lessons. She was proud of me when I went to a school dance and was able to dance once with one of my classmates. It was a stressful experience for me, as I did not relish the idea. As in the earlier grades, boys usually sat at the same desks with other boys and the girls did likewise. In the ninth grade the pattern was co-ed seating, which I found difficult to do.

Tenth grade at Hillside was the junior year. Three of the classes were fascinating for me: chemistry, biology and history. Chemistry was interesting because of the little lab experiments we had. I remember watching the sodium scooting through the water, the explanation of distillation and the making of a few compounds. Our teacher, a member of the Algonquin Tennis Club, often wore a yellow tennis jacket from West Virginia State. He also organized the first football team that Hillside had in many years. It was a rag-tag but enthusiastic bunch. I suppose football had been cut out during the depression. The former Hillside coach was coaching at the college. He had been fired because Hillside beat everybody. Rumor had it that they beat the college, too.

Distillation interested me because we had at least a half dozen bootleggers on our side of the tracks. Two of them belonged to our church, and they normally came to church in separate cars in case police decided to give chase. In those days, a car carrying non-taxed whiskey was confiscated and the occupants went to jail. Our chemistry teacher told us of going to his first teaching job in West Virginia where the locals took him out to see the still. They had pipes running under the sweet potato vines. Most of Durham's "moonshine" came from West Virginia. We held in awe the drivers who could elude the police through the West Virginia mountain roads. A "shooter" of whiskey was ten cents. Whiskey could be bought in the drug stores with a prescription. My dad's first stop when we went to Fayetteville would be at the doctor's office.

Although the bootleg establishments did get raided on rare occasions, I do not remember a raid taking place at either of the houses run by women. Both of them were in Hayti. Friday night was the big night because the tobacco factories paid on Friday. The bank was open half the day on Saturday. When the ABC stores were opened the bootleggers were not worried because the ABC stores would not wait until Friday to get paid. The community grocery stores operated on credit also. Two brothers, who worked at one of the factories, operated slush funds. They charged two dollars for a five-dollar loan. They drove twin black Oldsmobiles.

My fascination with biology was due to the teacher, who had come to Durham from Cincinnati. We were thrilled to know that he knew the Mills brothers. They were the rage then, along with Cab Calloway. One of my classmates was good at imitating Cab Calloway and was called upon to perform frequently.

History was also interesting because of the teacher. If the term had been in use then she would have been called a "glamour gal." She had the only raccoon coat on our side of the tracks. She disturbed me one day in class when she remarked that one believed in Sunday school and church until college days, and then didn't believe anymore.

The pressure to socialize increased. The junior-senior prom was coming up and I felt obligated to attend. With some timidity, I asked one of my classmates to attend it with me; she quickly agreed. She wore a pink gown and a pink ribbon in her hair. I had the use of the Chrysler, so I thought everything was alright, until I got home. My parents asked me about my date. I knew nothing except her name, address and relative position in the class. They were upset about her address, the fact that they had never heard of her family and that I had not invited a more "respectable" girl. I was glad the prom was over.

My first attempt to find a girlfriend failed because of that same kind of thinking on their part. She lived within a mile of us, but her dad worked in the tobacco factory. Sadly, I broke off the relationship with a full explanation. When I finally found someone willing and acceptable from a ninth grade class, she was harassed by friends of the rejected one. Nevertheless, we dated for several years, thus meeting societal expectations.

The Algonquin Tennis Club was unique for a Black community. Those who played tennis in Raleigh played on Dr. McCauley's court; in Fayetteville it was at St. Joseph's Episcopal Church; in Louisburg, Dr. Furlong had a court; in Roanoke the Drs. Downing did. In Lynchburg, Dr. "Whirlwind" Johnson, who trained Althea Gibson years later and lived to see her win at Wimbledon, was the patron. The Algonquin Club had first two, then three clay courts, a fulltime groundskeeper called "Lightning," because he talked and moved so slowly, a kitchen, and social halls in the clubhouse. It was there that all of the teen and many of the adult dances and other social functions were held. My dad was a member so I was eligible to play.

Every year Algonquin hosted a tournament, which attracted players from most of the eastern seaboard. There was always a junior section. I was a part of the winning doubles team one year and was written up in the Carolina Times. As was the case with the Boy Scouts and the dedicated leadership of Mr. Pendarvis and Dr. Evans, at the Algonquin, Mrs. B.A.J. Whitted, cashier of North Carolina Mutual and my mother's classmate at Kittrell College, made us her special project. "Miss Bessie" ran the tournaments, the dances, watched over us at all events, and saw that nobody and nothing got out of hand. With just a few exceptions, Blacks were not permitted to play in White tournaments. Somebody told me that Dr. Reginald Wier, who years later defeated me in a Black national tournament at Wilberforce University, had once won a New York open tournament.

In 1935, however, tennis segregation was complete. Nathaniel and Frank Jackson were the national champions. They, the Downings and the McGriffes of Portsmouth, Hubert Eaton and Harmon Fitch, the Black college champion, were regular visitors at the Algonquin. Regularly written about in the Black press, they provided inspiration for us.

The Algonquin was also the place for Black out-of-town visitors to appear. Possibly the most spectacular was Gretchen Branch, prodigy daughter of the Presbyterian pastor in Fayetteville. She was an accomplished violinist and concert vocalist while still in her teens. I remember the day she came to the Algonquin driving a cream colored Packard, wearing a cream suit and accessories. She now owns two funeral homes in the Philadelphia area.

My senior year at Hillside (1935-36) was memorable. The class I remember best was public speaking. I planned to make my speech on Isaiah 40:31, *"But they that wait upon the Lord shall renew their strength; they shall mount up with wings as eagles; they shall run, and not be weary; and they shall walk, and not faint."* The teacher saved my presentation until last, and then announced that my speech would be a sermon. It was the shortest sermon I ever preached, followed by an evaluation by the teacher and her theory on how I forgot most of it.

Therefore, our class sponsor for our graduation exercises decided not to take any chances on my valedictory speech. When I hedged on memorizing it, she had it memorized by another classmate and threatened to replace me if I failed to memorize it. Commencement was not held in the Hillside auditorium but in the Carolina Theatre downtown. For just this one time each year Blacks could sit on the main floor instead of in the colored balcony only. It was often called the "peanut gallery" or the "buzzard's roost." When I looked out over the footlights at what to me seemed a vast audience, I was fortunate that I had memorized the speech. At our 47th class reunion when I was making the banquet address, our sponsor was present, and I recounted our struggle. I also visited her at Duke Hospital two years later when she was terminally ill.

1936 was also the year driver's licenses were required in North Carolina. The legal age for drivers was 16, my age at the time. The law allowed licenses to be given without examination for those who had been driving four years. Since I had been driving since I was 12 I tried to escape the examination, but was told I could not since I was underage during those years. Fortunately, I remembered hearing a casual acquaintance say he had failed his test by making a U-turn at Five Points as directed by the examining policeman. When the examiner tried that same stunt on me I objected, saying it was against the law.

College Years

My largest graduation gift was $1,000 from my uncle, to see me through college. Tuition at his college was $36 per year; in Durham it was $75, so his gift seemed astronomical. In fact, I got through college and seminary with about $600 and several scholarships. I had planned to go to Johnson C. Smith University in Charlotte, the *alma mater* of my grandfather and uncle, but my parents asked me to become manager of Service Printing Company, the family business and the only Black print shop in town.

My father was quite impressed by Mr. McDougald, cashier of Mechanics and Farmers Bank, where my dad was trust officer. Mr. McDougald owned the Home Modernization Company and told my dad it would be advisable to own some kind of business in addition to his position at the bank, the N.C. Mutual, and his Real Estate Corporation. Therefore, he made an agreement with the *Carolina Times* to buy its job printing equipment, with the stipulation that the newspaper would no longer do any job printing and Service Printing Company would not go into the newspaper business. At my parents' request I left the Loftin Bakery where I had been working after school and learned the printing trade by working at it.

Mr. William Louis Loftin and his wife had come from Kinston, NC where they were employed by the local White bakery. Each of them borrowed $500 on N.C. Mutual Insurance policies, came to Durham, and opened a bakery in Hayti. I think Mr. Loftin was the most energetic man I ever met. In Kinston he had become interested in music, so began taking voice, piano and saxophone lessons from the same teacher. I heard him play piano and sing quite impressively for one who started so late. He complained to me that the jealousy of Mrs. Loftin and the very vivacious and beautiful teacher's husband caused him to give up his career in music. Their suspicions were groundless, or so he told me.

I began to learn the baking trade and was soon put on a commission basis to sell baked goods after normal shopping hours. I concentrated on the Friday night factory workers pay night and the Saturday "farmers coming to town" trade. I kept the oven on so that when the drunks came in asking what I had hot I could reply, "What do you want hot?" It only took a few minutes to heat whatever they liked.

Being local, the Loftins relied heavily upon me for advice. For some unknown reason they insisted on calling me "Jack." I suggested that they buy a flashy truck for bread delivery with the Loftin name in large two-color letters and drive a flashy car to create an image of success. I was just about to take over the delivery route when I had to move to the printing business. Fortunately, the print shop was in the same block so our consultations could continue.

Mr. Loftin wanted others to rush. When I protested that there was plenty of time to do what was needed, he said he would rather I rush through it, then sit down. I should do a job as best as I could, then, as fast as I could. He cracked eggs with both hands at the same time by cracking the eggs on the table and spreading the shells open as he dropped the yolks into a quart measure. Bakery recipes called for eggs by the quart, flour by the pound. We greased the baking pans with a cloth, thus wiping out any crumbs left from the last use instead of washing them. I enjoyed filling the doughnuts with jelly until Mr. Loftin noticed that I punctured the doughnuts twice to spread the jelly completely throughout the doughnut rather than on one side only. The machine worked like a hypodermic with a handle; I pushed down to squirt the jelly. It was instant jelly, made by pouring hot water into jelly powder in a wooden bucket. My favorite concoction was hot coconut pie topped with two inches of whipped cream.

Pans were put into and removed from the oven with a long handled spoon. It was my job to remove baked goods at the proper time, so I brought in an alarm clock. Mr. Loftin objected to the clock, saying I should know when to take things out. One day some cinnamon rolls with jelly topping burned. He would not allow the use of the term "burned," we had to say, "a little too brown." He took the pan from the oven and dashed it against the oven door, then told me to clean up the mess. I liked to bake eggs in a small round pan. One day when he saw me coming toward the oven he took the paddle, removed the little round pan and slammed it against the oven door. I rushed to the oven to find that he had substituted an empty pan for my eggs.

In North Carolina food establishments get inspected and the rating has to hang on the wall where customers can see it. We had an "A" rating. One day when the inspector came in, I was sweeping the floor. He said if I had not been sweeping at the time, he would have lowered our grade to "B." Thereafter, I could do no wrong. I thought it was providential because business might have failed with the reduced rating. The inspectors were serious. When I was working part-time as a dishwasher in Farmer's Cafe, I was told the cafe would lose its "A" if the inspector caught me wiping a dish.

Thirty years later when I was promoted to Navy Captain I got word that the Loftins had moved some years before to Virginia State College. They had read of me through the years and had my picture on the wall.

It was a heady experience to be manager of the Service Printing Company at 16. When business was good my salary was $15 per week. I paid my help ten cents an hour; my brother, Leo Townsend, son of the college coach; Gerald Edwards, of the National Science Foundation; and Walter Swann, North Carolina tennis champion. For a while Monroe Taylor remained with us. He had worked for the former manager, LeOtis Bracia, and had printed his own business cards showing himself to be the manager. I resented this at first, then obliquely confronted him about it and said, I thought it would be good to hold onto customers he knew well.

Mr. Bracia had been at the *Carolina Times* when Papa bought the job printing equipment, so he was hired as the first manager of Service Printing Company. When business did not develop as expected he moved from his rooming house to our home and took

An Affirmation of Faith

his meals with us to save money. When this really did not solve the problem, it seemed I was the best alternative.

It was taxing to run the print shop and keep up an "A" average in college. Since I was getting up at 6:30 a.m. anyway, to heat the house and cook the oatmeal, I began to get up at 4 a.m. to study. In the old days I could do my Latin while listening to Benny Goodman's half hour program. When he signed off with "Goodbye," I had finished. College courses required more concentration. Our house was closer to the classroom building than the boys' dormitory. The outdoor bell, which is still there, rang at 7:50 a.m. I could dress and get to school in time for class after the bell rang. If I happened to have the car, I parked just to the right of the entrance, otherwise I walked. Students who lived on campus could not keep cars. Bill Stafford who lived in Gary drove to Durham in a Model A Ford in September with Jake Blake, Melvin Sykes and his sister. Then he drained the radiator, disconnected the battery and put blocks under the axles. In June he filled the radiator, connected the battery, inflated the tires and drove back to Gary.

It was also against the rules for the campus girls to ride in cars. One day when I had given three of them a ride in the back seat they spotted the dean of women coming from the opposite direction. In a reflex movement they bowed from the waist behind the back of the front seat while I smiled at the dean in passing. I suspect she saw them but was being kind to me. On another occasion during an examination in her class, when I was tipped back in my chair, with the writing arm elevated so a classmate sitting behind me could read my answers, the dean simply walked over and pushed my hand down so the chair rested on all four legs. I had gone on a date with this classmate to the Carolina Theatre. We had walked both ways, so the whole evening, including milkshakes, had cost only two dollars. When we got to her door she blew me a kiss.

1936 was the year I entered the social security program. It came with a host of Roosevelt innovations designed for the general welfare. Until social security the only retirement plans we knew of were for railroad workers, government workers in Washington, Presbyterian and Episcopal clergy. We knew only two railroad workers, both firemen, one a Mr. Allen who had lived across the street from St. Titus Episcopal Church. I happened to be going down the street on my bicycle when they brought him home with his fatal heart attack. Mr. Trice, who lived with the Cox family across the street from us, was the other. I remember the time I was crossing the railroad tracks and saw him actually driving an engine with no cars connected. Blacks were not permitted to be engineers or conductors. The Cox son used to disturb us, when he got locked out of the house, by shooting into the air to wake someone to let him in. His marksmanship was useful to us one November day when our Thanksgiving turkey flew to the top branches of a tall pine tree. He brought him down handily.

Service Printing Company gave me prestige at the college. When the freshman class wanted me to be its president I declined, giving as excuse my business responsibilities. I often wore an oxford grey coat with hickory-striped trousers, nearly formal attire in those days. I frequented the pawnshops, picking up a double-breasted tuxedo for $15 and a single-breasted dinner jacket, a camel hair coat that I wore for 15 years. I watched for sales at the men's stores, particularly for pique bosomed formal shirts and starched collars. When we had company at home I would often wear a formal shirt and dinner jacket.

The college president, Dr. Shepard, who was also an ordained Baptist preacher, advised me to major in English and plan to go to Gammon, the Methodist Black seminary in Atlanta. When Adam Clayton Powell, Jr., congressman from New York and pastor of Abyssinia Baptist Church, the largest Black congregation, advised me to go to Virginia Union in Richmond, I took a dim view of his advice because he had gone to Colgate-Rochester, so I suspected he was belittling me. Now I imagine that having finished an eleven-grade high school and attending a non-accredited college, he was thinking more practically than I thought.

I did major in English, minored in history and joined the little symphony as second violinist. The college had hired Miss Margaret Demond as band director. As an Indiana resident, she had contacts that allowed her to bring the band with her.

The band members were quite popular on campus. Jake Blake organized a dance band to play commercially in the community. I was told I would not be useful to them because a violin did not make enough noise. My 8 p.m. bedtime would make this impossible anyway.

My religious involvement stepped up its pace. With my two sisters and brother, the Parham quartet was formed. The first number we learned was the familiar, "God So Loved the World." We sang it at an afternoon program at our church. It was common for churches then to have afternoon programs with musical selections by soloists, quartets or choirs and speeches or sermons by distinguished visitors. We really thought we had scooped the other churches when we booked Dr. Frank Porter Graham, president of the University of North Carolina at Chapel Hill. We were keenly disappointed when he did not appear. We assumed it was an oversight or a conflict in schedule.

I was invited to speak at a youth rally at the Hayes-Taylor YMCA in Greensboro. The building was made possible by a gift from the Cone family and was named for their two Black butlers. I preached at my own church and arranged for another of the NCC students to preach on Youth Sunday. When I was invited by Dr. Miles Mark Fisher to preach at White Rock Baptist Church at an evening service, my grandmother sent a telegram from Fayetteville. Telegrams and long distance telephone calls in those days were reserved for very important occasions or death. A customary part of the funeral service then was the reading of telegrams.

Dr. Fisher was an important role model for me. Except for Lincoln Hospital he was my best customer at Service Printing Company. In those days, before junk mail, a form letter was gladly received. He had a mailing list of 1500 and also used imprinted envelopes. He sent quarterly statements of contributions on forms we printed. My last job on Saturday was the White Rock Sunday bulletin, which carried advertisements of businesses owned by White Rock members, on the back page. Sometimes, when we were behind in our work, the White Rock Bulletin might not be finished until 9 a.m. Sunday morning. In such times I would still go to Sunday school and church, then get to bed after dinner and sleep until morning.

Dr. Fisher had a Ph.D. from the University of Chicago in church history. His dissertation on the Spirituals caused some controversy in Durham because he treated them as code songs. "Steal Away to Jesus," actually meant someone was going to escape. He said his grandmother had 22 children and was used by her owner as a breeder. He told me that I would have to become a Baptist or a Methodist if I intended to lead Negroes. There was a saying then that if a Negro did not belong to one of these two denominations, his religion had been tampered with. So when I went to seminary I majored in church history, joined the segregated Navy where I could be a Protestant chaplain for Black Baptist and Methodist sailors without making a switch. After World War II, I also entered the Ph.D. program at Chicago, majoring in church history. One of my classmates was Miles Mark Fisher, IV. When my mother died 44 years later I used as mortician "Pookey" Fisher instead of Ellis Jones, my classmate, or Scarboro, who buried my grandmother.

We did not get any business from the N.C. Mutual because it had a multigraph department that did all of the company work. We did very little for the bank because the Hunt Printing Company was next door in a building owned by the bank. We also had competition from the Norfolk Journal and Guide. But we did the printing for nearly all Black businesses, churches and professionals. We also did a brisk business with dance promoters, touring entertainers, markets run by Jews and some small White businesses. It was correctly assumed that our prices would be lower. My brother and his classmate earned only ten cents an hour.

The dance promoters used tobacco warehouses and booked name bands. The Regal Theatre booked prominent entertainers. I met Louis Armstrong, "Ma" Whitman of the Whitman Sisters, heard Ella Fitzgerald and Fats Waller at close range, and watched Mary Lou Williams do some arranging during intermission. We printed souvenir programs for the dances that carried more advertisements than pictures or copy. My most memorable religious experience in several decades involved the rough copy for one of those souvenir programs.

John Alan Foushee and Lindsay "Shorty" Davis had sold the ads for this program. It was summer, so I was wearing slacks and a polo shirt. When I went home by bicycle that evening I had the rough copy in my left shirt pocket. When I got home it was gone. Since it was past sunset I decided not to retrace my steps to find it. It was an emergency of the first magnitude, however, because there was no other record of who the advertisers were or the copy for their ads. If the two salesmen could remember whom they sold to they might take second thoughts about furnishing copy a second time and likely forget the whole thing. Furthermore, as usual the job had to be done the next day. I prayed that night as I never had before. The next morning at daybreak, before traffic got moving, I did retrace my route very slowly on the left-hand side of the street. I was halfway to the office when my heart sank; I met the street sweeper with the large rear brush, the two side brushes and sprinkler. Nevertheless, I continued to push on in near panic. Just two blocks later in front of the house of Dr. A.S. Hunter there was a dry spot. A car had been parked there when the sweeper came by. Before I got there the car was gone. In the middle of the dry spot was that piece of green paper, neatly folded. My joy and relief were indescribable.

Even today when I see a street sweeper I go into orbit. My eyes are brimming with tears even as I write this. I have told this story in every church and chapel to which I have been assigned. Since that time I have never doubted the willingness or the power of God to answer prayer. It was as though the Lord handed me that piece of paper on a silver platter. My feeling is that the Lord arranged for the car to cover the sheet soon after I dropped it and remain over it until the sweeper passed, then to move away slowly so a draft would not be created and to do so just before I arrived at the spot. There was also the need to keep the wind to a minimum all night and not to allow it to rain. I do not think Moses was any more relieved when the waters of the Red Sea parted or was Elijah more gratified when the Lord sent fire from heaven to burn up his sacrifice on Mount Carmel.

My second year of college was a disaster. One day when I was telling Mr. H.M. Michaux, head of the Union Insurance and Realty Company, about my schedule he said, "It will make a man out of you, but it might make a dead one." Soon afterward I came up with a headache, which lasted a week with no indication of abating. Dr. Evans gave me a chiropractic adjustment. Dr. Cordice told me to go

An Affirmation of Faith

to bed and stay there for at least a month. I withdrew from school and gave up Service Printing Company.

Fortunately for the company, there were two recent graduates of the Tuskegee printing curriculum in Durham, Joe E. Dillard and Julian Richardson. They and others were involved in a new enterprise, raising chickens for sale to hotels and restaurant hoping to be able to cut costs by raising their own feed and thus undercut competition. At the same time, other Tuskegee graduates came to set up our first photography studio; "Reuben and Rudolph," C. Reuben Freeman, C. Rudolph Stanback and E. Crescent Gleed. Richardson agreed to manage the print shop and moved into our home. Not long afterward, the company was sold to the White brothers, Nathaniel and George, who had finished printing at Hampton Institute. Service Printing Company was the last business to survive on Pettigrew Street until it was destroyed by fire in 1985. Dillard now runs a store in Durham; Stanback is still running a studio.

It was decided that it would be good for me to go to Fayetteville and stay with my grandmother. She did have a student living in the house with her, Claude Young of Louisburg. Since we were the same age and had similar interests we practically became brothers. It was a very pleasant six months for me since my uncle was president of the college. I drove for him, particularly at night, because his eyes were not the best. He used a magnifying glass to read the newspapers at times. In addition to the *Greensboro Observer, the Raleigh News* and *Observer*, he also subscribed to the *New York Times* as well as the *Fayetteville Observer*.

The *Fayetteville Observer* used to have a column titled "50 Years Ago." One day's article was on six vagrants who were arrested, three Whites who signed their names with an "X." The three Blacks could write their names, to the surprise of the police. When questioned they explained that they had learn to write at Dr. Smith's school out on Murchison Road. It was the predecessor of the college of which Dr. Smith was the first president. He hired my uncle as dean with right of succession and kept his word 22 years later. When Uncle retired, he was able to say that no graduate of the college had ever been jailed. The protest movement of the 60s was still a few years off.

An Affirmation of Faith

Uncle had the best mind in the family. He remembered his Latin and Greek with ease. When he finished Johnson C. Smith, in 1909, one of the requirements was a Latin oration. He used to listen to Hitler by shortwave because he admired his German oratory style. When the choir sang a translation of a Homeric poem, Uncle recited it on the spot in Latin. He told me that his philosophy teacher at Columbia did not like him but had to give him As anyway because his work was flawless. One night when I failed to decipher a scrambled word in a magazine puzzle, Uncle solved it instantaneously as the directions said a genius could do.

It was stimulating to be in his company. I enjoyed driving him to high school commencements for which he was the speaker. One night I saw him produce a speech from scratch after he got on the platform and saw the people in the audience. He decided they would not understand the speech he had written. A farmer who had a daughter at the college had invited us to dinner. One of the children stood at a corner of the table and fanned the flies away with a long stick on which was pasted streamers made of newspaper. Our host was anxious to be sure, Uncle understood that farming people need their children at planting and harvest times. It was the practice in rural areas to close schools at those two times and to open schools for several weeks in the summer.

Aunt Mae, Uncle's wife, was ideal for him. She was a close friend of his first wife, Aunt Mamie, who died with her son in childbirth after a fall down the back steps of the dean's residence. Grandmother somehow resented Aunt Mae's taking Aunt Mamie's place, but Aunt Mae never showed any anger or hostility because of it. I never heard Uncle call Aunt Mae by her name only; it was always "Mae Sweet" or "Mae Dear." She told me after his funeral that they never had an argument. He told me prominent speakers who made the circuit of the Black colleges always came to Fayetteville with delight because of her hospitality. Her handwriting slanted to the left, so she used to sign her correspondence to us, "Guess Who?" Aunt Mae is still the only one in the family with a Harvard degree. She taught biology at the college.

Males were at a premium on the campus. It was a teacher's college and teachers still are traditionally female. Therefore, I was as

An Affirmation of Faith

welcome on campus as a pig at a barbecue. The various clubs staggered their social functions so that the males would be available for each affair. Even then, the shortage was acute. Such a situation is, of course, ego supporting. Strict regulations kept most students out of trouble.

Two people outside of the family impressed me, the home economics teacher, Lula Lyles who later married Benjamin Booker of Durham, now a minister, and Dean Mays. Lula was such a radiant person as well as a striking beauty. Dean Mays was as my grandmother put it "the soul of thoughtfulness." He was my first example of positive reinforcement among supervisors. When any group did anything constructive, there would be a card on the bulletin board the next day signed by the dean and commending the group for its contribution.

So the fall of 1938 found me quite recovered and anxious to make up for lost time so that I could graduate before my 21st birthday. I also wanted to graduate *summa cum laude* in spite of the "F" in political science caused by cutting the class 22 times and the "F" in physical education caused by my lack of talent except in tennis (the school did not have a tennis team) and I suspected, by the teacher's and my common interest in the same girl.

Without the responsibilities of the Service Printing Company, I had more time for campus activities. I joined my dad's fraternity, Kappa Alpha Psi, and was elected editor of the campus newspaper, which was not published because of lack of funds. The next year one of the teachers brought out some issues by selling advertisements. I continued to look for opportunities to preach.

At a Mebane Presbyterian Church, I found the pulpit Bible and chair wet from the Saturday night rain. The situation was ameliorated for me when I found one of my mother's classmates on hand. I was inspired by the chemistry teacher, Noble Peyton, who became practically an atheist in college but regained his faith in graduate school and began considering the ministry as he went into the Ph.D. program. One day he lit a pile of sulphur on his lab table. When the fumes had us coughing he dismissed the class after he said, "This is the fire and brimstone the Bible talks about."

An Affirmation of Faith

Two new role models came into my life: the first was Rev. W. Tycer Nelson, the new pastor of our church, and the Rev. William Randolph Johnson, an employee in the social service division of the state department in Raleigh. Rev. Nelson was quite a contrast with our former pastor, Dr. Avant, whose daughter he married possibly his second year in Durham. Dr. Avant was 65; an old football injury caused his right hand to shake. He was not a dynamic preacher, having been an Episcopalian, then a Congregationalist, before coming to us. He was also the principal of Pearsontown School. Rev. Nelson was in his 20s, the son of an old admirer of my mother's pastor of Goodwill, the largest Black Presbyterian Church in South Carolina, with 1,000 members. He was tall with arms so long his shirtsleeves had to be pieced and quite dynamic with a good singing voice.

He saw to it that I was elected a deacon, ordained me and gave me my first Greek lesson. He received permission from the church to work on a Master's at the University of Pittsburgh, returning to Durham some weekends. In those days, one could go to Pittsburgh on the train with a clergy permit for about $10, including a Pullman berth. While he was out of town, I was his man Friday around the church.

On most of the Sundays that Rev. Nelson did not return, Rev. Johnson preached for us. He was more dynamic, dramatic and emotional. I still remember vividly his sermon on Saul on the Damascus road and have tried many times to reproduce it. When he preached, I hung onto his every word. A few years later after the war started and I was in seminary, I read a scathing editorial on him in the *Carolina Times*. Rev. Johnson had turned into the State Bureau of Investigation the name of someone he suspected of being a spy for the other side. Louis Austin said, "Everybody knows, including 'The Reverunt,' that no Negro has ever been disloyal to this country." Rev. Johnson was fired. I wrote him a letter expressing concern. He sent me copies of commendations by Thad Eure, Secretary of State, and others. Years ago, I read in a magazine of a William Randolph Johnson in an executive position of a tobacco company in Richmond. I wrote to him expressing my appreciation of his father as I assumed. He replied saying that his father was dead but he was forwarding my letter to his mother.

Rev. Nelson lived in the seminary dormitory in Pittsburgh and took some of his classes at the seminary. He prepared the way for me to enroll there. At the same time, my mother-in-law to be arranged an interview for me with Bishop Penic of the Episcopal Church because there was a shortage of Black priests. In fact, there was a feeling that there was no replacement in sight for Bishop Lanier who was retiring. I liked the St. Titus Church, where I was later married, and the rector, the Rev. Mr. Othello Doremus Stanley. I told the Bishop I would switch if he would get me a scholarship to Harvard. He countered with an offer of the Episcopal Seminary at Cambridge. To me it seemed a case of so near, yet so far. We parted in disagreement with his saying that it would be different if I were one of his own sons. I wondered if he would come up with Harvard if I switched first but didn't ask.

The senior year at North Carolina College (now North Carolina Central University) was frustrating in that I learned there would be no possibility of making summa cum laude. At NCC if one repeats a course and makes an "A" the second time, it does not replace the "F," but brings it up to a "C." As far as I knew, Eunice Rhoda Belle McClain had no mark lower than "A." However, I did complete all my required courses before my 21st birthday.

At this point, it seemed inevitable that we would go to war. My grandfather and my uncle had served during the war. I heard the Army was commissioning chaplains who had not gone to seminary. When I talked with my major professor about it, she said I should be more concerned with the needs of the soldiers than with my own wishes. I interpreted this as a slur. My attitude toward her was somewhat ambivalent anyway because she was so insistent about how inhumane the doctrine of predestination was and I knew Presbyterians believed in it. My appreciation for Dr. Newton really grew when I began preaching regularly. She had us memorize poetry so our minds would be full of beautiful thoughts. I have recited that poetry in sermons for years.

Disappointment came over my plans for the Army. Although non-seminarians were being commissioned, they had to be 24 years old, ordained, with four years of pastoral experience. I could not be ordained until seminary graduation, at which time I would be 24, but then I could qualify for the Navy, my preference. Since seminary would not have an entering class until fall, I registered in the graduate school, taking courses in John Milton, rural sociology, and one in race relations taught by Dr. N.C. Newbold, a White friend of my uncle after whom the nearest elementary school to the Fayetteville campus was named.

The graduate courses were scheduled in the afternoons and evenings for the convenience of local schoolteachers, the professors from Duke and Carolina and others who might be working during the day. Also taking graduate courses was Rivera Mitchell, who had come for law school, which had not opened as scheduled. I attended an orientation session led by Dean Van Hecke of the Carolina Law School. He gave us a sample problem to find the flaw in the statement of a man who said he found a coin dated 5004 B.C. The obvious solution that did not occur to me was that nobody would use B.C. before Christ appeared. I decided I had better not entertain thoughts of law. Furthermore, at that time I accepted the myths about lawyers as liars and crooks. We had a good example of this one block from our house. The lawyer was disbarred for deceiving a client who could not read. His defense was, "The whole legal profession is not above reproach."

Rev. Nelson was insistent that I go to Western Theological Seminary where he was taking a few courses and living in the dormitory while getting a M.Ed. in sociology at the University of Pittsburgh. I began saving for the first year by working in the meat department of the Big Star store at Five Points. My job was to clean and cut up chickens, grind sausage and hamburger, and act as a general "gofer" and do some cleaning. It was a better job than the previous temporary one at the Farmer's Cafe washing dishes, a washtub full at a time. There was a jukebox at the cafe that played, "You are my Sunshine" many times a day. It was the time of tobacco harvest. The cafe was across the street from one of the warehouses.

The cleanliness of the cafe was impressive. I was not allowed to dry a dish or a piece of silver. The dishes were placed in a deep sink. Then I hung a bucketful of strong soap in bars over the faucet

An Affirmation of Faith

and turned on the hot water full force. The bucket was full of holes so the hot soapy water poured out easily taking all food still sticking to the plates. I let the water out and stacked the plates in a wooden rack on the sink's drain board. Then I hosed them down with more scalding water, leaving them practically dry. I put the silverware in a larger bucket filled with holes, filled the sink again with hot soapy water, then vigorously shook the bucket in the soapy water until all food was gone. Then I hosed the bucket down with scalding water. This was a continuous operation.

The supermarket was interesting. My boss, Mr. C.A. Klutz, was sharp. He told me his salary was the same as the store manager's. I heard him refer to Mr. Richard Fowler, a barber in a shop nearby as "the nigger barber," and overheard him ask his assistant manager on returning from an errand if they "kept the niggers busy."

He surprised me by borrowing $15 and giving me his portable typewriter for security. I was disappointed when he repaid me several weeks later, since I did hope to take it to seminary instead of the Underwood upright that I had gotten in a pawnshop for $10. It was understood that I was not to wait on customers, although some of them would have preferred to have me serve them rather than to wait their turns. The meat had to be weighed, wrapped and priced, supposedly beyond a Black's capacity, certainly out of his place. I enjoyed the frustration of those who were inconvenienced by this system.

At times, Mr. Klutz would help me with the chickens when I got behind. I could cut up a chicken in one minute using a steak knife commonly known as a butcher knife. The butchers used a boning knife instead, about the size of a fruit knife. I was proud of the way I could whack a chicken breast in half, with half of the breastbone on each side. One day when Mr. Klutz was helping me, I unknowingly nicked the back of his hand. He asked if I knew I cut him. I said I did not and apologized. He said, "That's all right," and kept cutting with blood running down his hand.

The heads, feet and guts were dumped into large trashcans to be taken out behind the store. The owner of the Greek restaurant next door had permission to get as much of these items as he liked without paying. He used to come in, stand by me and help himself,

An Affirmation of Faith

using a meat tray that would hold about two pounds. I will never forget how sadly he would say, "Somebody could eat all of this." According to the news, there was not a cat, dog, or rat left in Greece; all had been eaten in a war occasioned food shortage.

Another interesting experience at the supermarket was the amount of listening that I did to the boss, the assistant manager, the butchers and the salesmen. They told me of their sexual exploits. One of them, Jimmie, talked a better game than all the rest, having serviced women in 45 of the then 48 states, all of the women married except for two. I heard him ask a customer when her husband was going to be out of town again. I saw another blush when he called her "Little Lady." Mrs. Chandler, who ran a boarding house, would not let anyone wait on her but Jimmie. One Saturday, Mr. Klutz had the checkout man handling Mrs. Chandler's meat to bring it back to be weighed. Jimmie had definitely under priced everything she bought, so he was fired. This was a relief to me because he was hostile to Mr. Klutz and told me that he would kill him if Mr. Klutz found the steak knife Jimmie kept hidden so nobody else would use it. I knew where it was hidden because I watched him retrieve it one day. How he was sure I would not tell the boss is a mystery to me. I tried to talk him out of the killing notion, but he said, "It's not wrong to kill the bastard." His excuse for his sexual exploits was that he was "keeping the home fires burning."

Mr. Klutz had a protégé named Rudisill working as a butcher who wanted to replace Mr. Walters as "box man." The box man worked in the cutting room all day, breaking down halves of beef and pork into the various roasts, steaks and chops. The temperature in the box was 40 degrees. I used to wear fur-lined leather gloves. Mr. Walters used antifreeze (alcohol), sometimes to excess. One afternoon after he had imbibed too much I heard Rudisill tell him, "F—k you Walters." Mr. Walters came unglued and began to whine. Mr. Klutz told Rudisill to apologize; Walters refused to take his extended hand, retreated into his box and cried, "F—k'em all." Rudisill and Walters were transferred to other stores in the chain.

The job occasioned many guilt feelings for me. In the first place, Mr. Klutz ordered me to put only half the chicken liver on the customer's tray, collecting the stolen halves on another tray to be sold separately. He would often come into the kitchen to ask how the livers were coming. Then I was to grind up all the molded bacon and hot dogs in the sausage. Into the sausage also went scraps of fat, which I kept soaking in water. The water clung to the fat, making the sausage weigh more. Bread and tomato juice (to keep it red) went into the hamburger. The butchers and clerks were adept at throwing meat on the scale and pricing it on the downswing to get a higher price. It looked as though they were just moving swiftly. The memorable incident involved a Thanksgiving turkey that was sold as a fresh turkey for Christmas to Miss Fannie Rosser, angel of the *Carolina Times*, an employee of the N.C. Mutual. The turkey started to smell before she got it home on the bus. She brought it back, much to Mr. Klutz's embarrassment. He cut the turkey up, froze it in salt water, and two weeks later took it out and cooked it for turkey salad in the delicatessen counter.

I rationalized my involvement in such dishonest procedures by reminding myself that I had no choice but to obey the boss, particularly since he was White. I was reminded of the sense of outrage Durham Blacks felt when Mr. Ramseur only got life imprisonment for having a Black kill his wife whereas the Black who cut her down with a shotgun through the screen door was electrocuted. My guilt continued to nag me; I was ashamed to go to church, but went anyway.

Seminary

Therefore, I was glad when September came and I left to go to Pittsburgh for seminary. I was able to pass my job to my "little brother," but he developed an allergy to chickens that persisted even when he wore rubber gloves. Last year I went to another Big Star in Durham, at a nearby location (the one where I worked was replaced by a business college). The butcher there had never heard of any of my coworkers. I never saw any of them again.

At the same time that I was working at Big Star, I was also working for "Sister Julia." Her husband, Dr. Warren, died that year soon after Professor Hawkins died. Both had colonostomies. It appeared that Dr. Warren was hopeful as long as Professor Hawkins lived. We knew that Dr. Warren was failing when we saw Dr. McCauley's car at the house. Dr. Mills, the attending physician, usually called Dr. McCauley from Raleigh in critical situations. Sister Julia replaced Dr. Warren's 1932 Chevrolet with a new Packard 120 and asked me to drive it for her. I tried to teach her to drive but she gave it up after running into a ditch in the cemetery, out of which she had to be towed.

The busy day was Sunday, beginning with Sunday school at St. Joseph's A.M.E. Church. Dr. Stephen Wright of the college directed the orchestra. He later became president of Fisk University, then president of the United Negro College Fund. I played second violin in the orchestra. At church time I went to Pine Street Presbyterian, getting back to St. Joseph's before the sermon ended. After church we went for a drive in the country, usually taking one of the widows with us, followed by dinner prepared by Sister Julia.

Erma Washington, a college student from Alabama, stayed at the house and served as a housekeeper and companion. She also went to Sunday school, for the rides and to the dinners. We began a superficial romantic interest, but I was reluctant because it seemed to me to be taking advantage of the situation. Sister Julia did not drink, but had a well-stocked cabinet of spirits; brandy for the fruitcake, champagne for the Jell-O, wine for the sweet potato casserole. The dinners were delicious.

I also did Sister Julia's correspondence for her. When her brother came from Canada to visit, I did his also. He was a retired Pullman porter, wore a Chesterfield coat with a velvet collar and pearl grey homburg hat. He had made a lot of money during the days of prohibition bringing in Canadian whiskey. I used to drive him to bootleggers' houses, and then pick him up later. His favorite was a widow who belonged to our church. Although she had expanded into the grocery business, she still sold a few drinks for old time's sake, although the ABC stores did most of the business.

I cannot remember any kind of salary from Sister Julia, but her generosity was unique. One day she gave me a check for $250, saying, "I know how stingy you are. When you get to Pittsburgh I want you to spend this for something foolish." I followed her advice partially by buying from Jose Medina, an upperclassman, a 1935 Ford roadster with a rumble seat for $50 and four recapped tires for $35. I paid Jose $25 down and $5 a month for five months. I so dreaded the coming of the first of the month that I promised myself I would never again buy a car on credit. I kept that promise until recently when interest rates on car notes dropped below interest income from investments. In addition, I got the tax deduction on the consumer interest. So I am still stingy.

Rev. Nelson loaned me his clergy permit so I went by Pullman to Pittsburgh for $10. He also alerted me to a vacant church in Youngstown Ohio, 60 miles from Pittsburgh, which could be reached by Pennsylvania and Lake Erie Railroad, roundtrip Sunday excursion for $1.25. Total cost of the seminary year was $329, reduced by a Presbyterian Board of Christian Education Scholarship of $100 and a seminary scholarship of $100, leaving $4 a week to be paid to the seminary. Before leaving Durham, I got a letter from the president, Dr. Kelso, suggesting that I make some preparation to pay my bills. I replied, "The Lord will provide." He wrote again that I should not come to Pittsburgh expecting some kind of miracle. Thereupon, I wrote him that I had $250 in the bank.

That $250 was imperiled one day when Papa brought in a promissory note from the bank for $200 for me to sign. He said I needed to establish credit for myself. Glad that I was 21, I refused the opportunity, reminding him it was all I had for the seminary. He was angry, disappointed; I was disgusted as well as angry. I remembered that he had insisted I take out a loan on the building and loan stock that Uncle gave me for college expenses, which loan had never been repaid. The money was used to buy a newspaper press for Service Printing Company and to repay him for money he had advanced for expenses. I felt relieved that this time he did not argue further, concluding the transaction with, "Well, good luck to you." I said to myself, "If I never come back to this place again it will be too soon."

The evening meal was being served in the third floor dining room when I arrived at Western Seminary. I stood in the dining room door transfixed; there was not another Black in the room. I heard invitations from each table, "Come on over and sit down." I had never sat with Whites anywhere; I had never eaten with any of them. At interracial conferences in Durham, the Blacks sat together in a corner. In my graduate classes at the college, the White teachers were behind their desks. My appetite was gone. Still my conditioning came to my aid. I did what I was told I sat down and ate.

From the first, I was befriended by George Slight Wilson, whose parents ran the company store in a nearby mining town. He said his parents did not allow him to use the word "nigger," that the family dentist was Dr. Garrett of Pittsburgh, a classmate of Uncle's at Johnson C. Smith. To my relief, I was not assigned a roommate. George spent so much time in my room that his roommate, Jack Greenawalt came to my room when he needed him. George and I shared confidences not shared with anyone else. I was the only one who knew it when he secretly married.

One other student, Albert Koontz, had no roommate; he lived next door to me. He was White but was so obnoxious that nobody wanted to room with him. It didn't seem to bother him. I was glad he never suggested we move together. Each suite had a large room for study between two bedrooms, separate bookcases, lamps and study tables so two people would not crowd a suite. Albert, whom we called "Koontz," in a manner that almost made it a cuss word, spent many hours standing in my door talking when both of us needed to be studying. He was chemistry major and had worked for Mine Safety Appliances Corporation in Pittsburgh. The students believed that his call to the ministry came from Uncle Sam rather than the Lord. Our class of 30 was twice the size of the class ahead of us. Seminary students were deferred from the draft. Koontz was fat, clumsy, and insisted he had to get along with people because he couldn't fight or run.

I knew his call was genuine. He wanted to be a missionary to China, and had worked at Mine Safety to get seminary expenses. He was learning Chinese, reading extensively in Chinese history and culture. Koontz liked to disagree. He was working on his senior thesis, an attempt to prove that Jesus did not descend into hell as the creed says. He argued that the Palm Sunday procession was a normal occurrence in which Jesus joined, rather than being the focal point. He carried around a Bible cover with no pages, saying it was all he had left after a course in textual criticism. He was in a running battle with the pastor of his church, Dr. Frederick Curtis Fowler, who was quite prominent in Pittsburgh. Although I felt imposed upon, I really liked him. Perhaps I felt he took a lot of guff I would have taken had he not been on the scene.

When he married after graduation, he brought Norma to visit me in Youngstown. I treasure the 8 X 10 enlargement of the three of us in front of the YMCA, where I lived. Soon afterward, they were both killed when he insisted upon passing a car on a curve going up a hill and met a truck. They were having problems in the marriage due to her extravagant shopping, buying lamb chops instead of pork chops. Their church had stopped his salary. They had painted over the walnut paneling in the parsonage with White enamel. I went with a few classmates to the wake. Koontz's mother welcomed me warmly because he had talked about me so much. She was wearing a hair net and did not seem to be grieving at all.

A study pattern from college days worked well at seminary. I got up at 4 a.m., studied until 8 a.m., got in an hour or so in the afternoon, and then went to bed at 8 p.m. In addition, we did not have classes on Monday or Friday, assuming that some students would be traveling from and to rural churches on those days. The weekly chapel was on Monday night. Since I did not go to Youngstown until Sunday morning and returned Sunday night, I had two extra study days, which I needed. Most of the students had finished church colleges, had taken courses in Bible, religious education, philosophy, and some even Greek. One classmate was a Greek major. All of these subjects were new to me. It was very difficult to learn Greek and Hebrew at the same time.

Pittsburgh was still a smoky city in 1941. Cars needed headlights on at all hours, except from 10 a.m. to 3 p.m. on foggy days. Clothes could not be hung outside. I used to blow little soot balls across my desk and watch the wind blow them back. A letter from a girlfriend in medical school in Michigan read "I was cutting up a cadaver the other day. He had Pittsburgh lung, so I thought of you." The Black section of Pittsburgh was called the Hill District; the main thoroughfares were Center and Wylie Avenues.

On Saturdays, I would take the 82nd Lincoln streetcar for a round trip to the area just to see some Black people. One day someone pointed out Lena Horne's house. I visited the office of The *Pittsburgh Courier*, a nationally circulated Black weekly newspaper and saw Crawford's Grill, owned by the family that sponsored the Pittsburgh Crawford's, a Black professional baseball team.

There were three Black Presbyterian churches in Pittsburgh; Bethesda, in the East Liberty section near the four million dollar East Liberty Presbyterian Church, called Mellon's Fire Escape since the Mellon family contributed heavily to keep it from going to Hell; Grace, in the Hill District; and Bidwell, near the seminary. Bidwell was twice the size of the other two combined with about 600 members due to the remarkable gifts of the founder, Dr. Benjamin F. Glasco. He was so spiritually powerful that he used to be called on to pray rather than one of the faculty when he was in seminary at Johnson C. Smith.

An Affirmation of Faith

When he visited in the community, he stopped at every house on the street, announcing as the door opened, "I am Dr. Glasco, and I came to pray with you." In the hospitals, he visited everyone on the wards where he had a member. He installed a baptistery for immersion. The baptismal font was the size of a birdbath. Every Sunday there was a woman in the pulpit, although she preached regularly only on Women's Day. He had people stand and pray in the congregation, several at a time. I visited his church after he moved to Philadelphia and heard him announce that he had preached that summer to more people than any preacher in Philadelphia by using a sound system on a flatbed truck. When I went to the organ to express my appreciation for the way his daughter wove a background for the entire service, she replied, "Wasn't the Lord wonderful today?"

Somebody at Bidwell introduced me to Lois Lee, who operated a funeral home on Brighton Road, near the seminary. I invited her to dinner at the seminary. She invited me to the Miss Pittsburgh Contest on the Hill, in which she was a contestant. Her garage opened manually. She gave me a cloth to wipe the dust off my hands, panties from someone she buried. She explained that the families never wanted the underwear, so she threw them in the washer and used them for rags. Lois later got married and her business boomed. She realized that many women did not want her to have their husbands even when they were dead. Now she had her own.

There was more spirituality at Pittsburgh Seminary than I had expected. The church history professor, Dr. Gaius Jackson, invited the entering class to his house for an evening of food and fellowship. He had each member of the class tell how his call to the ministry had come. Some of the stories were unusual. A Black classmate who did not live on campus but commuted from Sewickley told of a call that he had put on the back burner until the bank in Chicago, in which he was a teller, failed. He was James LeRoy Jones, son of the assistant pastor of Pilgrim Baptist Church, with a membership in the thousands. Sewickly at that time was reputed to be the richest community in the United States.

Dr. Slosser told of his religious pilgrimage through the Methodist system, his work on his Ph.D. at the University of London, the death of his first wife and his providential meeting with his second wife by backing into a seat on a speaker's platform in which she was sitting. His dissertation had been published, a history of church union movements, with a foreword by William Temple, the Archbishop of York, who by that time had become Archbishop of Canterbury. Dr. Slosser called it "My own volume." The students referred to it as "MOV." I was enchanted by his recount of his experiences and his international stature, as well as his piety. I decided to major in church history.

Spirituality was given a lift by the presence of a returned missionary from China, Rev. D. Kirkland West, who taught a course in missions. He held individual conferences with the students, prayer meetings and talk sessions. He had married a doctor with whom he worked at the same mission station. He also invited us to his home, where I accidentally stepped on the maid's button under the dining room table. She came in, wondering why she had been summoned.

Kirk West asked me how I was doing with my sins. I replied that I had none. He said I was the second person he had ever met with that opinion, the other was in China. After exploration with him I found myself to be as sinful as anybody else, perhaps more so because of my pride in my sinlessness. I also found myself to be quite dishonest according to Bible standards instead of the world's practicalities. So I had to write the Pullman Company and tell about using Rev. Nelson's clergy pass to buy my ticket to Pittsburgh. There were letters I had to write to teachers about using hidden notes during examinations; one, to a third grade classmate about a book of hers I had never returned. I had to apologize to a couple of students about whom I had made unkind snap judgments and another to whom I had forgotten to deliver an important message.

Another student made me feel quite guilty when he informed the group that he had asked me to pray with him at 6 a.m. but I had refused because it was during my time for study. This student, John Morris, made a great impression on me because he was wealthy and handsome with a very sharp mind. Somehow, I just did not feel he needed my prayers and was certain that my studying was more important. Much to my relief he did not repeat his request for prayer time. My studying was a matter of obsession. I had to make good. My guilt was intensified when John was asked to leave because he

An Affirmation of Faith

was not approved by Pittsburgh Presbytery. We felt that it was a result of a feud with his pastor whom we felt John threatened by his superior ability. The pastor said he was unstable.

Classes at seminary began with prayer by the professor. The Monday evening service had a choir of professional quality. Faculty and seniors did the preaching, it was excellent. My only touch of homesickness came one Monday night at communion when the organist played some old hymns as background music. John Morris comforted me at that time. Perhaps his request for prayer was for my benefit.

The study schedule reinforced by prayer began to pay off. All my marks on test were at least A's, as well as the course grades. I began to take extra courses, particularly in Old Testament. As so many Blacks did, I had identified with the Children of Israel and their struggles against captivity, slavery, and even the discriminations of those days. Our Old Testament professor, Dr. Culley, who was also the dean, said one of the attractions the real estate agent mentioned about his neighborhood was that there were no Negroes and no Jews. It did not occur to me to question why he bought there. I was pleased that he had the courage to mention it. I liked Dr. Culley.

Since most of the students complained about Hebrew, I took extra work in it. Because I wore Homburg hats, they began calling me "Rabbi." I defended Dr. Slosser when students complained about his topical method of teaching, his weight, and his personal references. They called him the "Cisco Kid," fat in the can. They complained about Dr. Culley's yellowed notes and his wry humor, his Old Testament notebook that required four Bibles to get sufficient scripture clippings to fill the notebooks. He said they could copy all the scripture references if they preferred. In 1941, Bibles cost only 25 cents at the dime store. I was awed by Dr. Culley's scholarship and the fact that his Ph.D. was from Leipsig where the classes were in German. It was said that he knew ten languages.

Really, at Pittsburgh I felt like Alice in Wonderland. Excited about Dr. Culley's language skills, I found that Dr. Kelso, the president, knew eighteen languages. He had been born in India of missionary parents, came to America to attend college, and also went to

Leipzig and majored in philology. He told us of his association with the Carnegie family.

Once when Dr. Kelso feared some of the board members would not attend a meeting, he had Carnegie send out the invitations. Not a single member was absent. His most interesting story was the deathbed conversation when Andrew was ill. Mrs. Carnegie told her husband that she wanted him to give most of his money to his favorite charities and leave her only fifteen million, which he did. Within ten years that fifteen million had grown to twenty-five million. The house next to the seminary dormitory was the home of Mr. Jones of the Jones and Laughlin Steel Co. The seminary custodian, Frank Sams, often had been used as chauffer for Mr. Jones when he fired his own chauffer for hitting too many bumps in the street. He gave the fired employee thirty days severance pay. Frank would drive for him until he hired another. The Jones mansion was the first I saw containing an elevator.

My classmate, Al Becces, was the first Catholic priest I had ever met. He had been a missionary in China seven years but had married when he came home on furlough. The seminary required him to do his whole seminary course over. He used to get into arguments in theology class because he followed scholastic theology. His Hebrew script was the prettiest I ever saw, so was his wife. Jose Medina was the first Spanish-America I had ever met. I bought his 1935 Ford V-8 for fifty dollars, my first car, and was able to drive to Youngstown on Sundays thereafter. It was a roadster with a rumble seat. It was originally tan but Jose had repainted it blue. The blue paint was peeling in large sections, making it look like a two-toned cow.

Surjit Singh, in the class ahead of me was the first Indian (from India) with whom I talked. He was from Punjab, a Sikh, whose life was threatened when he became a Christian. He was brought to Pittsburgh by Dr. John Wick Bowman, New Testament professor, who taught many years in India. Surjit was far beyond us in intellect and later joined Dr. Bowman on the staff at San Francisco Seminary. Dr. Paul Leo, a Jewish-Lutheran refugee from Hitler's Germany, taught us Greek. One day when I forgot to put my name on an assignment, I was complimented when he recognized my Greek handwriting. He told in chapel of the friend who also had trouble

An Affirmation of Faith

with English who preached a sermon on the Devil based on three questions: "Who the Devil is he, what the Devil does he do, and why the Devil does he do it?" One afternoon, not knowing he was in the room, I pounded on the door of a classmate with the palm of my hand. Dr. Leo almost went into a panic, saying the Gestapo practiced this method.

So much of the material from the seminary classes found its way into my sermons in Youngstown. Now I realize that this helped me to remember so much of it for the examinations. I soon became sought out by my classmates around exam time because I seemed to know what to study. The truth of the matter is that I learned it all. One day Dr. Bowman announced a test on three chapters of Ephesians, remarking that we could almost memorize that much. My rejoinder was "What do you mean, almost?" One upper classman with whom I was taking an elective sought my help. He had a photographic mind, so saw no need to attend class. He would read somebody's notebook the night before the exam and make "A." This time there was a conspiracy against him to refuse to let him read a notebook. Fortunately, for him I was not party to the conspiracy so he got his "A."

His name was John Paul Baker. He wore overcoats tailored to match his suits but in a heavier material. He apologized to Dr. Slosser for forgetting to bring an assignment because he had left it in one of the other cars he drove the day before. One day when he got home, he found that his wife had changed all the cars except the one he was driving. John was a good actor and spent as much time at the Pittsburgh Playhouse as we would spend in class.

The class was invited to dinner by Mr. Glunt, of the Presbyterian Ministers Fund, the first insurance company in the world. I bought a $1,000 policy with my mother as beneficiary with a premium of $25.38 annually for twenty years. I had bought an identical policy from a North Carolina Mutual salesman on the train to Youngstown for $32.48 annually. I was willing to keep the policy with the Black company out of a sense of loyalty.

There was another non-resident Black student in our class, Rev. Doyle John Thomas, pastor of a Baptist Church in a Pittsburgh suburb. He brought his gospel choir to seminary to sing one evening.

An Affirmation of Faith

This was a new music form for me, which I found interesting. Doyle was an expert gospel pianist and had a voice that could be heard for blocks. I visited his church and stayed overnight with Doyle and his mother learning a new type of religious expression. Doyle preached in cadence, clapping his hands at the end of a measure. Perspiring profusely, he said he ruined several suits each year by sweating them out. His church had no hymnals because everyone knew the words. I had heard shouting in church before but not to the extent at this church. He also anointed people with oil and prayed for healing. He now preaches in Danville, VA at Loyal Baptist Church.

Healing was a current subject in Pittsburgh that year because of the arrival of Kathryn Kuhlman to work with Dr. Jack Munyan and Dorothy Jean on their radio program and at People's Central Church not far from the seminary. She became the prominent figure of the broadcast and the church very quickly to the extent that Jack and Dorothy faded from view. Kathryn is dead now; I heard Jack on the radio in Pittsburgh two years ago.

At a Kuhlman meeting my eyes were opened in two respects. First, I lost all aversion to women preachers. With reddish blond hair, she wore a blue dress, red rose corsage and Black baby doll shoes. I remember how she stamped her foot as she quoted the Lord of the fig orchard, "Cut it down," in reference to the unfruitful fig tree. Then, I saw my first healing. A deaf woman came to the platform to testify that she had just been healed. She was grinning from ear to ear. She told how embarrassed she had been not to understand what people were saying and how happy she was that she had taken the long drive.

From that time, Kathryn went into orbit. Ambulances brought patients to the Carnegie auditorium. When the auditorium was being repaired, she was invited to use the prestigious First Presbyterian Church. She moved to the Stambaugh auditorium in Youngstown and the Shrine auditorium in Los Angeles on a regular schedule. She built Faith Temple in Franklin, PA and sponsored 22 other churches. Her radio network expanded. I was delighted when I heard her quote from a letter I had written one day. Her books, *Believe in Miracles* and *God Can Do It Again*, were thrilling reading for me some years later.

Pastor, Butler Memorial

At the end of an exciting year, the Board of National Missions agreed to supplement my five dollars per week at the Youngstown church so that I could spend the summer there. I became an Ohio resident when I moved into the West Federal Street YMCA. The executive secretary was Rev. Simeon Simon Booker, a Red Cross Army representative in World War I and one of the founders of Alpha Phi Alpha, the first Black fraternity. His daughter, Carolyn, I found attractive, but fearing that her family was pushing her on me I backed away, assuming I was doing her a favor.

By the time I found that this was not the case; Carolyn had become interested in the Rev. Curtis Vincent Holland, a Fisk graduate and baritone soloist, working at a mill as a summer job. His accompanist was Edna Wheeler, a Fisk graduate and music teacher at Palmer Memorial Institute in Sedalia, NC, founded and headed by Dr. Charlotte Hawkins Brown. The affluent Durham Blacks sent their children to Palmer rather than unaccredited Hillside, which I finished. So Curtis, Carolyn, Edna and I had a time of it in the spotted Ford roadster with the rumble seat. Carolyn had a concert quality, soprano voice. I was best man at their wedding and officiated at their daughter's, at which their maid of honor was the organist.

My Butler Memorial Presbyterian Church was five blocks from the city square, but most of the members lived five miles away in a section called the Sharon Line because it was on the streetcar route from Youngstown to Sharon, PA. Older residents might say, "I live at stop 19," rather than saying Karl Street for example. The big church activity for summer was Bible school. One of the members, James Thomas, had constructed a trailer out of a Model T Ford chassis, which he attached to the spotted Ford. It had rails around it and folding Sunday school chairs in two rows. I could get ten kids in the trailer, five in the rumble seat and five in front with me comfortably. I often carried twenty. Guardian angels were diligent because we never had a mishap of any kind. The Ford had no trailer hitch, the trailer had no brakes or signal lights, and the trailer chairs were not secured to the floor. We made the round trip from the Sharon Line daily for two weeks.

Butler Memorial had once been a Welsh Congregational Church, but was vacated when the neighborhood became predominantly Italian. In 1942, many Blacks had moved into the "Bottom" as it was called and others were following. There was a storefront church in the Bottom whose pastor had a speech impediment. The Spiritualist Church, two blocks from ours, had a woman pastor. I was all set to make it a community church in short order. My first new member came from the Sharon Line, and she was the bride at my first wedding. I learned there was a certain attraction to coming to church in town; in addition to coming to church in town, the members could use the church parking lot during the week. I also learned that the Sharon Line members offered strong resistance when Presbytery thought the church should relocate to where a community center, owned by the Presbytery, was already operating on property given by Mr. Butler, for whom the church was named.

Therefore, I spent as much, or more time, on the Sharon Line as I did in the Bottom. The Sharon Line people furnished the leadership for the congregation. The former pastor lived there in retirement. Most of the residents were homeowners. Lots were sold for twenty-five dollars. A good house could be bought for two thousand dollars. Men at the steel mills with good jobs earned twenty dollars a day.

Youngstown was a strange city in many ways. When Rev. Dusenbury, the founder of our church, told me about it before I came to town, he said it looked as though the town was on fire at night. The blast furnaces and converters did light up the sky. Mills moved there from Pittsburgh to get a lower tax rate. Blacks were recruited by steel mills in Anniston, Alabama and shipped to Youngstown in cattle cars, which unloaded them in the mill yards in Youngstown.

They were given slips verifying they had jobs then were released to go into town to find housing. A member of our congregation was the daughter of a recruiter who got a stipulated price for each man recruited. All of this took place in the twenty's. Yet when I arrived in 1941, one of the largest social clubs was The Bama Boys. Most of my congregation was from Alabama.

The contrasts between Youngstown and Durham were hard to believe. There were only three Black schoolteachers in Youngstown, although the population of Blacks was about the same, twenty-five thousand. There was nothing comparable to White Rock Baptist Church or St. Joseph's AME Church in Durham in size or prestige. There was not a Black bank, insurance company, high school or college. There was one auto repair shop and one Taxi Company, both owned by Underwood, several barber shops, social clubs and bars. Of the doctors, one was a native. The funeral directors did well. In general, anyone with ambition looked toward Pittsburgh or Cleveland except for those planning on a legal career. Black lawyers did well. Many years ago, Attorney Stewart had been Clerk of Courts. In 1941, Attorney Crumpler was assistant District Attorney.

Colliers magazine published an article calling Youngstown "Murder town USA." It told of the high incidence of murders by car bombs. The penalty for manslaughter then was one to ten years in prison. One could hear someone say, "I'll do a year in Columbus to get you out of the way."

One thing that distressed me was the long line of wives at the mill gates on payday afternoon. They were waiting for their husbands to come out with their checks so that together they could pay the bills and shop. I asked when I saw some of my acquaintances in line why this was done. The answer was that if they did not get in line some other woman would and then the bills would not get paid. Another line I found unusual formed outside the jail at the end of the day shift. Judges sentenced offenders to so many nights in jail so they could keep their jobs and support their families. The wives gathered there for a few minutes conversation with their husbands before they were locked up for the night.

It was difficult to motivate young people to continue in school. Boys were glad to get old enough to get a job in the mill and quit school. In the years since, my memory may have failed me, but I think there was only one graduate in the Youngstown College procession at my first commencement in Youngstown, a young woman, Ann Black. There was an active NAACP pushed by Attorney Maynard Dickerson, the publisher of the weekly *Buckeye Review*. One of his employees later studied law and became national counsel for the NAACP, Attorney Nathaniel Jones.

For a small church of eighty-two members, it was unusual that three medical doctors attended there. Dr. Thomas A. Lander, from South Carolina, had his office building just across the street from the church. One Sharon Line patient of his told me that she wished two people would never die and they are Dr. Lander and President Roosevelt. Dr. Lander treated her at no cost to her. She was a beneficiary of the Roosevelt social programs. Dr. William R. Smith was the brother of the president of one of our Presbyterian Colleges. Dr. Wallace was the third physician we saw often.

One lawyer succeeded in industry. Attorney Clarence Robinson was vice-president of the Poland Scrap Yard, a pillar of St. Augustine's Episcopal Church and perhaps the most prominent person in the Black community.

In 1986 when one of my NCC students received a three-year scholarship to Marquette Law School I suggested she call Mrs. Mary Scott, daughter of Attorney Clarence Robinson. She was invited to dinner by the Scotts.

The Presbyterian Church during the 40s was a growing movement. The denomination wide New Life Movement was designed to add a million members. *Catholic Digest* found in a survey that a Presbyterian would be more likely to attempt to evangelize a stranger than a member of any other denomination. We organized our visiting teams at Butler Memorial and visited the homes in the "Bottom." I was standing in the Bottom with some young female residents when a fellow walked up and wanted to know what was on my clipboard. When I told him it was the church roll, he asked if his name, Andrew Brown, was listed. When I could not find it, I offered to add it, to which he agreed. The females joined later during a Sunday morning altar call. In a few years, we doubled the membership of the church.

It was important to me to be known as approachable. One way I attempted to do this was by visiting the nightclubs. Although I did not drink or smoke, I had the impression that food was cheaper at such places because the money was made on alcohol. I usually went alone wearing clericals. Often there was somebody who wanted to talk at length. The bartenders seemed happy to have me come in. Some of these places had peepholes to identify prospective entrants.

It was advantageous to own a car in those days. Many of the members from the Sharon Line took the bus to church and to town so an occasional ride was welcomed. At the YMCA we did not have a dozen cars in the driveway. It was easy to get someone to ride with me to make calls on the church members and then to become a part of the congregation. One day, an obese woman and her pregnant obese daughter hailed me as I was about to turn into the driveway. The mother placed the daughter in the center of the seat beside me, grabbed the steering wheel with her left hand and the door handle with her right, and then with great effort shut the door. Nobody breathed easily until we pulled up at the hospital emergency door.

When September came I moved from the YMCA back into the seminary dormitory. We had lost several classmates. One who was an Army Air Corps pilot had been recalled to duty. Another, John Morris, had gone to Chicago Theological Seminary. Nobody had failed any courses. Our return was like the reunion of a family. Study patterns that served me so well the first year were resumed.

I felt threatened one day when Mrs. Read, the seminary secretary, sent word to me that I would have a roommate. He came over shortly afterward carrying a portable typewriter. He was older, the pastor of a church near Charlotte, NC, and a candidate for a Master of Sacred Theology degree (S.T.M.). In those days, the usual seminary degree at Western was a Bachelor of Sacred Theology (S.T.B.). I saw the end of my splendid isolation in a suite of rooms newly redecorated. It also bothered me that he was missing a tooth or two in front of his mouth. As we talked about the expense of attending two schools (he also wanted a Master's from the University of Pittsburgh); we differed over the probable cost. Thereupon he decided to spend the night with a friend, so as not to incur any obligation to the seminary

An Affirmation of Faith

and check the matter out the next day. I breathed a sigh of relief and had a happy feeling when he left.

Although I never saw or heard from him again, one of my classmates, Ralph "Lucky" Logan led me to a realization of how selfish I had been. From what I know now about body language and affect communicated through the nuances of speech, I am sure that he was the one who felt threatened. "In as much as ye have done it unto one of the least of these, my brethren, ye have done it unto me," never crossed my mind. Even though my assessment of the financial picture was likely correct I had rejected him whether he knew it or not.

The next Black student to register at Western was not sent to my room and I did not ask why. He would have been welcome because he was a family friend. His father, Dr. Henry Lawrence McCrorey, was president of Johnson C. Smith University. After serving several churches and going through two divorces, he, too, wanted the S.T.M. I had heard about his churches, his divorces and his Lincoln automobile. The only other Black person I knew who owned a Lincoln was a Youngstown mortician, Horace Greeley Emerson. I had also heard that "Mac," as he asked us to call him, had named his two sons from his two marriages, Henry Lawrence III and IV. He was H.L. Jr.

I took Mac with me to Youngstown on Communion Sundays. He did baptisms for us also. It did not bother me that he was a much better preacher than I because I enjoyed listening to him. He was the soul of congeniality and helpfulness.

The seminary admitted to classes a Black female pastor of the Fellowship Spiritual Church of Youngstown, just one block from Butler Memorial. She came with her secretary, who took notes in class. In Youngstown, she was known as Madame Posey. She also gave spiritual readings in her home. A member of the Butler Memorial family went to her when he was out of a job. She folded her Bible over his hands and asked if he knew somewhere they were making concrete. When he replied, "Raymond Concrete," she told him they had a job for him. He was hired.

Madame Posey got Mac to do a lot of Christian education for her church. He had the use of one of her cars. Finally, he got spooked one night in church when the guest preacher greeted a newly arrived worshipper with, "Come in Brother Jones, I see you have three dollars and sixty-four cent in your right trouser pocket. I want you to come up and lay it on the offering table. Mac was afraid he would start around the sanctuary revealing things about those present, and he did not want to be embarrassed. Mac told me the Madame said if he left her she would die. He left and she died. Later so did he.

Because my study program was going so well I decided to try for the S.T.B. and S.T.M. by the end of the following year thus saving a year of study. I majored in church history for the S.T.B. and Old Testament history for the S.T.M. I heard that many years ago someone had done this. It seemed unfair to me to work for three years and get another bachelors whereas some sharp students in other fields were getting Ph.D. degrees in that length of time. In addition, law schools were moving from the LL.B. to the J.D. as the first degree in the field.

Dr. Slosser suggested that I write a chronology of American Church History for my S.T.B. thesis. I cleared it with Dr. Culley to write on Jeremiah and the Deuteronomic Reform for the S.T.M. There was a sense of gratification in now being a Middler (the name for those in the second year) rather than a junior (label for first year students). I felt that I knew my way around. There was a certain amount of status in being a student pastor.

Much attention was being given to the war. Navy Chaplain Staunton W. Salisbury, came from Washington to give a recruiting speech. We were told he was a Captain but I was not impressed because I had seen many Army Captains. Then George Wilson told me a Navy Captain is equivalent to an Army Colonel. I had no inkling that the same Chaplain Salisbury, would one day be my Chief of Chaplains, pave the way for me to be a Navy Captain and baptize two of my three children. I read the Scripture at his first wife's funeral and marched beside the current Chief of Chaplains at his funeral. As the band struck up Onward Christian Soldiers, the Chief of Chaplains, Admiral James W. Kelly, said, "Dave, this is the way to go."

Several members of the senior class became Navy Chaplains. George Wilson took a semester's work at Princeton that summer so he could enter the Navy the next December. Members of the Youngstown church were being drafted. I kept up correspondence with them. Still I felt no compulsion to plan for participation, likely because of the low esteem in which soldiers were held in Fayetteville because of the proximity of Fort Bragg. Seminary students were still classified 4F, a draft exempt category.

Early in December, a note was posted on the seminary bulletin board inviting the students to apply for positions at the Pittsburgh Post Office. I went down and was assigned to railway mail service sorting packages for large cities in Indiana. I worked from 11 p.m. to 7 a.m. Monday through Friday, thus not interfering with the few class days left or the Youngstown weekends. There was so much dust in the large room that the overhead lights looked like full moons trying to shine through the clouds. It was difficult to find an empty stall in the rest room because men sat on the commodes and rested without dropping their trousers. I fell asleep sitting on a mail truck one night. The boss touched me and asked, "How about doing some work now?"

The sorting procedure was to dump the bags of packages onto a conveyor belt then remove the packages individually to throw into separate bags suspended from a rack for the various towns. I closed the bags as they became full and loaded them onto a nearby truck. I was surprised by the lack of attention to such stickers on packages as, "Handle with Care," "This Side Up" and "Fragile," but the careful handling of anything marked "Glass." I was told that the slots that could be seen along the overhead beams were peepholes for inspectors. One clerk was caught removing quarters from envelopes addressed to a film processing company.

My supervisor was very appreciative of my work. He was suffering with a cold aggravated by the dust. Many of the workers wore nasal cotton inserts manipulated by a stainless steel loop that lay on the upper lip. They reminded one of bulls with rings in their noses.

Perhaps the most impressive visitor that year was Dr. Clarence Edward McCartney, pastor of First Presbyterian Church Pittsburgh. He talked to us on "Preaching without Notes." He had written several books of sermons which some of us used extensively, especially *Great Nights in the Bible*. His most famous sermon was *Come Before Winter*, which was not in print at that time. Several of us went to his church one Sunday night because one could not get a seat on

An Affirmation of Faith

Sunday morning. Most of the seats were reserved through the pew rent system; the few seats for visitors were taken long before 11 a.m. The pew rent practice guaranteed the church's income. The rate of the rent varied with the location in the sanctuary. Mac had told us that the reason he lost his church in Philadelphia was that he removed the locks from the pew doors. At the North Presbyterian Church on the outside bulletin there was a line that read, "All Seats Free." On the First Presbyterian Church Bulletin a line read, "Those who would like to engage a pew are invited to see the church treasurer."

After seeing Dr. McCartney in action, I decided to adopt his method. It seemed to be relatively simple. He kept the big pulpit Bible open to his text. Since his sermon was essentially a story from the Bible, he had it there before him. Dr. McCartney was unmarried and lived in the Duquesne Club across the street from the church. He announced his sermon subjects on cloth signs the size of two bed sheets in front of the church. Dean Moore at the Episcopal Cathedral next door to First Presbyterian did likewise.

Dr. Clausen at First Baptist Church Pittsburgh also used the no notes method, but without a Bible. His pulpit had no book rest at all. Dr. Robert Schuler is comparable to him, forceful, dashing, and photogenic. We also went to First Baptist for an evening service and were surprised that the ushers were what we called then "Sweater Girls," pretty young ladies wearing sweaters with the sleeves pushed halfway up the forearm. We speculated on the amount such ushers collected as compared to middle-aged men.

Another impressive visitor was Dr. Hugh Thompson Kerr, pastor of Shadyside Presbyterian Church in the East Liberty section of Pittsburgh. We heard that eighteen millionaires belonged there. For years, Dr. Kerr had been on radio station KDKA, which could be heard as far south as Durham. They said a Pennsylvania farmer wrote Dr. Kerr a note on a piece of wrapping paper asking him to visit. When he did so, the farmer gave him an astonishing amount of money for his work.

The Youngstown weekends continued to give me a sense of fulfillment. Except for one snowy Sunday morning there had never been any trouble. On this particular morning the fuel pump went out. I had a classmate with me, James Francis Rowe, who was to preach at a rural church. By the time we got help, church was over at both places, although we went by to explain. I felt responsible, so I lent Jim the fifteen dollars the rural church would have paid him. I was really affluent at this time because of the post office job.

If I did not have anyone with me then my first concern was to find a hitchhiker for the trip. I liked the company; there was no danger in those days. One night on a return trip, the hitchhiker recognized me as one who had given him a ride some months previously

Two students impressed me as being unusually Christ-like this year. One of them was Virgil Moccia, a senior who told me that he had hoped to take the Butler Memorial Church if I had not appeared. I was not sure he meant this until I got to know him better. Then I became convinced that he would give you the shirt off his back. He had an aunt who lived in the Bottom. Perhaps he would have been better for Butler Memorial than I was. A few years later when he was pastor of the Manchester Presbyterian Church near the seminary, the Bidwell Church was looking for a pastor. Some of the Bidwell members heard him say that he would apply for the position. This remark was made by M. Edwards Breed. Edwards showed his descent from Jonathan Edwards, the foremost theologian, philosopher and revivalist of the colonial era. Dr. David R. Breed, M. Edwards' grandfather, had been pastor of First Presbyterian Church of Pittsburgh. Years later when I saw Ed at the Evangelism Explosion in Cincinnati he welcomed me like a long lost brother. He was holding a balloon. When I said I wanted to take one to my son he gave me his without hesitation.

There was another sobering thought at commencement. Three of us had taken a competitive examination for Presbyterian seminary seniors that offered a thousand dollar prize. I thought I did well except for the Hebrew, which I checked after the exam on the eighty-fifth Psalm. Dave Young had trouble with the Greek passage about Paul being caught up into the third Heaven. The prize was won by Tom Goslin of Princeton. I received a book, implying to me that I was lacking in theological sophistication.

By using the rumble seat, the space over the seat inside around the window, the seat beside me and the floor I was able to get all my belongings into the car with scarcely enough room for me. As

I started for Youngstown, I began to cry as I realized that a wonderful era had ended. George Wilson, the closest friend I ever had, was already in the Navy. I would miss Dr. Slosser and Dr. Culley. The seminary had become a family to me, most likely never to be reunited in this life. Some of them I have not seen since. I don't remember how long I cried. I know I was not ashamed, but I did feel guilty about not being disturbed this way when I left Durham and my real family.

The seminary taught me that family is where you find it, so I have tried to create family everywhere I have gone since then. The practice in Black churches of calling men "Brother" and women "Sister" facilitates this. We also have our church "Mothers." It seemed strange to me when I learned that members of First Presbyterian Church in Pittsburgh called Dr. Macartney "Clarence," but I learned to value those relationships in which I was called "David."

My first order of business in Youngstown was to get ordained. There was no longer an impediment due to my graduation. Presbytery set a date in June, less than thirty days from commencement, with the ceremony to be held at Butler Memorial. I said that I did not want to be installed as pastor, perhaps supposing I could find a larger church once ordained.

It did not occur to me to ask any of the family to come to commencement nor to the ordination. Since the ceremony was to be in the afternoon, Edna, Carolyn and Curtis could be on hand. Dr. Paul Gauss of Westminster Presbyterian was the preacher; Rev. Samuel J. Purvis of Memorial Presbyterian gave the charge to the pastor. His language sounded quaint to us each time in the ritual he addressed me as "Thomas David Parham, Jr., Sir."

The text of Dr. Gauss' sermon was Matthew 16:18, "And I say also unto thee, thou art Peter, and upon this rock I will build my church; and the gates of Hell shall not prevail against it." I have never lost the sense of the eternal quality of my ministry nor of the church as an institution.

Edna and Carolyn were disappointed after the ceremony because I did not experience some kind of surge of power or some kind of difference in self-awareness after it was over. I was disappointed because the members of Presbytery followed the full ritual of installation in addition to the ordination. Then it was my time to say silently, "Yes Sir" in appropriate deference to my superiors in the church. I never said anything about this contravention of my wishes to anyone until now. It seemed likely to me that the senior clergy were doing what they thought best for Butler Memorial and for me. Years later, I found that a candidate for ordination normally would not be ordained until he (no women then) received a call to a church as pastor. They may have supposed that I knew this or did not want to expose my ignorance having so recently graduated.

My first wedding was not long in coming; my first Communion was in two weeks. The first baptism was twelve months after the first wedding. I told the couple that I was thankful that I had already had my first funeral since the wife was the first new member who joined the church after I came to Youngstown.

The second wedding was more influential in my life. Whereas the first groom was in the Army and was married in uniform, the second was already called up in the draft making an extensive honeymoon impossible. I went to the Pennsylvania and Lake Erie Station to see him and the other draftees off. The window of the railroad coach near him was stuck so somebody removed the glass with his fist, making it possible to wave through it as the train moved away.

As I stood there watching the train, others turned and were leaving. One tall, beautiful Brown skinned young woman looked at me with tears streaming down her face and asked in frustration, possibly anger, "And what's wrong with you?" She could see I was wearing a clerical collar, but might not have known I was draft exempt. My reply was, "Nothing."

I began to think about my reply to this grief stricken wife or girlfriend and realized how true my statement was. Superb health, no family responsibilities, pastor of a small church that could easily get another seminary student from Pittsburgh, fully qualified to be a chaplain, so I decided to join the Navy forthwith. The recruiting office informed me that the Office of Naval Officer Procurement was in Pittsburgh, so back down that familiar highway I went.

The LT serving as procurement officer was very cordial as he informed me that he did not have authority to accept my application because of my race. I was stunned because I had seen Black Army

An Affirmation of Faith

chaplains practically all of my life. My aunt had a classmate who was a chaplain at Fort Bragg at the time. The LT did not tell me that the Navy had no Black officers at all. He likely did not know that the first Black Ensigns were in training at the time as was the first Black chaplain. I was somewhat naive about the Navy racial policy.

Two months later when I saw a picture in the *Pittsburgh Courier* of the first Black Navy Chaplain, James Russell Brown I went back to Pittsburgh. The same LT remembered me and said, "I can take your application now." It was then necessary to go to Philadelphia for ecclesiastical endorsement. The Presbyterian General Assembly Office was located there. The Stated Clerk, Dr. William Barrow Pugh, of the family that endowed Grove City College, was the endorsing agent. Dr. Pugh asked if I would consent to go into the Army because the need was greater. I told him before I would go in the Army I would stay in Youngstown so he endorsed me for the Navy.

The low esteem in which soldiers from Fort Bragg were held in Fayetteville and similar attitudes toward those from Camp Leonard in Youngstown had prejudiced me against them. I am now ashamed that I rejected the area of greater need and that I reacted negatively to Dr. Pugh because he was wearing a blue shirt. I think I had never seen a clergyman wearing a blue shirt.

My next task was to be interviewed by an active duty chaplain. A letter from Washington informed me that a Catholic Chaplain who was on leave in Cleveland would be attending the Indians game on a certain day and I could meet him at the stadium. So I attended my first major league game wearing clericals so the chaplain might recognize me with the help of my paint job. We found each other in the stands after the game of which I had seen almost nothing and couldn't remember the other team's name. The only topic I remember of our conversation was how appropriate a clerical collar would be for a chaplain in dress blues. Chaplain Casey told me that the old Navy dress blues had military collars, as Marine dress blues still do, very similar to a clerical collar.

From then on it was a matter of waiting until I received word that I would be commissioned September 22nd and report for active duty December 5th. I did not say anything to anyone about it in

An Affirmation of Faith

Youngstown or in Durham. One day an investigator went to the house in Durham asking about a LT Parham. My mother told him there was no such person to her knowledge. He insisted I had given that address. When she saw the full name, she knew.

In November, I went to the seminary to find a Black student to take my church. The four of them discussed it for about five minutes then agreed that Casper Glenn would take it because he seemed interested. The week before I was to leave one of the members saw me in the bank in uniform. I had come to close my account and did not think any of the congregation would be in town that early in the morning. On Sunday three days later, I announced my departure and the coming of Casper the next Sunday. As I look back, my conduct appears high-minded and inconsiderate, even though there would have been little resistance to the move because of the popularity of the war. I promised Casper and the church that I would return after the war, not suspecting that they might not want me back; so full of myself was I in those days.

I left books and the car with the Baskins family, my fluorescent lamp, typewriter and reading stand with Eleanor, a high school student who lived nearby, and other articles in the church. Chaplain School was on the campus of the College of William and Mary in Williamsburg, VA. By train and bus, I arrived a day early, excited to be again in my native state.

Having never read Goffmans' *Asylums* nor having ever heard of the concept "total institution," I was quite unprepared for the following weeks. In a total institution, most decisions are made by higher authority with the resultant depersonalization and devaluation of the one who enters it on the lowest level. In addition to the military, other total institutions include some hospitals and prisons. The culture shock I experienced may be easier understood by remembering the theme of a senior thesis at the seminary, "The Black Preacher is the Freest Man Alive." In Youngstown, I was almost completely self-determining. I would tell the church what I was going to do. I moved as I liked, wore and ate what I chose, rose and retired when convenient for me.

The next morning I rose at 0600 hours, put on dress blues and reported to the barbershop where I was relieved of my moustache, which I had worn for nine years, and was shorn of my nine-inch long hair. Later our class was subjected to a harangue by the Officer in Charge, CAPT William H. (Pat) Rafferty, CHC, USN. He told us how fortunate we were to be in the Navy with better pay than we were accustomed to having, $2,000 a year. One of my classmates, Lauriston Scaife, had just come from Newport where his church paid him $10,000 (an Episcopal church). Four years ago, I read a book because the introduction was by Bishop Lauriston Scaife.

Chaplain Rafferty also told us not to run to sickbay because if we were at home we would not go to a doctor because we would have to pay. The next morning I woke up with a sore throat and fever so I drank some water and returned to bed. At 0800 hours, the duty chaplain came for me because I had missed quarters. I told our executive officer, Chaplain Irwin W. Schultz that I was sick and could not go to sickbay because Chaplain Rafferty said so. Chaplain Schultz said Chaplain Rafferty did not mean it the way I took it, that I should go to sickbay. But for missing quarters I was given two hours extra duty, which consisted of marching a rectangular course on the athletic field in the mud.

My next problem came with a fire drill held at 0200 hours. Somehow, I did not hear the alarm. Everybody was out, except me. Again, the duty chaplain came to get me out of bed. I have always been a sound sleeper. On a Scout camp out, I walked in my sleep and almost got hit by a bottle. In Youngstown, the YMCA was on highway 422, and my room was on the side with the stoplight where the 18-wheelers had to gun their engines to get started again. Later in Guam, somebody went berserk and fired a carbine through the tents in officer's country without my hearing it. Also in Youngstown, I was asked what was wrong with me over the telephone the night before; I didn't make sense. I had answered the telephone and later hung up without waking.

My final problem came with the first room inspection. I was in my room studying when the chaplain came in with his hat on, saying he was inspecting. So I watched him as he walked around the room, wondering what it all meant. Chaplain Buck then informed me that he had his hat on because he was inspecting, and the next time somebody came in with a hat on I should sort of stand up. I promised him I would certainly do so. He called attention to the books on the bunk that I was using; this was called gear adrift. He struck me as being quite personable as contrasted with the CO and XO. I last saw him many years later as Dean of St. Paul's Cathedral in Boston where Bishop Burgess was being installed head of the Diocese of Massachusetts. Senator Edward Brooke read the Gospel.

It irked me that I was designated a seminarian, and so I had to stay at the school for 12 weeks. Those with two years pastoral experience were finished in eight. I had been preaching since I was 16 and was at Butler Memorial for three years as a student pastor, 6 months after ordination. The regulation proved to be a blessing, however, because the extra four weeks were given to two-week field assignments at some nearby command. My first assignment was to the Service School Command at Hampton Institute (now University). Black service school selectees were sent there because they were not allowed in the comparable classes at Great Lakes. The recruit camps were separate at Great Lakes but there was only one service school.

Part II.
Moving Mountains

Chaplain School

Hampton was quite prestigious in the Black community. Booker T. Washington had attended there before founding Tuskegee. Hampton has the largest endowment of any predominantly Black university. When our family sold the Service Printing Company in 1938, it was sold to three Hampton graduates of the printing department. The other trade schools on campus made it a natural setting for a service school.

There was one Black officer on the staff, Ensign Cooper, a Hampton graduate. As a LTJG, I was the ranking Black officer in Tidewater. Several Black petty officers were used as teachers. One of them, PO1 Eastmon, had a Masters from Columbia University. He applied for a commission but the doctor refused to give him the physical examination until ordered to do so by the CO. Then the doctor falsified his chest measurements and other data sufficiently to disqualify him. When he found this out after his rejection and complained to the CO, the reply was that it made no sense to put the doctor on report because he would be on report to other doctors who would do nothing. It reminded me of Colonel Young of Xenia, Ohio, who in like manner failed the physical for general. He rode his horse to Washington to demonstrate his good health, but to no avail. Let me hasten to say, however, that these two doctors were unique. I have the highest regard for all the doctors who have examined, treated, or served with me.

The Hampton chaplain, Rev. Chazzaud, was employed because he had been a missionary in Africa. He invited me to preach in the chapel. The choir director, Noah Ryder, had been choir director at

An Affirmation of Faith

Hampton before he entered the Navy. He was allowed to remain at Hampton on active duty until the war ended. It was thrilling to listen to the Hampton choir being directed by a Navy seaman in bell-bottoms. A similar arrangement was made for the administrative officer of Chaplain School, Professor J.W. Lambert, of the William and Mary faculty. Dr. Georgia Ryder, Noah's widow, recently retired as head of the Music and Fine Arts Departments at Norfolk State University.

The two weeks ended all too quickly. I immediately requested to have the same assignment for my second two weeks and was elated by the affirmative response. I had made Youngstown a promise, so I could not hope to stay at Hampton the rest of my life.

Some of the Chaplains teaching at Chaplain School had been in combat situations. Chaplain Glynn Jones had been shot five times by a Japanese sniper while conducting a funeral on a South Pacific beach. The sniper saw he was wearing an officer's insignia. Chaplain Fitzgerald had served with Marines, and had glowing reports to make of their intense loyalty. Chaplain Rafferty had been on the USS Ranger and had received personal decorations. I've had movies of the Pearl Harbor attack and other early engagements. We were well motivated to push for victory.

The second Hampton tour was even more interesting. I enjoyed the officer's mess; the 24 of us were served by six stewards. They worked three at a time, so each steward had every other day off. The meals were outstanding. Guests were permitted, so I brought several female members of the Hampton staff, a classmate from N.C. College, and a Hampton teacher in the Commerce Department who had a student from our church in Durham. I met Dolly Davidson, great-granddaughter of Captain Robert Smalls, the first Black Navy Captain. I had no idea I would be the second.

The most interesting officer was LT. Arthur Hazard Dakin, an author from New England, who had written a book on the colonial period involving the clergy of that day. He was surprised that I did not have several jealously guarded hours every morning for serious study. I found that the complement at Hampton was not large enough to warrant a chaplain even if Chaplain Chazzaud had not been at the Institute, so I sadly gave up hope of even a short tour of duty there. It was a sadness like that seen on the many murals throughout the Navy spaces on the campus of enlisted men painted by John Biggers, who was there at the time. The CO approached him about this, so the next mural had one sailor smiling ever so faintly. When I saw Dr. Biggers at an exhibition of his work in Richmond last year, he told me all the murals were destroyed after he left Hampton to embark on his career. His show was prominent nationally.

Back at Chaplain School we began wondering what kind of orders would be coming. A representative from the Office of the Chief of Chaplains came down to do interviews. I was pointedly asked how I would work in a religiously diverse situation and specifically what I could do for Catholics. I had Catholic religious articles that had been blessed by Chaplain Fitzgerald when I left Williamsburg. I was told that I would likely be stationed at Great Lakes, so I made it my first preference on the choice of duty form. Great Lakes it was.

Great Lakes, IL

Fortunately, I did not get to Great Lakes until March, when the weather was a little milder. I was assigned to Camp Robert Smalls in an adjoining office to Chaplain Brown. He told me how the Navy had asked Bishop Gregg of the AME Church to nominate a suitable chaplain to be the Navy's first Black one. He had been dean of a small church college, but was an expert swimmer and lifeguard, an accomplished musician, voice and piano, and had some experience in drama. He was happily married, but without children. Hence, he was able to move on short notice. Bishop Gregg had made a good choice. We were in the 19th Regiment, all Black except for the senior officers of the line, who were also LTJG's.

The commanding officer of the regiment was LTJG Yoas, whom I saw only during the orientation speech he made to new recruits. I remember only that he cautioned them against "playing the dozens." This was a verbal interchange in which one would insult the other and the other would reply, "your mamma," or sometimes "your mammy." My office adjoined Chaplain Brown's. We shared a clerk, Wilburt Russell, who did such a good job of answering the phone that many civilians who called thought he was the chaplain. Chaplain Brown and his wife lived in town, in nearby Waukegan, IL. There was no statue to Jack Benny, as I supposed there would be since it was his hometown. I lived there also in a room I rented at the Irvins on Utica Street. We were denied on-base housing, even in the bachelor officers' quarters. We could not go to the officers club, get a haircut in the officers' barbershop nor eat in the officers' mess. We were allowed to eat in the second-class petty officers' mess, so we did not have to leave the camp for lunch. We could also eat at the Navy Exchange cafeteria in the headquarters building 1911, but the cost was higher.

Several of the first 13 Black ensigns commissioned were still at Great Lakes, along with Dr. Wharton, Dr. Frazier (MD and DDS), and the second dentist, Dr. Tom Watkins of Charlotte. The most colorful was ENS Dennis D. Nelson, head of the Special Training Unit, an entire battalion of illiterates. On paydays, the Navy was paying in cash in return for a pay chit that had to be signed and fingerprinted. Payday was a very busy day for us chaplains as we signed the pay chits for many men who could not write and watched them mark an "X" beside the signature. These men looked as alert and intelligent as anyone else; many of them had families. We called theirs the knucklehead battalion and we called STU Knucklehead University. I was struck by the air of determination with which they marked those "X's," and was convinced that I would not have to perform this task for the same man again.

This battalion won all of the competitions that did not involve reading: the drill competitions, the athletic contests, the barracks and personnel inspections. You never had to tell one of these men anything twice; he would never forget anything he was told. The purpose of the unit was to bring the men up to a third grade level in twelve weeks.

I was so impressed with the program and the materials that I sent a packet to my uncle, who was president of Fayetteville State at the time, an elementary teacher training institution. The first primer had a sailor's picture with the caption, "This is a sailor. He has on a hat." This was more practical than my primer, which began, "Baby Ray has a dog. The dog is little. Baby Ray loves his little dog. The little dog loves Baby Ray." I never had a dog, nor were any of my friends called "Baby" anything. It would have seemed demeaning. I supposed White people talked this way.

ENS Nelson was called "Lord Nelson" by the Black teachers who worked for him, enlisted non-rated personnel who were called from new draftees because of their college educations. My best friend in childhood, Marion Fleming, was one of them. He had a Masters in math from Michigan when he was nineteen years old, and was teaching at St. Paul's College when drafted. He was allowed to strike for radio technician, and made third class before he accumulated enough points for discharge. He and most of the rest would have been commissioned if the Navy had been fair in those days. Marion became a dentist later.

Another teacher was Loftin Mitchell, a relative of the Durham Spauldings, now a New York playwright. ENS Goodwin also had Durham connections; his brother was married to Margaret Kennedy Goodwin, whose mother was C.C. Spaulding's sister. Much of my free time during the day was spent with the teachers or the ensigns and the off duty time with Marion.

My first attraction to him was that we were practically the same age; I was one day older. He lived in Fayetteville, went to Haymount Presbyterian Church, and his grandmother and mother were in the same women's church circle with my grandmother, the "Willing Workers." He was named after his grandfather, Elder Marion Stevens, who was still wearing a wing collar in 1930. Mr. Stevens ran a barbershop for Whites; Marion's dad ran a barber supply agency. There were four Fleming boys; Kermit, Alan, and Harry were all older. I decided I would have four sons when I grew up because they seemed to have more fun than I did with just one brother.

My second attraction to Marion was his intellect. He skipped from the fourth to the sixth grade, then from the sixth to the eighth. He finished Johnson C. Smith in three years, so he graduated from high school at fourteen, college at seventeen. In the early years, I hung onto every word he said as being the last word on any subject. I named my cat after him and when I married, it was to someone with the same name. Still I never felt that I caught up with him intellectually, although I tried. In the days at Great Lakes, I suspect he enjoyed our association because I outranked him considerably and was comparably affluent.

Marion was also very sociable. He seemed to know an inexhaustible supply of very pretty girls in Chicago so he arranged double dates for us. We by-passed Waukegan, which was called "Bear Town" in those days, because the girls supposedly looked-like bears. It was my theory that Great Lakes had drained off the pretty ones as sailors married them and left, just as I thought Johnson C. Smith had done to Charlotte over the years before it became a co-ed school in the 30's.

Downtown Chicago could be reached in an hour on the electric trains that came within easy walking distance of anywhere in the city. The fare was one dollar round trip with trains running on the half hour. One day en-route to Chicago Marion wondered how the trains were grounded because there was no third rail. I didn't understand what he was talking about. He wanted to know if I took physics. I asserted that I had, so he repeated his original question, to which I replied that I did not know. I should have said that I did not know any physics.

The fastest of the three sets of electric trains was the Electroliner, on which my cousin Tommy worked as bartender. When I got on his train, I was careful not to make any sign of recognition because I had not asked the relatives if he passed for White. Any time I went to Chicago to visit relatives they always met at Cousin Rosa Lillian's house. She was named for my mother and was darker in complexion than the rest. I was given to understand that some of the other cousins could not be visited. Many years later when Tommy and Rosa were the only ones still living they still lived separately, but used to talk by telephone every day. One Sunday when I was invited to preach at a church near his home, I called him by phone before I left the church. I had never visited his home.

I found a cousin stationed with me at Camp Robert Smalls, Johnny, a hospital corpsman. His mother was the daughter of Uncle Bob, one of my paternal grandfather's ten siblings. I had met Uncle Bob at Uncle Willie's funeral in Freehold, N.J. The Burts lived in Buffalo. My brother met them by answering an ad in the Black weekly newspaper for a room for rent when he went to Buffalo to work for Union Carbide on a summer job during his college days.

The most exciting experience of the Great Lakes adventure was the Sunday preaching. Chaplain Brown and I alternated on Sundays, preaching in the drill hall at Robert Smalls. There were two Protestant Services, 0830 hour and 0930 hour with a compulsory attendance of 1500 at each. The men were marched in by companies and seated on folding chairs facing a worship center on one wall that was covered

An Affirmation of Faith

by sliding doors during the week. There was a Hammond organ and bleachers for a choir of about sixty voices trained by a sailor named Ross from the rather large music department, which included the band. Our organist was Don who could skillfully combine Bach and Gospel in medleys for preludes and postludes. One Sunday he did a rendition of Bach's "Come Sweet Death" and Thomas A. Dorsey's "He Knows How Much You Can Bear" that I found particularly moving. We also were quite excited when Leroy Gentry came to boot camp. He had just made a picture in Hollywood, so we had a movie star organist for a few Sundays. I was flattered when he sent me an invitation to his marriage to a New Orleans doctor's daughter some years later.

Chaplain Brown preached the same sermon at both services; I used different ones. His notion was that if the sermon was good it should be repeated. My feeling was that the choir, organist, and in my case, the preacher would be bored the second time around. My sermons were folksier, colloquial and a little louder than his, so they received a better reception until he changed his style somewhat with his sermon "Accentuate the Positive," from the current popular song by Bing Crosby

It was the practice to have guards in the aisles watching for sleepers. If one was spotted the guard touched the man on the end, who in turn touched the next one until the touch got to the sleeper. My challenge was to carry no sleepers. I was also motivated by the realization that some of the men had never been to church before, had never talked to a clergyperson. Our senior chaplain, John E. Johnson, who retired and built the Bayside Presbyterian Church in Virginia Beach, said we had the greatest preaching opportunity in America. I believed him, and I used to give an altar call after each sermon. One Sunday the lights went off during the altar call. When they came back on I found eighteen men standing at the rail, the largest response I ever had even to this day.

Some who answered the altar call had not been baptized. The swimming pool in 1911 was the only facility that could be used for immersion. Pool rules required that all swimmers be naked, but an exception was made for chaplains. Therefore, I baptized the naked men wearing a black bathing suit and a cross. I had never done an immersion baptism before arriving at Great Lakes.

Chaplain Brown was transferred to Hawaii and was replaced by Chaplain Berg, a White Norwegian Lutheran. We alternated Sundays also.

He told me how he became blind while in seminary. He could find no medical help. He prayed in desperation and in complaint over the disruption and likely end of his ministry. Then he accepted his blindness, sang in the choir and had classmates to read to him so that he could continue his studies. Then his sight returned. I used to listen to him preach, enthralled by his experience. In Chaplain School he bumped into an old friend who exclaimed that he was a spitting image of a friend of his named Berg. When Chaplain Berg affirmed he was Berg the friend said "You can't be; Berg is blind as a bat." He reluctantly accepted the Navy Identification Card as proof.

With the recruit load decreasing consolidations were taking place at Great Lakes. One of them involved moving a White battalion into Camp Robert Smalls. After cleaning the barracks vacated by Black sailors, the wooden, double-decked bunks were brought outside in the sunlight and completely sandpapered. I expected that I would be getting orders soon, which was the case. No other Black chaplain had been commissioned. We were assigned a White choir director.

One day Chaplain Berg brought in a White sailor who wanted to be baptized by immersion. He told the sailor that if he had to be baptized that way I would have to do it because he could find no scriptural warrant for immersion. I had always wondered why John the Baptist needed the Jordan River if he sprinkled people and why the Ethiopian eunuch and Philip seized on the "Water" near the road on which they were riding. So the sailor and I went to the swimming pool for my first White baptism. He was quite appreciative, said I had "led him to Christ." I had never expected this kind of thing to ever happen anywhere or any time. A few weeks later, I got a letter from the sailor's father wanting to know what "faith and order I was." I answered that I was of the Presbyterian faith and had used the order for baptism in the *Book of Common Worship*. The letter was from Mississippi, as I remember. I never heard anything else.

Waukegan was not the closest town to Great Lakes. North Chicago was just outside the gate at 22nd Street; although 85 percent Polish there was a small Black population. The First Baptist Church had as its pastor the father of Nat King Cole. Several of the Navy Exchange saleswomen were members there. Since my 0930 hour service was over at 1030 hour, I had plenty of time to walk to First Baptist. The Cole family was very much in evidence there. Rev. Cole did the preaching. His wife directed the choir in which a daughter sang. I also saw a son people called "Fats."

The thing that impressed me most about First Baptist was the expression of sheer contentment on the face of one old overweight deacon after he had made his way down the aisle laboriously to his seat. I used him in a sermon illustration for the text, "I was glad when they said unto me, let us go into the house of the Lord." He was still alive on a subsequent tour at Great Lakes when I had the opportunity to tell him of the way I remembered him.

Transit to Hawaii

Just as I had followed Chaplain Brown to Great Lakes, I followed him to Hawaii. En-route there by train, I had a layover while I waited for a ship in San Francisco. A tennis enthusiast at Great Lakes had told me to look up Lulu Chapman, YMCA secretary, in Oakland. She became the first woman to defeat me on the court. She was just as sharp on the ping-pong table. She kept two cars because she could get a gas ration book for each, an Olds and a Packard. Lulu knew everybody, and she highly recommended Rev. Roy Nichols who later became a United Methodist Bishop. We played tennis with Rev. Henry Mitchell, who had just moved from the post of Campus Minister at NCCU where my baby sister was his organist. He just retired as Dean of the School of Religion, Virginia Union University where I taught several courses for him. I met Rev. John Dillingham who so impressed me that I advised my brother to do an internship under him at Faith Presbyterian Church. He did, later succeeding him. I had a room on Sutter Street in San Francisco, so I took the "A" train across the bay.

V-J Day came before my ship assignment came. I watched people drive old cars into store windows, then empty the windows of their displayed merchandise and loot the stores. A beautiful woman came out of a bank with a glass of whiskey in her hand. Seeing me in uniform, she offered it to me. One fellow had climbed a lamp pole and broken one of the glass covers that protected the bulb so he could place his bottle inside. He would wave his free hand and yell, then take a swig from the bottle. A group of celebrants grabbed a cable car at the top of the hill and spun it around, making a merry-go-round of it.

One of our yeomen from Great Lakes now stationed in San Francisco, Petty Officer Thompson, told me that a Navy Captain dragged him in a doorway and pushed a bottle into his face saying, "Sailor, you are not drunk enough." The *Chronicle* the next day reported a number of rapes and other acts of violence. I saw a big sign on one broken store window the next morning, "God Bless America."

Although it had been a year since the first Black officers had been commissioned, we were still novelties. It irked me to be walking along Sutter Street at night and to be hailed by Blacks on the other side of the street, "Hey Stu." They thought I was a petty officer in the Stewards Branch of the Navy. Although all other enlisted men below the rate of Chief Petty Officer wore the bell-bottoms or cracker jacks, stewards from third-class up wore officer type uniforms without insignia on the raincoat and a small USN on the cap where the officer's crest belongs for those below CPO. Chief Steward's wore the chief's anchor there. I felt that if they could see well enough to tell I was Black they could also see the shiny gold and silver officers' crest on my cap. On one occasion, I crossed the street and showed the fellows the stripes on my sleeve. Somewhat bemused they apologized. The custodian at the cleaners I patronized in Durham greeted me with "Hi Chief." I was now past the complaining stage.

"Lord Nelson" was very anxious to get the stewards' special uniform changed. The rationale for it was that they would not look out of place in areas restricted to officers. Nelson's opinion was that it deprived them of being really in the Navy. At Chaplain School when I took the course on Navy Regulations it was specified that only a steward in the Navy could be called "Boy." When this regulation was later changed, the tradition died hard. As late as 1951, when a White officer said to a steward first-class, "Boy, bring me a towel," he replied, "Sir, there are no boys in the Navy; we are men. And as long as your ass points to the ground you will never get a towel." The officer complained to the BOQ officer but no disciplinary action was taken.

An Affirmation of Faith

This First Class steward, Pinkney, had a forceful personality, good judgment, and fine rapport with his superiors. The Chief Steward assigned to the BOQ worked for him and accepted the fact. Everybody knew Simmons ran the BOQ. Years later when stationed in Japan I wanted to help a White sailor who came to me from a destroyer. I went aboard, talked to the PO on watch and was told that the best person to see was the first class steward. I found he had been on board seven years. He was in the officers' wardroom smoking a cigar. He listened to me and told me he would take care of it. I noticed that when the executive officer came in he called him "XO," without the "Sir," in the way peers address each other. When I returned to my office I called our chief steward who told me, "Yes he runs that ship."

Years later in my study of sociology I learned how the informal structure of authority works alongside the formal structure and is often more effective. In two instances, I found chaplains whose influence was extraordinary. One of them told me, "I don't work for my Colonel, he works for me." It was a fact that when there were baptisms in his chapel the Colonel was on station holding the bowl for the chaplain. The other chaplain told me his battalion Colonel complained to him that he could not get a pet project approved. He asked the Colonel to brief him on it and promised to take it up with the general that Thursday night when he would be having dinner with him. The project was approved. The next week the Colonel in question said to me, "You know it certainly is handy to have a chaplain on your staff," then told me the story. This chaplain was a LT, the other a LCDR. Somewhat more modest was the chaplain who reported to a Chief of Chaplain seminar in Norfolk how he was helping his boss in Vietnam, a General, to do his job. The Colonel retired from the Marine Corps and enrolled in a theological seminary.

When I did get assigned to a ship for transportation to Hawaii it turned out to be a Coast Guard landing ship, tank, 1ST 761, now used as a barge on the Elizabeth River in Norfolk with all its superstructure gone. I look down on it from the bridge leading from Portsmouth. I was assigned to be roommate of the unofficial ship's chaplain, a LT who in civilian life had been a magician. They thought this made him the nearest thing to a chaplain they had. He took his work seriously.

An Affirmation of Faith

When appointed he had gone to the fleet chaplain's office and picked up supplies for the three major faith groups, made up packets for each man according to his religious preference, and called them in individually and presented the packets. Since I was a professional chaplain, he invited me to preach on Sundays.

This LST was my first at sea experience. The morning after we shoved off there was an announcement on the bulletin board, "The uniform of the day is optional." Most of the men changed into bathing trunks and shower shoes.

The ship was returning to Pearl Harbor for another load of ammunition. Bins had been made on the tank deck for such storage. The empty ship with its flat bottom also provided me with my first rock and roll experience and the preliminary nausea that can develop into seasickness. I found that if I got into my bunk or if I stood so that the motion was side to side instead of front to back I had no problem. One day, after greasy sausages for lunch, only the bunk could stave off the nausea. To this day, I am thankful never to have been seasick.

There were many "firsts" for me on this cruise. My first shipboard Sunday was most memorable. The chaplain asked me to conduct the service and supported my efforts in handsome style. I felt that many of the worshippers came out of curiosity. All of us were thankful that the war was over. It was a novel experience to do counseling at sea in a stateroom instead of an office. Nearly all of the Black steward's mates came in to explain why they were in the steward's branch of the Coast Guard and were very anxious for my approval.

For the first time in the Navy, I was a victim of theft. I lost a fore and aft blue cover that could be worn with dress blues instead of the frame type cap with the blue cover in winter, white in summer. Chaplain Albert, district chaplain in Philadelphia, was the only other chaplain I knew to wear the blue fore and aft, so I was proud of it. Another novel idea I picked up from Chaplain Albert that served me well was to reply to letters with the opening sentence, "Your letter of (date) arrived today and I hasten to reply." I asked the stewards mates if they knew where the cap was but got no leads. By the time I returned to the States the cap was no longer being worn.

Pearl Harbor

I arrived in Pearl Harbor without incident. My orders were to Manana Barracks, near Pearl City. The usual way we gave directions to it was to say one should go through Pearl City and turn right at the corner were there was a little naked boy playing in the yard. He played in the yard all day and was as brown as a cocoanut.

Manana was a barracks area for 3,000 Black stevedores, organized into logistics support companies or Seabee Special units. They were loaded into cattle cars each morning and transported to the piers at Pearl Harbor where they unloaded ships all day, then were returned at the end of the day.

There was a very interesting game being played by the supply personnel and the stevedores, a kind of treasure hunt. The most highly prized treasure was whiskey. The day that they found whiskey in a carton of Post Toasties was a red-letter day. It was easy to see that every carton of Post Toasties got dropped and broken open so that those closest could help themselves. Then it was necessary to change the labels on the whiskey cartons. They told me that they had also discovered the false label for the altar wine and caused a shortage in Hawaii. One of the members of my Bible class was quite proud of the leather attaché case he liberated.

At Manana liberty expired at 1800 hours. In addition to the guards on the gate there were others patrolling the fence armed with carbines. The barbed wire on the fence was turned inward to keep the sailors from escaping. I was told that there had been a race riot after the accused rapist identified in a lineup was found to have had

An Affirmation of Faith

duty at the time of the crime. The barbed wire, guards and early liberty expiation were all measures intended to prevent a second riot.

There were other measures taken to keep the lid on things. I was the third chaplain on the staff. There was a resident Red Cross representative. We also had Charles Flax, a civilian chorus director from the Black service school at Hampton. My roommate was LT. Edward S. Hope, son of Dr. John Hope of Atlanta University, and the highest ranking Black in the Navy Line. He was given temporary additional duty to Okinawa to serve on a court martial of a Black sailor for rape. On board also were two Black dentists, Dr. Frazier and Dr. Watkins, and a Black M.D., Dr. Wharton. Other Blacks included LTJG Fort, who was reputed to head the largest rum company in New England, ENS G.D. Smith, who had worked his way up from steward, and WO4 Willie Powell, a submariner and ex-steward, who was the highest paid officer on the station. He was conspicuous for his many gold crowns and his congenial manner. He taught me to soft boil an egg by putting it in a cup of boiling water and letting it cool down enough to be eaten.

ENS Garrett was the youngest of the Black officers. The senior medical officer was LCDR Goldberg, a Jew, so quite acceptable to most of the Blacks, except for the few who felt that he had been assigned to Black troops because he was primarily a physical therapist rather than some kind of surgeon.

Black petty officers, were common, some of them were prominent. LTJG Fort's brother, an athletic specialist, was there to remind me that when he and others were shipped out from Great Lakes I had told them I would be on hand when they got back. Wendell Smith, sportscaster from Chicago, married to Wyonella Hicks of Durham, was somewhat of a celebrity. Mrs. Berry Davis of my Youngstown church wrote that her son George's address was quite similar to mine, so I found him as easily. Jim Bargainer, the first Black in Ohio to get an electrician's license, also from the Youngstown church, was with us.

The Black band, which had been recruited from A&T College in Greensboro and NC College in Durham with the promise that they would be stationed at the pre-flight unit at the University of North Carolina until they were discharged, had been shipped to Manana when the pre-flight school was closed. Judge Parsons of Chicago had been head of the band but was discharged before I got to Manana; the current leader was "Lanky" Coles, of Hillside High in Durham and my mother's next-door neighbor. Two other Durhamites were still with the band, Silas James, a VA pharmacist until his death several yeas ago and George Boyd.

Another boost to morale had occurred just before I arrived. CDR Grady Avant had been relieved as CO by LCDR Starnes, a former football coach from Ohio. As I remember, they told me CDR Avant was from Mississippi, which was enough in itself to stack the popularity deck against him. In like manner, a football coach from Ohio would certainly commend himself to Blacks of that era. It was received favorably by all. Although the 1800 hour liberty expiration did not apply to officers, it was annoying to have to log in and out. If one forgot to log in at night, he received a call.

When I checked in at the fleet chaplain's office before getting transportation to Manana, a specialist (W) or chaplain's assistant sang the praises of the senior chaplain, Neal Ellis, for having 1,500 men at church services. I was impressed until I found that the services were held in the outdoor theater right before movie time. Since there were 3,000 men and 1,500 seats, it was wise to go to church and remain for the movie. Chaplain Ellis assigned me and Chaplain Richard Manwell to the chapel where we took turns with the morning service, which attracted about 50. I was scheduled once in the theatre. I am not sure Chaplain Manwell ever was.

Ellis was LCDR and Southern Baptist; Manwell was LT, Congregationalist, and a graduate of Yale. There was a vast theological difference between the conservative Ellis and the liberal Manwell.

Chaplain Ellis felt that Chaplain Manwell did not have a Holy Bible, but a Bible full of holes because of certain beliefs he did not accept, Chaplain Manwell said when I reported this to him "That's exactly what it is." When I mentioned that I wanted to use my fellowship from seminary at Yale, Chaplain Ellis said, "I would not go to a leper colony and not expect to catch leprosy." I considered myself a conservative, but a co-existing type.

An Affirmation of Faith

Chaplain Ellis was leaving, so he gave me his Bible Class, which met nightly except on Sundays. It consisted of about 18 men derisively known as "The Chaplain's Boys." Brother Council was said to carry a Bible "on his hip." He was accused of throwing his Bible down in the middle of a crap game, denouncing the sinners. Brother Mosby preached from the steps of the library until he was hoarse. When Chaplain Manwell was scheduled to preach, Brother Mosby would sit outside in the swing and read his Bible. I have often told of the incident in which somebody tried to tell him a dirty joke. He replied, "My mind is no trash can and I am careful what I put in it."

The "Chaplain's Boys" had really organized themselves into a church. They excommunicated one of the members who remained for the movie after Sunday night service.

His excuse was that he missed his wife. Brother Houston jumped me one day in the library for reading the comics. Since it was before Peanuts, I had to agree that they were not spiritual. When I was detached to go to Guam Brother Houston said, "Chaplain, I don't want any stuff out of you when I get to Heaven; I want to see you there." I fully intend to keep my promise to Brother Houston that I will be there. Hopefully he expects to live out his three score and ten plus a few more. Heaven is my home but I am not homesick yet. I would like to see my daughter get the M.D. she has just started.

I tried without success to convince the Bible Class that one catches more flies with honey and that the sinners they wanted to convert were turned off by their abrasive speech and conduct. Since they all wanted to enter the ministry, I began their theological training with classes in theology, church history, ethics and Bible, Old and New Testament. I gave them file folders and mimeographed the instructional material for them to keep. I lived to see Brother Hensley finish college and seminary, become an Army chaplain, to be invited to preach in a large Baptist church in Baltimore where Brother Reid is pastor and to have Brother Elijah Jones walk into my office at Portsmouth Naval Hospital 31 years later, bringing his folder with him. He helped me as a volunteer in my hospital ministry.

An exception was made to the 1800 hours liberty expiration for those who were out with church parties. In Honolulu there were two churches that we frequented, both of them Pentecostal. Bishop and

Mrs. Baker headed one of them, Sister Mahoi the other. All three of them were large and jolly. On Saturday nights delegations from both churches and soldiers from one of the Army chapels came to bring guitars and tambourines. Sister Mahoi was more energetic and younger so it seemed that we visited her "Church in the Valley" more often. In addition, Sister Mahoi was of Portuguese extraction and a dark brown, even darker than the full-blooded Hawaiians; we felt her to be almost one of us. She and Brother Houston received the gift of tongues one night after Sister Mahoi's sermon. I have never seen a happier man than Brother Houston at that moment. Only once had I seen a smile as wide. It was on the face of a Black paratrooper at Fort Bragg on the front page of the *Fayetteville Observer*. He had saved the life of a White paratrooper by grabbing him as he passed downward when his chute failed to open. The picture had them hugging each other.

The Army had turned over Chapel #2 to the civilian Blacks who worked for the government in Pearl Harbor. The pastor was also in civil service. I took a church party there one night because a friend had introduced me to the organist, Ada Lemon. I took it personally when the pastor told the congregation that the Lord was tired of cute preachers, since I was in dress whites. Surmising that he felt threatened or at least annoyed, we did not visit there again.

Ada and her husband, Lawrence, introduced me to some other Blacks, who for the most part disappointed me. Some drank too much, another reportedly killed his wife after I left and was sent to prison. We had some crime at Manana also. Chaplain Manwell and I went to see some sailors accused of raping a White WAVE. Each one said he was not guilty but the others were. One characterized himself as a "slow mover," and as such was unable to accomplish anything. He further stated that he had been at Manana so long with the early expiration time that when he got in line at the whore house, he always had to leave before he got to the head of the line. When he saw the WAVE laying there, his nature started going to his head, so that he did not know whether to get it or to eat it. Chaplain Manwell blushed when this was said; a wave of sadness swept over me for the amorality of such a lifestyle. The doctor who examined the WAVE said she was a 32 years old virgin before the rape.

An Affirmation of Faith

The first stage of Navy disciplinary action is "Captain's Mast," derived from the days when the CO held court at the mast of his ship. One day our CO had at mast a sailor accused of homosexual conduct. His hair was much longer than regulations permitted and unkempt as well, so that his white hat did not fit properly. His trousers were four inches too short and tight at his hips. He stood there crying. The accusing petty officer said, "I found him lying on the floor with his ass up in the air crying. This fellow (pointing to another sailor) was standing there with his dick in his hand. He said he was going to fuck him." The CO asked the other fellow if he took the accused pants down. The answer was affirmative. When the CO asked why, the reply was "Everybody else did it."

The accused became suspect when he was assigned a different bunk in the barracks. The new occupant of the bunk was repeatedly awakened throughout the night by men expecting to have intercourse with the former occupant.

At one of the smaller commands on the island, I found additional friends from my Hampton four weeks. At the radio station at Lualualei there were remnants of the Youngstown Company at boot camp at Great Lakes 261. Chief Petty Officer Dr. Noble Peyton, my chemistry professor from NCC, was there. The Navy had used him as one of the instructors for the 13 original Black ensigns. He said the Navy had offered him 2½ stripes but he did not want a Navy career. I could not understand his not taking the stripes, which would have made him the ranking Black in the Navy. PO1 Eastmon was there also and still had not been commissioned.

The Red Cross in Hawaii had many field workers. Ours was White, but very zealous for the men's welfare. He told one Captain, "I don't care about those dickey birds on your collar. I want this man to have leave." I was delighted to find Ed and Ruth Spurlock in Red Cross uniforms. Ruth was of the Edwards family in Durham and a ravishing beauty. Compared to her most of the Hawaiians we saw looked plain. An exception to this plainness was Patricia Molokini, who came on base to see Dr. Tom Watkins. When she entered the main gate in her Packard Clipper, the whole base came to attention.

We came to attention, too, when Admiral Chester Nimitz visited. He had received his fifth star. As junior chaplain my office was at the end of the row. For some unexplained reason I was the only chaplain he stopped to see. I was so excited that I could not remember if he had on a tie. The only thing I remember he asked was if we had a choir. For days, I was walking around the base with outstretched arm saying, "Who wants to shake the hand that shook the hand of Nimitz?"

The other chaplains were very eager to do all the counseling they could. Since they had more rank and were White like the administration, they could likely get more done for the men. They would also have to pass the other two offices with their doors invitingly open as Admiral Nimitz had done to get to me. I had my ministerial group every night and they were free, so I spent less time in the office. One week I did not come in until Thursday and I wondered why I came in then; I spent time in sickbay, supply and admin offices, then started finding someone who could go swimming with me at Soldiers' Beach. My roommate and I played tennis in the afternoons. Dr. Goldberg liked to play also. So I developed a routine of swimming in the mornings, tennis in the afternoons and Honolulu at night, unless the Honolulu churches were to visit us.

On the tennis court, I received my only wound of 37 years in the Navy by cutting my middle finger on my right hand trying to open a can of tennis balls. One stitch was required, so I asked about a purple heart. The answer was that since they were American tennis balls rather than Japanese I was not wounded by enemy action. I still carry the scar. My compulsiveness made me uncomfortable with my daily routine. At dinner one evening I told the Chief of Staff of the Pacific Fleet that if the Navy didn't have any more for me to do I would just as soon go back to Youngstown. The other officers were shocked.

On another occasion they were shocked again. We were having a meeting of all officers with a discussion of the rapes, crap games, etc. among the enlisted personnel. In a fit of what I considered righteous indignation, I told them they could expect no better as long as they played poker in the club and frequented the whorehouse across the street. Actually, it was not a whorehouse, but a barracks for female civil servants. My roommate told me my only mistake was using that term for it. The special services officer called me

An Affirmation of Faith

aside and reminded me that many Christians do not consider gambling sinful and that churches that did not have bingo and raffles were so poor that they were inconsequential. The poker games were discontinued for about a week. There had been some discontent on one occasion because ENS G.D. Smith won all the money.

One family from Bishop Baker's church, the Miners, was very close to me. Mrs. Miner had a daughter who was in Tennessee as a missionary. In her pre-Christian days, she had taken hula girls on entertainment tours across the US in a bus. When the girls saw their first snow in Chicago they ran out in their pajamas to throw snowballs. They were given valuable assistance by Joe Louis when they were accused of being bogus. He vouched for them, thereby assuring the success of their tour. Mrs. Miner kept a granddaughter, Philomena, about 3 years old. Philomena wore Chinese pajamas. She called her grandmother "Apo," Chinese for grandmother. Every night when Mrs. Miner prayed with her Philomena would say, "Apo, don't forget to pray for the chaplain." I still remember the wonder in Philomena's face when I gave her a bracelet with her name on one side, mine on the other.

Years later when Philomena was a teenager I was privileged to arrive at the Miner's house just as they were beginning evening prayers. Mrs. Miner was sitting on the floor with them playing her ukulele. A younger brother, whom I had not remembered, Joe was singing lustily:

> *"I've found all I needed in Jesus*
> *I've found all I needed in Him.*
> *He will give me power, in my trying hour,*
> *I've found all I needed in him."*

"This was one of the most precious moments in my life. This is my life, Chaplain," Mrs. Miner said, "my grandchildren and I."

Upon arriving in Hawaii, I was delighted to find that the radio did not play a continuous stream of Hawaiian steel guitar music and Hawaiian songs. After hearing one rendition of "What a Friend We Have in Jesus" jokingly done in Hawaiian style I was also delighted that church music was rendered largely as written. The section of

Waikiki Beach, chosen for the combined picnic, was disappointing. There were large stones underfoot and the girls swam in ankle length dresses. I had never heard of muumuus and did not ask why they dressed that way, assuming it was modesty. A muumuu is quite a costume for a high diving board. The soldiers brought the food and refreshments in a truck we called a six-by, so a good time was had by all. Still I was restless.

Guam

It is likely that the Chief of Staff talked to the Fleet Chaplain because I got orders to Guam. Chaplain Brown was there, having left Manana before I arrived. The response of the other officers was, "See what you get when you shoot off your mouth?" I was excited about the change and justifiably so. I was given three camps, Camp Knox, Camp Wise and Camp Piti. I lived at Camp Knox in a tent in officer's country. The shower was a helmet with holes in the bottom. The tent sported a wooden floor and mosquito netting around the sides. There was another mosquito net suspended over the bed so that the sides of the netting could be tucked under the mattress on all four sides after getting into bed.

The feature I liked most about Camp Knox was the chapel, built by Seabees at the end of the road leading into the camp from the main gate. Strangely, it did not have the same sobering effect on everyone, including some members of the choir who disturbed officers' country one night, by riding through singing "Hey Ba Ba Rebop." I slept so soundly that I missed the impromptu concert even as I did not hear the rounds fired from a carbine in the same area one night by a disturbed sailor.

Sunday morning was busy for me, three services at three camps in three hours. I wore a robe, stole and hood in spite of the heat with all three streaming behind me as we dashed from camp to camp in my jeep. Two of the camps had choir directors. Soloists were plentiful also. Claude Finney in particular did most of the solos for us. Camp Knox had a complete print shop with letterpress and hand set type so we had printed church bulletins and stationery.

In Guam, I had my first experience in running a chaplain's office. Two librarians, two drivers, two yeoman (secretaries) and a mechanic, Wilbur LaBorde (called "Labrador"), were assigned to me. I let them work day on and day off. The jeep was fitted with fender skirts, whitewall tires and a robin egg blue paint job, including the canvas top. An extension was welded to the front passenger seat to make a bench seat all the way across the front. The seats were upholstered in leatherette. Across the panel below the windshield "CHAPLAIN" was painted in large white letters with a cross at both ends of it. There was no other like it on the island. I also had a Dodge Command car that we used for our departmental picnic every Thursday at Tumon Bay. This was also the site for baptisms.

On Easter Sunday morning, I baptized five men by immersion in Tumon Bay. Twenty-five years later on Easter Sunday morning at LaJolla, California I went down to the beach from my motel to put my hands in the waters of the Pacific in memory of that incident.

Although the war was over there were some Japanese still hold up in the caves. It was difficult for us to distinguish between them and the Guamanians, a fact that angered the Guamanians. The atmosphere was so relaxed that nobody complained if Japanese or Guamanians got into the chow lines since Guamanians did some work around the camps. The men were irritated when they stole clothes off the drying lines. They used to sit on the fences and watch the soldiers work on the airstrips, but the Army Air Force General ordered them hunted for capture after it was suspected that they planted a mine that blew up a bulldozer. Leaflets in Japanese were dropped from the air announcing the war's end and a promise not to kill anyone who would surrender. One day eight of them marched into Camp Knox in formation and officially surrendered. Others surrendered at other locations. We had a prisoner of war camp from which the men were taken on work details. They were allowed to go to church on Sundays.

One day I was driving behind a POW truck with a female Red Cross worker. One of the prisoners gestured by pushing his right index finger through a circle made of his left index finger and thumb. I shook my head negatively. He gave a wave off gesture of unbelief. The prisoners seemed to be a happy lot.

An Affirmation of Faith

Red Cross had seven Black females on Guam. Counting marines and soldiers, we had 7,000 Blacks on the island. Regulations permitted the women to go out with officers only. I was the only Black officer left on the island. Every night I took a different one to the movies at one of the camps in its outdoor theatre. I invited them to the weekly departmental picnic. I took them to dinners arranged by senior petty officers. They came to church at the Knox Chapel. Some White officers showed up at church one Sunday when they were singing. They also attended the Marine and Army Air Force chapels. Regulations required that the escorts be armed so I was issued a .45. At each main gate the guard inspected the .45 and returned it to me. I jokingly told the women that there were only a few chaplains and the Chaplain Corps was very anxious to protect them. Actually, the .45 was to protect the women from any men who might decide to take undue liberties.

There were some Black Army officers in Saipan, who used to get liberty to come to Guam. I never asked the women about the conduct of the Army officers but I did refuse them my command car so I would not be an accessory if they got out of hand. The women were proud of their reputation on the island and so was I, even though I told them I was glad they were not my relatives since at that time I thought the situation lacked propriety.

The Army officers on Saipan were useful to the Black Naval personnel there. The White marines were involved in a dispute with the Black sailors over some native women. It was rumored that the marines would storm the Naval Base. The sailors enlisted Army help to set up gun emplacements so that when the marines drove up they evaluated the situation and left. Someone got the bright idea of settling the dispute with a football game. I got orders to Saipan, arriving in time for the football game. The referee wore a .45. One sailor raised his fist at a marine on the line but the marine did not reciprocate. I don't even remember who won the game.

The reason I gave for wanting to make the Saipan trip was to visit some of the units of Black Seabees who had been transferred there from Guam. The island commander asked me when I arrived how long I would stay. When I told him five days he said I could leave before then if I wanted to. He had his chaplain give me a tour of the island which included the units I had wanted to visit. I was impressed by the statue of the Japanese graduate of Louisiana State University who had developed the rice industry on Saipan.

Rumor had it that the island commander was really in a kind of exile for questionable practices at a stateside command, including ownership of the liberty bus, feeding base garbage to his own pigs, taking kickbacks from Navy dentists who treated civilian personnel, etc. If so, his annoyance at my visit was not solely social. I left his island early, taking an entire hand of bananas, which we used to make ice cream in Guam.

The racial situation really made me a powerful figure in Guam. I can't remember anything I ever requested that was denied. When one of my choir members was put on report the legal yeoman tore up the report chit. When the officers at the mess complained that we had lemonade every day the stewards told them I liked lemonade. One of the officers asked if I minded having tea sometimes, I magnanimously consented. Film was developed for me at no cost. Never before, nor since, have I received such deferential treatment.

A point system had been devised to determine the eligibility of personnel to be sent stateside and released. Points were assigned for dependents, time in service, and time overseas. Since the other Black officers arrived there before I did and were mostly married with children, I was the only Black left soon after I arrived. The men delighted in asking me how many points I had because I had fewer than most.

The Red Cross compound was on Commander Marianas Hill. After depositing the movie companion of the evening, I used to drive to the top of the hill for the view of the ocean and sky. It was the most beautiful setting for prayer I ever saw. It remains my most precious memory of Guam.

In about six months the point requirement had gotten so low that even I qualified for transfer and release. I was reluctant to go, naturally because of my pivotal situation. It was also pleasant to be in an environment of plenty.

My first death occurred in Guam. The men liked to have plenty of food in their tents. Beer was rationed and so was Toddy, a chocolate canned drink. A well-stocked tent eliminated the necessity of going

An Affirmation of Faith

to the mess hall. One of the sailors stole a ham from the mess hall and was making his get away in a jeep. It turned over and crushed him. He was considered not to have died as the result of misconduct.

My first contact with Youth for Christ was in Guam. There were Saturday night rallies led primarily by Southern Baptist Chaplains. My Red Cross companions accompanied me, careful not to wear stockings lest they be blood streaked from swatting mosquitoes. Chris LaConta was the most talented tenor I had heard by then, except for Roland Hayes. He sang every Saturday night. For years afterward, I corresponded with one of the Youth for Christ ensigns who got out and went to the LeTouneau School for flying missionaries. Religious commitment among the servicemen on the island was very strong, partially in opposition to the prostitution that was in vogue throughout the Pacific.

The going rate for prostitutes was $20. There were all kinds of stories going around about nurses who were earning thousands and shipping the money home through money orders. We were told of a two-doctor, two-nurse team in Okinawa that used an ambulance just outside the gate of the various camps on payday. One day at one of the camps the paymaster did not arrive before the ambulance did but the men insisted on lining up anyhow. The team protested without success. The doctors were badly beaten, one fatally. At one area chaplains meeting, I heard a chaplain from one of the islands complaining about a semi-official house of prostitution with military guards and military medical inspections. I can still hear him pleading, "But what can one of those guards tell his parents he is doing?" Some of the sailors complained that the procedure was to collect the $20 as one entered the house, and then submit to the inspection. If in the opinion of the medic the man's penis was too large he was ushered out without a refund.

In Guam there was a wide circulation of a pornographic collection called the "G-I Bible." The Commander Marianas chaplains thought that the island commander was not sufficiently diligent in stemming the circulation of the material. I never saw it but talked to some who had. The Island Commander got the upper hand in the argument when the next chaplain he received outranked the Marianas chaplain.

An Affirmation of Faith

Disciplinary problems were common. I loaned one officer my portable organ to play in his tent because he was confined to quarters for selling whiskey to an enlisted man. One sailor staged "wedding" with one of the native women with a buddy of his wearing chaplain's insignia. The next time she came to the base she wanted to know why there was a chaplain driving a bulldozer. Another native woman complained to her sailor boyfriend that her best friend's boyfriend had her house wired with electricity. The sailor reported it, and the boyfriend was brought back to Guam from stateside to stand court martial.

Life in general was relaxed. The Red Cross had a Butler Hut, much larger and sturdier than a Quonset Hut, in which there was a piano, record players, games and refreshments, and most important, decent female companionship. Dress was casual, khaki shorts, short sleeved shirts, pith helmets and boon Dockers (an over the ankle suede finish rubber soled shoe). Sailors wore dungarees, often bleached almost white to contrast with the blue buttons and white hats. They often painted their boon Dockers blue or white and blue. I wore my dress whites no more than twice, on Christmas Day, as I rode all over the island telling people I was having a white Christmas, and possibly at the Easter Sunrise Service in the largest outdoor theatre, a very special event in Guam.

The weather was warm all year and it rained every day. One was usually wet either with perspiration or rain. If it rained during a movie nobody moved. The difference rainy season made was that it rained all day everyday. To retard mildew all closets contained an electric bulb, which was never turned off. We had one typhoon to come by with minimum inconvenience. We had to assemble in Butler Huts. I saw one Quonset Hut roof sail by as a glider would. Nobody was injured.

We were told that much of the material for the war could not be returned stateside, because of prior agreements with the manufacturers that the domestic market would not be flooded with military surplus. We heard accounts of trucks and other vehicles being dumped at sea that still had the plastic covers over the seats.

We heard of jeeps being driven off piers and being buried along with other material still in the shipping cartons. Years later, I saw a picture in a Black magazine of a Black millionaire who had gotten rich by recovering such material and selling it for scrap. One day I heard a radio appeal for all vehicle drivers to fill up with gasoline because a new shipment had arrived with nowhere to offload it. That afternoon a storage tank caught fire.

One strange souvenir of the Guam experience was a fifth of Three Feathers whiskey. One day soon after my arrival there Dr. Jones said, "Give me $1.20, we are going to have a party and invite some native women; the money is for whiskey." I gave him the money. A week later he handed me the fifth of Three Feathers with the explanation that they were not permitted to invite the women. I kept it with me until I was released, and then recalled, until one day in 1958, 12 years later. I gave it to Chaplain George Paulson, Greek Orthodox, with four sons who wrote the history of the bottle on its label. I was satisfied that the bottle would not present a problem for him or for me.

Although a non-drinker, I suppose I have spent thousands on alcohol through similar contributions to parties, receptions, officer's club dues and entertainment in my home. I never picked up the tobacco habit but have bought cigars when promoted and, always kept ashtrays in my office and home. In my attempt to be non-judgmental, I may have been too permissive.

Transportation stateside was arranged for me on a military sea transport ship. Most of the passengers were returning soldiers. A Navy chaplain, Fred Lau, was attached to it. Again, I found life at sea much to my liking. Fred was anxious to get off the ship, out of the Navy, and enter graduate school at the University of Copenhagen. Since my replacement at Youngstown was in no hurry to leave, I was in no hurry to get back, so we agreed that I would request orders to replace him.

We talked to the district chaplain about it. He said, "Fred is just starting his sea tour and he wants to leave. That isn't fair, you have finished yours and you want to go back. That doesn't make sense. Even if you were White, I wouldn't let you do it." We were both disappointed. It was with this decision in mind that I wrote in my letter of proposal of marriage to Marion that she would be spared the inconvenience of other Navy wives with husbands at sea because

I would never be assigned to a ship. I did not think I would have Marine duty either.

I heard in Guam that when a Marine general saw the globe and anchor on a Black man he said he knew the United States was in trouble. Providentially both of these assumptions proved to be wrong, ten and twelve years later.

Charleston, SC

My new duty station was Charleston Navy Yard in the home of my maternal ancestors. I was excited over the prospect of finding relatives and family friends. It was not surprising that I was not allowed to live in the BOQ or eat at the officers' mess because this had been the situation at Great Lakes, and Charleston was where the Civil War started. I found a room with a Seventh Day Adventist family on Ashley Avenue near where the hanging tree stood. I thought the $4 per week rent was reasonable until I found that families in the projects paid $2.50. The landlady and her daughter sat up all night after I said a statement they quoted was not in the Bible. They found it by piecing together two verses from different chapters.

They told me the hanging tree was the site of the hanging of maybe 17 men, some White, some Black, following some kind of disturbance. The street went around the tree, which was protected by a concrete wall. It was also said that more people had been killed by running into the wall than were hung on the tree. It is my impression that the tree has since been removed.

The senior chaplain at the Navy yard was the brother of the Presbyterian Ministers Fund representative who sold me my first insurance policy. Chaplain Glunt assigned me to preach in the brig and to have an office in the steward's barracks. He wanted me to organize a Black Sunday Service in the steward's barracks. Neither I nor the stewards had any enthusiasm for such a project. I passed the word and set a time, but nobody showed. He told me he could have requested my retention if the Black service had panned out, but since it didn't there was no reason to keep me. I would be ordered to Norfolk for separation.

The prospect of separation had me feeling ambivalent. I enjoyed being in Charleston. I found many relatives. I was in the three Black Presbyterian churches as guest preacher or visitor. Rev. Perry Metz, grandson of "Uncle Billy" Metz, a close friend and ministerial colleague of my grandfather, Rev. M. J. Seabrook, escorted me everywhere I wanted to go, including the Seabrook homestead on Seabrook Plantation. He knew the current occupants of the house. We were told that the grave of my great grandfather, Governor Whitmarsh Seabrook, was on Gun Bluff Plantation, which was so overgrown that it would require horses to go through the underbrush. I had hoped to take a picture of the grave for my mother and grandmother. At the school on James Island where my mother taught, I found an old gentleman who said she taught him, so I took his picture.

At Zion Presbyterian Church, I met the McCottrey family and found a daughter, Cynthia, to be a delightful person. At Second Presbyterian Church I heard my first Presbyterian Gospel Choir. The pastor, Rev. Simon Scott, had a son and namesake, then in high school, who became my predecessor at Messiah.

My only function in the Navy Yard Chapel was to perform a wedding for one of the stewards. I assumed I would not be welcome in the Sunday congregation. It was the strangest wedding I ever had. The bride had none of the joyfulness one would expect. When the groom tried to kiss her after the ceremony she pushed him away. That evening I saw him handing her a package over the fence. It looked like a small ham or shoulder. He said, "Chaplain you know I have to support my family." My feeling then was that any Black in South Carolina in the Navy was entitled, under the principle of equity, to just about anything that he could liberate.

I did not relish being in Norfolk again so I was glad when the separation was not a lengthy process. Not to have been promoted was a disappointment. In those days promotion was by ALLNAV, a notice sent to every command in the Navy, announcing that all officers with a certain date of rank were thereby promoted. For LTJGs the date of rank was twelve months before the date of ALLNAV when I first came on active duty.

When I was near 12 months, the period was increased to 18 months; when I got to 22 months promotions were discontinued. I was a LTJG for seven years.

Youngstown, OH

After separation, I spent some time in Durham, then back to Youngstown, where my replacement, Miles McKenzie, still had two months to run on his contract. I went to the employment office and registered for what was called 52-20, $20 a week for 52 weeks, a special program for returned servicemen. The interviewer asked if I would agree to take a job if offered. I told him I would take any Presbyterian Church that became available.

A single room at the West Federal Street YMCA was still only $4 per week. Meals in the cafeteria could be had for $.50 or at Mrs. Epperson boarding house on Belmont Avenue for $.35. A week's bus pass was $1.25. I had my $300 mustering out pay and some terminal leave pay, so I could well afford the two months wait. It was great to be back in Youngstown.

The thing that struck me most after my return to Butler Memorial was the sound of female voices in worship. After two years of Navy choirs and quartets, as well as male soloists, except for the Red Cross workers in Guam, it was refreshing to hear sopranos and altos again. Particularly gratifying was the junior choir, which repeated its special selection, sung the last Sunday before I went to the Navy, "For You I Am Praying." I had been gone such a short time that the choir still had all the original members. That Sunday was one of my most memorable.

Others were quick to say they had been praying for me also, particularly Penny Sidney, who as a 3-year-old asked her grandmother's help to pray for me nightly, that I would come back to Youngstown safely.

An Affirmation of Faith

My first priority was to rehabilitate the church. The men of the church helped a contractor and me to repaint the church inside and out, and to begin a building fund to brick veneer the outside. We promised that everyone who would give $25.00 would be listed on a plaque in the church vestibule. I also solicited contributors for stained glass windows, which would have memorial panes near the bottom. The first donor was "Doc" White, who wanted his window inscribed, "Illustrious Sir Domingo Napoleon White, A.A.O. Noble of the Mystic Shrine." The second family donor was the Davis family, whose son was with me at Manana Barracks. The church had not looked so dingy and un-kept to me before I left, but after so many Navy chapels maintained in excellent shape, I was ashamed for my Navy buddies to visit Youngstown and see the church as it was.

The visitors did come. Ed Bessley, who had been one of my drivers in Guam, came on a night from Pittsburgh with a carload of friends. I took them to one of the Black nightclubs where they were much impressed when the doorman said through the peephole, "Bring them in if they are with you, Reverend." Wilburt Russell, our yeoman from Great Lakes, came for a visit of several days and worshipped with us on Sunday. It was a far cry from the 1500 sailors at Great Lakes in that drill hall but meaningful in other ways.

Other Great Lakes buddies had returned to Youngstown. Several members of the all Youngstown Company 261 were back in town. Herbert Allison was in the hotel business. Brother Faucette, who washed the clothes of the rest of the company while he was sick to keep him from being dropped from the company, was in good health. Emmett Wright called cadence for our contingent in the Fourth of July and Memorial Day parades.

I had a large enough ego when I went to the Navy, but now as the ranking Black to return, I needed a larger hat size. For anything involving the military or veterans, I was the self-appointed authority. There was also a kind of aura that was attached to veterans in those days that Vietnam veterans could not believe. For the populace of Youngstown the war was very popular; the unconditional victory was heavily relished because Youngstown's steel was vitally involved. We were close to Ambridge, PA where LSTs could be seen in various stages of completion, close to Warren, Ohio, where McKenzie muffler made gas tanks for planes. Before I left for the Navy, the daily noon services in the Chapel of Friendly Bells in Trinity Methodist Church always concluded with a prayer for those in the Armed Forces. Because of nearby Camp Reynolds, the West Federal Street YMCA was practically a USO, allowing the soldiers to sleep on the lounge furniture in the lobby when all rooms had been filled. Now that the war was over the YWCA was not as crowded. I was permitted to install a telephone in my room because I was pastor. All the staff I had left was still in place. My new room was across the hall from Cal Smith, a policeman, Prof. Thomas Mumford, who gave up college teaching because of failing eyesight and now worked in one of the mills, and Ernie Leshore, who ran an automobile garage. In those days one could get a new Ford every year for $250 and the trade-in. Ernie did this every year until 1947 then the prices increased dramatically because of the shortage of new automobiles as compared to the demand. It was common practice to give a new car salesman $300 under the table to jump you to the top of the waiting list. I settled for a 1938 Buick sedan that Joe Cooper, a saxophonist who lived at the Y, sold me for $325 so he could buy a new stereo.

Another remnant from pre-Navy days, still living in the Y, was Melvin Flowers, maybe the youngest resident there, still in his 20s, medically discharged from the Army with respiratory problems. Still, he had been somewhat of a companion as I visited members of the congregation, since he lived on his disability pension and had nothing pressing to do with his time. I soon picked up another fellow traveler, Herman Aikens, unemployable because of severe sickle-cell anemia. If it had not been for the blood bank at the mill where his father worked he would long since have been dead.

At the same time I was picked up by two White Presbyterian pastors, as a fellow traveler, Logan Barnes, from Evergreen Presbyterian on Youngstown south side and W. Frederic Miller of First Presbyterian in then Youngstown. Logan, who had finished Pittsburgh Seminary, was a classmate of Harold Tolliver, pastor of Grace, one of three Black Presbyterian Churches in Pittsburgh. Fred had majored in church music at Union Seminary, and was an accomplished organist and director. He gave me my first opportunity to preach at any First Presbyterian Church anywhere when he invited me to substitute for him in Youngstown on the Sunday that he directed Bach's St. Matthew Passion with the Youngstown Symphony and his own choir, with out of town soloists, at an evening concert in his church. He said he wanted to save his energy that morning for the concert. He also paid me to make a wire recording of the concert (before the advent of tape recorders). One day, enroute to some church function, I addressed him as "Rev. Miller." He replied firmly, "The name is Fred." He was the first White man older than I, except for classmates, that I ever addressed by his given name. It was very difficult for me, and I wished he had not been so positive about it, but was afraid to disobey. It was ten year's later in California when I was back on active duty that I reached a first name relationship with Logan Barnes. I was the only Black pastor in Mahoning Presbytery until I left Youngstown for good, a kind of permanent token.

One of the opportunities for such a token came with the summer program for youth. In the Synod of Ohio, a geographical region including most of the state, I was often called upon to be on the faculty of the summer camps, held at Bethany College and at the College of Wooster. Summer camp in those days afforded opportunities for the young people to really become acquainted with the widespread ministries and mission of the church, often foreign missionaries on leave were faculty personnel. Decisions were often made by the young people for Christian vocations. One of the young fellows, Perry, who showed promise, became a Navy doctor years later.

In the Durham days, I had been invited to become involved in an interracial relationship by an acquaintance that was enamored of the practice. Soon afterward he and his girlfriend were arrested and convicted by the court of being a common nuisance. In addition to the immorality of the situation, as he pictured it, I was actually afraid of being lynched. When the sister of one of my Wooster students, being older, a professional and the owner of a Cadillac, seemed friendly in a more than casual way, I invited her to Youngstown where she worshipped at our church and met my friends. I was encouraged, but after leaving Carolyn's house when she said, "Dave, Carolyn is almost as White as I am," I cooled down immediately, deciding that the millennium had not arrived. Then when I was invited to her town, I met her friends, but did not stay at her family's home, nor did I raise the issue. Years later, I talked to a former Wooster camp faculty member, then a missionary in Japan, who had my former friend to write. She was to get married, so I invited her to honeymoon in Japan. This was our last contact, and my last temptation to think of a serious interracial relationship. Without the Ford rumble seat, the foursome of Curtis, Carolyn, Dave and Edna never revived. Curtis went to Hartford to work and study. Floyd came home from the Army, but he and Edna somehow did not hit it off as formerly. Carolyn invited Pat Garrett from Pittsburgh over for a visit. Her dad was one of the four surviving members of the Johnson C. Smith class of 1909, Dr. Garrett a dentist. The others were Rev. Dusenbury, the founder of Butler Memorial, my uncle, Dr. J.W. Seabrook, president of Fayetteville State College, and Dr. Elwood Downing, dentist of Roanoke, VA.

I was really attracted to Pat; I began to call her long distance, made trips to Pittsburgh until one day she told me she wanted so badly to get out of social work. She was "so tired of pounding those bricks." I knew that on my salary I could not support a wife, so if she did not want to work we had no future. I never mentioned this to her; I just stopped driving to Pittsburgh. Another attraction for me was the Black branch of the YWCA. My cousin's wife, Alice Parham, was secretary there for years. One of her protégées, Bea Hayes, belonged to our church. Her father was White but married to her mother.

When my cousin Clarence went to the Urban League job in Warren, Alice went, too, and pinch-hit for him when he was drafted by the Army. Alice was replaced in Youngstown by Mrs. Sanoma Nixon, who later became Mary Frances Eaves, with a beautiful soprano voice, who became the star of the Butler Memorial Choir. Then Sara Alice Phillips, a war widow, came to the Belmont Branch. She had visited her husband's grave in Europe at the Army's expense. When Emmett Wright asked me at Carolyn's wedding reception, "What about that Sara Alice Phillips?" I told him of her intellect, wit, taste in furnishings and pretty new car; it was not long afterward that they married. Sara Alice became executive secretary of the national YWCA office in New York. Emmett is pastor of a church in Long Island. They live near my brother-in-law, Dr. J.W.V. Cordice, who removed the letter opener from the chest of Martin Luther King, Jr.

Carolyn did marry Curtis, with me as best man and Gwen Belcher of Nashville as maid of honor. Carolyn's dad, Dr. S.S. Booker, a founder of Alpha Phi Alpha, the first Black fraternity, married them at Third Baptist Church, the Baptist church of prestige rather than numbers. The ceremony had a phrase for the man to repeat that I never heard anywhere else, "and with all my worldly goods I thee endow." The newlyweds went to Wilberforce University; there Curtis was to head the Wesley Foundation. Years later, I officiated at their daughter Beth's wedding at a Lutheran Church in Washington. This time Gwen was the organist.

Doc White seemed not to be any nearer death than when I left. In my absence an old friend of his, Captain James, a retired fireman, had written me often for him. I had answered the letters religiously. Now Doc wanted to give his house to me; I demurred, but suggested that he give it to Butler Memorial, which he did. Then he applied for old age assistance. He was rejected because of the recent gift of the house. It did not seem to even annoy him; perhaps the move had come at the request of his attorney. In any event, it seemed to be understood that he would occupy the house for life anyhow and his allowance from the lawyer would continue.

It seemed to me that it would extend my ministry to the community if I participated in several local organizations. Therefore, I joined the alumni chapter of my college fraternity, Kappa Alpha Psi, and at Doc's urging made application to the oldest Black Masonic Lodge, Covenant 59. In the next few years I advanced through the Scottish rite to the 32nd Degree. My participation in fraternity life was constant also. I was the only clergyman in either, as I remember.

So often when on active duty I would sign official forms with the "R" of "USNR" twice as large as the "USN." I had a copy of a poem by a dentist entitled, "Don't Take Away My R;" some years later that expressed my sentiment exactly. When asked if I would stay in after the war my reply was St. Paul's "Me Genoite!" "God forbid."

An Affirmation of Faith

After a few months of freedom, the Navy did not look as bad as it had. The hero worship helped. I found a reserve chaplains unit that drilled regularly at Newcastle, PA, not far from Youngstown. We had a nice lunch in a downtown hotel. The CO of the unit was much friendlier than the senior chaplains for whom I had worked. He even offered help with correspondence courses. The other chaplains were quite congenial also. An invitation came to the annual meeting of the Military Chaplains Association in Washington, which I attended in uniform. It was quite pleasant to be in uniform without the discipline and responsibilities to command.

While in Washington, I visited Dolly Davidson, great granddaughter of Captain Robert Smalls, whom I had met at Hampton. Seeing her brought back the pleasant memories of the Hampton experience. The next time I saw her a year later she remarked that it was the first time she had seen me in Jody clothes, with quite a bit of upset. I told her that I would send her a shoulder board from my grey uniform, sensing she had completely lost interest in me, now being a civilian. Meanwhile the work at the church continued. We were given a lift by the arrival in Youngstown and the church of Rev. A. James Reaves and Mrs. Reaves, up from Sanford, NC to live with a daughter on Poland Avenue. He had been ordained by the United Church of Christ and had long since retired. I put him in a robe and asked him to do the pastoral prayer every Sunday, and to preach on occasion. The congregation was enthralled by his prayers and the bearing of this adorable old couple. My only disappointment with this couple was the Sunday they invited me to have dinner with them. The entree was chitterlings, which I had never before eaten, because when in Durham, Mrs. Cox across the street used to clean them with the odor permeating the whole neighborhood. Happily, the Reaves chitterlings did not taste the way Mrs. Cox's chitterlings smelled. On a visit to Durham I went to Sanford, looked up the Reaves family and made a wire recording with greetings by his nephews to bring back to Youngstown. I also looked up the father of the Red Cross worker at Great Lakes, John Ballard.

Another project I undertook was the construction of an office in the basement of the church where I could do counseling. I retrieved my typewriter, typing stand, file cabinet and some of my books.

With a few pieces of furniture, studio couch, desk and a sermon file, I was in business. Rev. Gibson of Centenary Methodist Church sold me his platen press and type. Virgil Moccia of Manchester Presbyterian Church in Pittsburgh sold me his Multilith. So with the old Mimeograph I was off and running as far as printing was concerned.

The printing equipment was located in the ladies rest room, which had no use during the week except on Wednesday evening at prayer meeting time or Thursday evening at choir practice time. This rest room had the most unusual concrete floor. When I called the health department for the procedure to apply for a permit to install a ladies rest room the official asked how many rest rooms we had. When I said there is one, he said they would make me put in another one and no permit was needed. Since concrete was $9.00 per yard, and that was the smallest load delivered, I ordered it, after the men of the church installed the plumbing. There was so much concrete that the commode base and four inches above it were covered. Therefore, I scooped the concrete out in a semi-circle to provide access to the base of the commode in case plumbing difficulties developed. If a tornado should strike, Butler Memorial's ladies rest room floor would survive.

With everything now organized to my satisfaction I began planning to return to school. The University of Pittsburgh had an extension course in counseling taught in Youngstown by Dr. Zahniser, which I took. I wrote the seminary requesting living space while attending the University of Pittsburgh full-time in a Ph.D. program in religious education. Dr. Jarvis Cotton denied my request on the grounds that Youngstown had a greater need of me so I should give full time to my ministry. Then I wrote the University of Chicago and was assigned dormitory space. The seminary agreed that I could use the Sylvester Marvin Fellowship, which I won at graduation for having the highest average in the class, even though the Chicago theological position was suspect in conservative and fundamentalist circles.

University of Chicago

Therefore in September I went to Chicago on the train, took the elevated city train to 63rd and University, and a taxi to the Divinity School. There were two disappointments. Both of my roommates were Black, Scarlette of the staff of Bennett College in Greensboro and Long of Miles College in Alabama. I had my friends to send my mail addressed to the "Colored Room" but never heard anything from it. I told Shelton Key, a classmate about my unhappiness so he suggested that I apply at the Congregational Theological Seminary, which was closer to the Divinity School anyhow. I got the room then requested a refund from the university, which I never got. Once when an alumni representative called me for a donation I told him about this and suggested I had already given.

The other disappointment was that I had to take entrance examinations. Since I was an honor graduate of college and seminary, I thought this was unfair. If there was a graduate record examination then, I did not hear of it. Nevertheless, I did fail the entrance examination in two areas: biology and humanities.

Because I missed the biology by just one point, I was administratively passed. For the humanities deficiency I had to take a course, Humanities II, and the following examination. In college I did not have art appreciation, which was not offered until after I had graduated (by my wife-to-be), music appreciation, which was not required if taught nor philosophy, of which the one course was taught by one I considered dumb, dumb, dumb. I was pleased that I had passed economics since I never had a course in that subject either. I supposed that hearing my dad talk about his work as trust officer at the bank stood me in good stead.

The University of Chicago in those days was unique. If one could pass the entrance examination, one could matriculate after the second year of high school. Class attendance was not required, only that the examination be passed. Anyone who thought he/she could pass the examination without taking the course was welcome to try, and the tuition was $25 a semester hour instead of the $40 charged if one went to class. While I was there a YMCA secretary's son who had finished high school in Switzerland took all the examinations for his B.A. in a week. He decided then to enter graduate school since he was settled in. There were many 18-year-old B.A.s, who had come in after their sophomore year and finished in two years. These were the famous whiz kids.

It was quite stressful to be a 26 year old in a class of 18 whiz kids. My heart went out to the teachers who had better have their facts straight. One of them, Dr. Axelrod, sat cross-legged on the desk and took on all comers. The other, whose name I have forgotten, was a recently released Army Chaplain who later was on the staff of Faith at Work in Columbia, Maryland with Bruce Larsen and Lloyd Ogilvie and the president of a Midwestern college. You can believe that I listened well, read voluminously and was well prepared for the 6 hour open book examination. After it, I ached all over but was thankful for the assurance of success.

The University of Chicago at that time was host to the Federated Faculty of four theological schools, the Divinity School of the University of Chicago (Northern American Baptist), Meadville Theological School (Unitarian), Disciples Divinity House and Congregational Theological Seminary. Such a pluralistic structure allowed a liberal view not possible at the usual denominational seminary. The fact that one of the schools was Unitarian also made a difference. Particularly was this true because the best-known Unitarian teacher was Dr. James Luther Adams, a translator of Paul Tillich. Dr. Adams had been a Pentecostal Preacher before he went to Harvard for graduate work. Often in his class, he might be waxing eloquently about Jesus when he would stop and say, "But remember I am a Unitarian." One evening I drove all the way from

An Affirmation of Faith

Great Lakes to hear Dr. Adams lecture on "The Christian Myth and Bach's St. Matthew Passion." In the lecture, he considered most of the Christian story as myth in the sense of not being true in a scientific sense but conveying truth. We used to say Dr. Adams lectured in public but preached in class.

There were several ex-chaplains in Chicago then. One of them came back to the dormitory one day in great agitation. One of the professors had called Jesus a bastard, so he was packing his clothes to leave the school. I tried to argue that it should make no difference what those clowns said because what he really wanted was a Chicago Ph.D. He said he could not stay in a school that would allow such a statement to be made, so he left. At the orientation for new students, Dean Loomer outlined the liberal theological position of the school as contrast with the fundamentalist position. My reply was that those who faced combat needed more faith than that. The next day I received a snide compliment on my heckling of the dean. I accepted personally and still accept the fundamentalist principles or doctrines of the Virgin Birth, Divine Inspiration of Scripture, Divinity of Christ, Substitutionary Theory, The Trinity, The Resurrection of the Body, and God as Creator of All that Is. None of these was an essential doctrine for graduation from Chicago.

On the other hand, Dr. James Hastings Nichols, eminent church historian, began his chapel sermon with "Jesus is God." The liberalism extended both ways. Even Dean Loomer did not tell me to leave. In my interview with him, he wondered why I wanted an additional degree if I did not want to teach. When I told him I wanted a Ph.D. for the prestige he suggested that there were easier schools where one could be secured.

It was really thrilling for me to be in the company of worldwide scholars. Dr. Amos Wilder, brother of Thornton Wilder, author of *The Bridge at San Louis Rey,* taught New Testament. He was much impressed by the term paper I did for him on the miracles of Jesus on my Vari-Typer, using several typefaces. Dr. Wilhelm Pauck, who later went to Harvard, was in theology. Other scholars included Dr. Daniel Day Williams, who came out of the church pastored by Hartzell Spence, about whom the movie *One Foot in Heaven* was made, and Dr. Joakim Wach who expanded the categories of Ernst Troeltsch.

Dr. J. Coert Rylaarsdam was in Old Testament; Albert Schweitzer, whose *Quest of the Historical Jesus* nearly created a theological revolution, came to play the organ at the Rockefeller Chapel of the University during the Bach festival. Anders Nygren who wrote *The Idea of the Holy* came to lecture. It was also at Chicago that I heard Bishop Martin Dibeliusa of East Germany talk about the difficulties of living under a Communist regime as a Christian.

There were many communists at Chicago in those days. At the Woodlawn house where I ate lunch one could hear complaints about *Time* magazine, the comic strip Little Orphan Annie and Colonel McCormick, publisher of the *Chicago Tribune*. I liked Woodlawn House because it was designed by Frank Lloyd Wright. At Chicago, there was much support for the Rosenbergs, who had sold atomic secrets to Russia. One day when I went to vote in student elections, a volunteer asked if I needed help. I told him I wanted to know who the community candidates were. He cheerfully pointed them out on my ballot.

Although a full time student, I still took care of the church in Youngstown with the help of the convenient railroad schedule. I would leave Youngstown Sunday night after the evening service, sleep all night on the coach, wake up when the train stopped at Gary, not far from Chicago. Not until the train became crowded after the Christmas holidays and I had to stand, did I find out that the train stopped at Kent, OH, maybe 50 miles from Youngstown. I could go to sleep very quickly with my ticket between my fingers as my hands were clasped on my chest. The conductor would just slide the ticket out without waking me.

On Fridays after class there was a convenient train to Youngstown from Chicago. It did not take long to catch up with the week's mail and happenings. Then I could make visits on Saturday and Sunday afternoons. The Sunday afternoon visits usually included a stop at the Mahoning County Tuberculosis Sanitarium on Kirk Road. I used to record our morning Service on a wire recorder and take it out to be played during the week by Edward Bailey, a member of our choir who was a patient there. The wards were segregated as to sex and race. It was there that the expression "beauty rest" became understandable to me because it seemed that the women were unusually beautiful. It may have been due to other causes, such as attractive sleepwear or time to carefully dress, do hair, or put on makeup. The men told me that such prolonged bed rest strengthened their sexual urges

The death rate at the sanitarian was rather high. The primary treatment was the bed rest. Sometimes a lung was collapsed to allow it to heal faster. On other occasions, a lung was removed. I did not like to see the long curved scar from such surgery because it meant only one lung was left. Marguerite Armstrong was one of the prettiest who died. Her boyfriend, Joe Baldwin said to me, "Don't come telling me about any kind of God after what happened to Marguerite. She never did anything to hurt anybody except herself." I failed Joe in not taking the time to explain a possible way out of his theological dilemma. He was killed not long afterward.

My friend Herman Aikens, possibly because of his acute sickle-cell anemia, always refused to go with me to visit the sanitarium. It was the only place I went that he was afraid to visit. He developed tuberculosis himself and was taken there. He lasted only long enough for me to visit him once. When I asked the congregation on Sunday morning to join me in prayer for him, I saw Margie Henderson in the back of the church shaking her head. She was also a friend of his and had been informed he had died.

The Aiken's family asked me to have something to say at his funeral, although he did not belong to our church. I talked of his suffering with patience and the identity of Jesus with such suffering. When I had finished the pastor said, "I will let that go for the eulogy." Then he began what I considered a tirade against Herman for all the things he could have done for the church that he didn't do as a way of warning other young people that they had better get busy about the Lord's work, because they did not know how much time they had. My friends and I were disgusted at what we considered very harsh treatment. Some of them intimated that they would come to my church but never did. Now as I think about the composition of the audience and the life styles of so many of them the pastor did have a point. Herman's mother thanked me for my words as reported to her by other relatives. She had already collapsed before I got up to speak.

Two of my fellow students at Chicago became prominent in later years. Frank Madison Reid, Jr., whose father was an African Methodist Episcopal Bishop, is now a Bishop himself. Dennis Bennett is credited with beginning the Charismatic movement in the Episcopal Church, from which it spread to other main-line Protestant Churches and to the Catholic Church.

In addition to the Sylvester Marvin Fellowship, I was supported by the G-I Bill, which paid all tuition and fees, bought books and gave a monthly allowance. The secretary in the Veterans Affairs was Mrs. Doris Lloyd, whose husband Gil was also a veteran and aspiring minister. I kept in contact with them over the years until recently. The last I heard, he had been made president of a national organization of Black clergy. They settled in Seattle, WA. At Western Seminary, (now Pittsburgh) there were no women in the student body. At Chicago there was a contingent of about 20, including Kyo Kasai, who became engaged in a neat little ceremony at a student party to Victor Fujiu, Martha Hayes, Davida Blake and Ardis Tiedt. Somehow, I started inviting one of them to have lunch with me on Wednesdays. One Thursday a male classmate whose name escapes me asked, "Dave, how come you had lunch with Ardis yesterday?" I answered, "Because it was Wednesday." He wanted to know what that had to do with it. I told him it was just a custom I had. He then said that he accepted the theological position of the school but not the social. He was also an out-spoken pacifist, remarking one day that if we had another war he hoped all of us ex-servicemen would get to go.

Somehow a solicitous attitude or my suspicion of one was annoying to me. One day I got the message that Davida wanted to see me. I suspected that she wanted to invite me to accompany her to a school dance. My reply was that she could find me. She thereupon invited a graduate student in another field who was also Black and lived in our dormitory. The other females thought she was doing a nice thing.

Rebecca Woodson, a high school classmate, was on the campus as a lab tech for Dr. Allen, who had hired her when he was at Duke.

They were doing research on urine. Students were asked to bring urine to a large marble-like round container that stood outside their office. It looked as though it could hold 100 gallons. Sometimes I had lunch with Rebecca and her friend, Lois High.

The Chicago theological curriculum was as novel as the college curriculum, but not as freewheeling. Class attendance was expected. I heard of nobody finishing the degree program in a week of examinations. There was a core curriculum that was common to the B.D. and Ph.D. programs. Upon completing the core with the examinations, one could go either way. It seemed stupid to me to work for another bachelors if one could get a Ph.D. in practically the same time except for the dissertation. After the core, one took courses in a specific area after which there was a field examination for Ph.D. students or graduation for B.D. students. After the field examination, the Ph.D. students took qualifying examinations in French and German then wrote a dissertation. I did not finish the two-year core the first year because my prior work was not considered up to Chicago standards.

In fact, I was denied admission to a class taught by Seward Hiltner, because he did not think the work I had done at Chicago, under two professors for whom he did not have the highest regard, adequately prepared me for his class. He permitted me to audit the class, however. He said he did not want me to go out and say I had studied under Hiltner. After auditing the class, I still had no notion of where I was inadequate, but maybe that is proof that he was right.

It reminded me of my visit to Northwestern University to see Dr. Carroll Wise and ask for admission as a Ph.D. student. He said he already had four Ph.D. students, but I could come and get a Master's. I told him I already had one, and considered it enough. Years later when I began to supervise doctoral candidates I understood how one could have too many.

In Chicago at this time there was a family situation. Two of my siblings were with me in the same city. My baby sister Ella was at Northwestern taking music therapy and my little brother Ward was at McCormick Seminary. We even shared one professor, Dr. Joseph Harotounian of the McCormick faculty, as guest lecturer at Chicago. He was unique on the Chicago campus, an avowed

Calvinist. He gave as reason for his theological position, "If a man as smart as John Calvin could believe the way he did he must have been right." Dr. Harotounian had many stories to tell of his experiences as a chaplain at Wellesley. After a class the student we used to call "Stick" Bennett because he walked with a cane, said to Dr. Harotounian, "Doctor, you will have to admit that the Bible is only human experience." The reply was, "Yes, but it wasn't your experience and it wasn't mine."

On my first visit to the McCormick campus, I found my brother in the gym shooting baskets. He said he also had a job working in the dining hall as a waiter. He had just been to see a Veterans Administration psychiatrist to try to determine why he did not get better grades. He was used to good grades for little work in college when he majored in Chemistry. I used to get up at 4 a.m. to study; he got up at 7:30 a.m. when he had a class at 8 a.m.

My brother had access to a VA psychiatrist because he served about a month in the army. He and about a dozen of his senior classmates at NC Central were drafted and sent to Fort Bragg. There the White mess hall had a breakdown, so all the White soldiers were fed in the Black mess hall at regular meal times, the Blacks were fed afterward. My brother and his friends organized a hunger strike, refusing to eat in the mess hall at any time. All of them were ordered to the hospital, were examined, declared physically unqualified for service and honorably discharged. Therefore, he was not eligible for the GI bill benefits in a school.

Brother Ward did not get better grades, but the students credited him with having the best mind on the campus. In addition to his work and exercise, McCormick had female students also. They included Jean Jackson, daughter of Attorney T. Lamar Jackson, of Youngstown, Jean Muir, a movie star type, and Castle Williams, a Black student who was working on a master's in Christian Education. They introduced me to a local general practitioner, Dr. Love, unmarried, who was somewhat interested in Jean Muir but thought her parents might object. He was sure his parents would object to her also, since they lived in Mississippi, as most Black parents would. Dr. Love drove a Buick with trumpet horns outside the hood on each side.

Brother Ward also had a Sunday job as assistant at Grace Presbyterian Church. The pastor, Dr. Augustus Eugene Bennett, was a rarity, a Black graduate of Princeton Seminary. I gave my brother a cutaway suit, then had a picture made of the three of us in cutaways. One Sunday I missed going to Youngstown so I could preach at Grace. Sister Ella Lucy brought her boyfriend to church that Sunday, Dr. Charles D. Proctor, who later became her husband.

When the school term ended I returned to full time ministry in Youngstown. As usual, we had vacation Bible School, June weddings, Junior High and High School, Presbytery and Synod conferences. With Curtis and Carolyn married and at Wilberforce, Pat Garrett, out of the picture, I was glad to hear from Marion, my wife to be, that she would be coming to Pittsburgh for Alice Wanzer's wedding. I invited her to visit Youngstown. I was quite interested in why she communicated at all, since I assumed she was still engaged. When she arrived, I found that she had broken the engagement, because the fiancé did not seem interested in setting an early date for the wedding. As I remembered it, he was thinking of seminary anyhow.

I showed Marion the whole of Youngstown, or my part of it, the church, the sanitarium, and the homes of the more active members, the St. Augustine's Episcopal Church, its rector and his wife. She seemed to enjoy the visit and to be impressed by everything she saw. I had always believed that she would not do as a pastor's wife; now I was having second thoughts. I knew that my salary was woefully inadequate for two and her position as head of the art department was tied to NCC, but it was something to think about. We began to correspond more frequently and I went to see her when I visited Durham. I learned that she was teaching a Sunday school class at St. Titus Episcopal Church where her father was on the Vestry.

This summer had its sadder experiences also. One of our teenagers contracted syphilis from her husband while she was carrying twins. Both twins died in childbirth as did she. The three of them were placed in the coffin, one baby in each of her arms. It was the most heart-rending funeral I ever had. One of my friends who belonged to our church got angry and shot his wife's boyfriend in her house. The wounded man died, but not in the time period in which the assailant could be automatically guilty of manslaughter. I made a sizable contribution to his defense fund. Another friend and supporter, a local insurance agent, C.H. Nelson, was taken to the sanitarium where he died, but not before commending me to the staff. When September came, I was ready to go back to Chicago.

This was my last year of eligibility under the G-I Bill, so I intended to complete the core, take some courses to help on the field examination and pass the German language exam. The course work went well on schedule. I bought a German grammar and began to study with a classmate, Marvin Maris. He was from a German speaking family. He used to go to the library in the afternoons and read German newspapers

I began to get apprehensive, so I engaged a tutor, Savel Kliatchko. He wanted to teach me to speak the language, but I mistakenly refused this approach because the examination was a reading one. I know now from experience with Japanese that it would have helped really, if I had learned to speak the language. Sadly, enough, when the day came and I went in for the examination, I was given a book, from which I was to translate two pages from different sections of the work. I could not even translate the title of the book, *Monasticism in Protestant Church Life*. Since dictionaries were permitted, I did the best I could with the two pages but not satisfactorily in the opinion of the examiner. When the names of those who had passed were listed mine was not included. I read and re-read the list many times. The French had been so much easier, a book on the reunion of various branches of the Methodist Church in America. In addition, I had taken French two years in high school and two years in college. Also, I had passed a reading examination for a master's in education at NCC. I still have never had a single class in German, but I had a real sense of failure. Savel complained that I had embarrassed him because people knew he was my tutor.

The university allowed one failure, but with the second failure sufficient explanation had to be given before one could try the third time. I was afraid to try the second time because I could not think of a logical reason I should be allowed to make the third try. I never took another German examination. When I got to the language requirement stage at American University only one language was required, so I passed the French again after taking a cram course. So nearly 30 years after starting on a Ph.D. program I finally completed it. Nevertheless, I continued to study German, bought a German Bible, which I began to read with much interest since it was Luther's translation. Marion and I began to write in German. An assistant secretary at the YMCA in Youngstown had majored in German and recommended the *Hagboldt* Series for study. I subscribed to the German version of *Reader's Digest, Das Beste*. When I went back on active Navy duty I had enough nerve to ask to be assigned to the only Navy billet for a chaplain in Germany, Bremerhaven. Instead I was ordered to Japan since the Bremerhaven chaplain got an extension because his son was being assigned to Germany with an Army Unit. In Sasebo, Japan I found a German speaking Presbyterian Pastor named Zenno who studied under Karl Barth. I invited him to the club for dinner and took great delight in the bewilderment of the Japanese waitresses as they heard us conversing in German.

Youngstown was losing its attractiveness for me for several reasons. It seemed as though after doubling the membership we had reached a plateau from which advancement did not appear to be forthcoming. I had been there nearly ten years, off and on, so it seemed to me that someone else should be having a try. It began to bother me that I was not married, and therefore, as I saw it, not a man of responsibility. My mother had married when she was 30; the next March I would be 31.

There were two vacant Black Presbyterian churches, Bethesda in Pittsburgh and St Mark's in Cleveland, both twice the size of Butler Memorial. A committee from Bethesda came to hear me one rainy Sunday morning but left with a tinge of sadness at my performance as I sensed it. St Mark's never responded to my overtures. The resigning pastor at Bethesda, Rev. Robert Pierre Johnson told me that I had been in Youngstown too long. He was moving to Washington and Fifteenth Street Presbyterian. St. Mark's called Rev. Isaiah P. Pugue, who had been succeeded at Trinity in Rochester, NY by my brother-in-law, Rev. Charles G. Kearns. Even though Trinity had desired Rev. Pogue to be discontinued as pastor, he and his wife remained in the congregation and sang in the choir until the call to

Cleveland came. I felt that he deserved St. Mark's much more so than I for his unusual Christian attitude.

Meanwhile I was getting notes from the Navy asking if I'd like to return to active duty. I felt that I could not move to another church at the age of 30; heaven help me at age 40. It also seemed an opportunity to get married, since the Navy pay and allowances would provide adequate financial support for a childless family. A further advantage would be that the Navy would not require a chaplain's wife to perform the pastor's wife rule, which role I was not convinced Marion could comfortably perform. So I agreed to return to the Navy.

My sister, who was a year younger, had been married for some time and had several children. My baby sister, who was five years younger, also had one daughter. My little brother invited me to come to Salisbury, NC to perform the wedding ceremony for him and Gerry in the church where he had served as assistant in her hometown where he met her. It was scheduled for the Sunday before Vacation Bible School started so I chartered a small plane to make the round trip on the same Sunday after morning worship. We sat down at Clarksburg, VA to refuel. As the pilot checked his magnetos he found the left one was missing and needed minor repair. I had misgivings about continuing the trip. The pilot offered to do a circle over the airport and then land to pick me up. I told him if he got airborne to keep on his way back to Youngstown because I was taking a bus home. I called my brother and he got the senior pastor to do the wedding. So I was the last unmarried one of the family and the oldest.

Providentially, Jimmie and Dorothy Woodson visited Butler Memorial one Sunday. He was working in the mill even though he had a Masters in history and was working on a Ph.D. at the University of Wisconsin. He was a graduate of Tuskegee, who knew many of the alumni I knew in Durham. Dorothy was such a delightful person that I was even more drawn toward Marion because she reminded me of Dorothy. On my first visit to their home they decided to join Butler Memorial. I was overjoyed. As the days passed I felt that I had found another brother in Jimmie as I had with Marion Fleming when I was a preteen and with George Wilson in seminary.

Jimmie was of course interested in German, also Spanish and Italian. The church was in an Italian neighborhood. Youngstown was getting an influx of Latinos. It soon became apparent to me that I could leave Butler Memorial with Jimmie in charge until another pastor could be found. He was not interested in commuting to Pittsburgh Seminary to enter the ministry as such. But he was willing to accept responsibility for the church program and the preaching. So I wrote Marion a letter of proposal on my Vari-Typer, using the church text font similar to Old English print, telling her that I would be returning to active duty in the Navy on 1 January and that I would like to be married before my 31st birthday on 21 March. I promised her that she would not have the separation problem common to other chaplain wives since I would never go to sea.

As I remember it I waited patiently a week for a reply. When I had heard nothing for two weeks, I was talking about it with Jimmie in the office one evening when we decided that a call would be appropriate. I called, asking Marion if she had received my letter, with some degree of anxiety. She had received it, had talked it over with her parents and had decided in the affirmative as to the marriage. But the date would have to be at the end of the school year because with her job she did not have time to buy clothes and make other necessary arrangements. Somewhere in the conversation she said, "I don't have anything to wear," a refrain I have heard many times through the years.

Although I was disappointed by the delay, I felt that the wait was worth it because Jimmie and I agreed that I was in love and I knew nobody else that I thought would do as well as a Navy wife. In later correspondence, I suggested 1 June as a date that would be easy to remember. I happily informed the congregation, family and friends. In the congregation there was some disappointment and a little grumbling about turning everything over to the "Layman in Charge." But family and friends were joyous with me. It would the first wedding in Durham for the Cordice family. Marion's brother and sister had married in New York.

Part III.
At Peace with God: Stepping Out in Faith

Great Lakes, IL 2

And so on New Year's Eve in 1950, I caught the very familiar Baltimore and Ohio train for Chicago, this time with a one way ticket. When I arrived at Great Lakes this time I was welcome at the Bachelor Officers Quarters, the Commissioned Officers' Mess and the Officers' Barber Shop.

Again I was assigned to Camp Robert Small but it was no longer a locus of training for Black recruits. The Black proportion, as in the rest of the Navy, was less than 5%. When I checked in I was told that I was eligible for promotion from my original rank of LTJG, which I had held for seven years, to full LT. This was a pleasant surprise and perhaps the last of the ALLNAV promotions in which everyone with the same date of rank was promoted by directive, or one of the last selection board promotions in which everyone in the zone was promoted. With my record it had to be either one or the other because I was not competitive at that time. In 1951, even the promotions to CAPT were with "100" opportunity.

CAPT Frederick W. Meeling, an unusual Catholic, was Center Chaplain. He had a missing finger but could play the piano well, especially Protestant Hymns which he delighted in singing with other chaplains. A Marine Colonel told me that he was responsible for his unit's sanity during the war. They were on a small island in the South Pacific. Each evening Chaplain Meeling used to gather everyone down on the beach to tell sea stories. Even during official calls at his office he would say, "One more story and I'll let you go."

My assignment was to the receiving station, where I worked under Chaplain Karl Petersen, a Lutheran. The receiving station was filled with men who were reserves and had been recalled to active duty. Many of them did not want to be on active duty and applied for hardship discharges. Most of our time was spent counseling with such men and helping them to get their papers in order. We had a yeoman (secretary or clerk) who could produce an application for hardship discharge with 7 copies in record time. Any application we sent to the board by 1100 would be decided upon by 1500. So every day at 1500 there was rejoicing as well as disappointment.

I remember one non-rated married man with 7 children who had allotted 100% of his pay to his wife. He used to hitchhike to the Naval Air Station Glenview, then try to get a hop to Memphis, where his family lived. One of the pilots promised him that any time he could get to Glenville he would find him a ride to Memphis and return. I asked him why he joined the reserves with such a family; his answer was that he needed the money. I used to say that the board would release anyone with three children and a pregnant wife; this man was released as soon as he got the necessary affidavits from home attesting to his circumstances and a job guarantee exceeding his Navy pay.

There were some who were glad to be recalled. I remember one seaman who came in asking for enough New Testaments to fill up the rest of his sea bag. He had been ordered to a small ship without a chaplain, and he intended to witness to the men aboard at every opportunity. My saddest experience there involved a sailor who noticed that someone had left an electric iron. He spoke to the Master at Arms about it who told him to help himself to it. The fellow who owned the iron missed his train and came back for it. The fellow who had it was reported for wrongful possession and given a bad conduct discharge.

In the temporary absence of the assigned chaplain I was sent over to the WAVES barracks. At that time the WAVES had to be 21. It was frustrating for them because the 17-Year-old male recruits would say "Yes Ma'am" to them. It was even more frustrating when the Protestant WAVE Sunday Service was organized since there were no men on hand. Large numbers of them switched to the Catholic Church Part until the innovation was discontinued. In interviewing

An Affirmation of Faith

a WAVE one day I asked for her religious preference. She said that she did not know what kind of guy she might meet.

My most unique experience with WAVES involved the little city of Zion, IL near Great Lakes. Zion was founded by two former Episcopal Priests, father and son who set up the Christian Catholic Church. Zion had no alcoholic beverages, no movies, no smoking even in rental property. Annually the residents staged the Zion Passion Play which drew large crowds from many miles away. On a Saturday night two sailors took two WAVES for a ride then issued an ultimatum, "give in or walk back." With some difficulty one WAVE persuaded the other to get out as they were passing through Zion. In short order the police wanted to know what they were doing walking through town. When informed, they radioed for the sailors to be picked up and jailed. Then they took the WAVES back to Great Lakes. Sunday morning before church the WAVE who got angry over that ultimatum called and asked me to get the fellows out of jail because they needed to be with their families on Sunday. On another day a very effervescent WAVE I had interviewed waved at me as her platoon was marching down the street. Her petty officer warned her that she could be put on report for such. Her reply was "Go ahead bitch, put me on report," which she did, leading to her discharge. I wondered if she ever paid for her car, the reason she joined the Navy. Another WAVE was discharged as a paranoid-schizophrenic after she reported another wave for massaging her back as she requested, then moving to massage the front side. The offending WAVE was discharged also. The psychologist at that time was liberal with his diagnoses of neuroses and psychoses for WAVES. The most colorful WAVE was, LT Mabel Hughes, who played the organ for several of the Sunday services. They used to call her 6:00 o'clock Mabel because she began with a 0600 hour Catholic Mass after a few hours of sleep Saturday night. Her husband came from Maryland for a visit. As he was leaving he said to me "keep an eye on Mabel." I replied smiling "That would be like watching a ping pong game." Her favorite quip to get a choir moving was "Quick like a bunny."

The WAVE experience left me enamored of the WAVES and very happy to get one or more assigned to me. Years later I tried to get each of my daughters to join the Navy without success.

An Affirmation of Faith

My next move was to the station brig, operated as usual by a Marine detachment. It was my first working relationship with this elite organization. The commanding officer had majored in art. He felt it was obligatory for him to "chew" people out on occasion, so had developed the appropriate vocabulary for such occasions. Many of the inmates were marines or sailors who did not want to go to Korea and had been told that one could get a bad conduct discharge after the third court martial. So they would go AWOL after each release. One private who had worked very hard for his BCD got placed on disciplinary status for a brig infraction. When his discharge papers came the master sergeant waved them in his face and told him he would never get them although he eventually did.

Others who did not want a BCD had gone AWOL in California and hitchhiked to the east, hoping for trial and confinement safely away from the debarking point for Korea. They also hoped that the police action in Korea would soon be over.

Sunday Services in the brig were of marathon quality. We had a favorite hymns period in which the inmates requested "The Old Rugged Cross," "Come to the Church in the Valley by the Wildwood," and similar numbers every Sunday without fail. Then we welcomed all the new arrivals and said farewell to all who would be leaving before the next Sunday. Then we got to the usual order of service with more hymns, prayers, scripture, sermon and Communion on the first Sundays. Nobody had anywhere to go except to lunch at noon. Some of the prisoners attended Catholic Masses also. We had a request for a Catholic hymn during the song service. It seemed to me to be a good idea when a group of prisoners wanted to outfit a meditation chapel in an unused room in the brig. They outfitted it with an altar in the center, repairing the whole space tastefully. Then one morning we found that they had cut a hole in the floor under the altar and escaped from the brig. This act closed the meditation chapel. Another prisoner waited until it snowed and then crawled under a chest to the fence, went over, stole a car and drove out the gate. He wrote the master sergeant a letter saying he would return after some rest and that he would like to accompany him in combat. He rested over 30 days, so when he was caught he was charged with desertion. He wanted to use his letter to the master sergeant as evidence that he intended to return but sergeant said it was his personal property and the prisoner could not use it.

Another private who worked in the tailor shop of the brig dressed up in an officer's uniform and saluted his way out. We often said that if such devious people would expend the same energy in constructive ways they would be outstanding. As I was enamored of the WAVES I was also enamored of the Marines

My sad experience in the brig came one night when one of the prisoners had oral sex with 17 other prisoners. His father came up from Chicago and met him in my office. "Why did you do it son?" The father asked. "I don't know Dad." I felt that the words, "Son and Dad" said it all. I was witness to a divine encounter in which the forgiveness Christ came to bring was again actualized. The son was a mousey little fellow. The father was tall and distinguished looking already, but I remember him as ten feet tall.

Meanwhile, time was racing toward 1 June. George Wilson had agreed to be my best man. I had written Marion that I did not need any pre-marital instructions and that it would not bother me if St. Titus decided to fumigate after having so many non-Episcopalians in the chancel. The Rev. Mr. Othello Doremus Stanley, former priest at St. Titus, had gotten permission from the bishop to perform the ceremony. He had prepared Marion, her brother and sisters for confirmation. George and I would be in dress whites and would spend Friday night before the Saturday wedding at our house. George would drive to Durham; I would go by train as usual. We planned a honeymoon at Niagara Falls using Marion's 1949 Desoto. I thought it would be an easy matter to go up to Niagara from Rochester where my sister was living. I had made several trips there to baptize their children in Trinity Presbyterian Church, where a former organist had been R. Nathaniel Dett, who became famous for his "Listen to the Lambs" at Hampton Institute. A prior organist had been Cab Calloway's mother.

In Durham extensive preparations were made. The Cordice home at 1503 Fayetteville Street was partially remodeled and redecorated. The side-by-side living room and parlor were changed into a living room extending the width of the house. Our reception was to be held there since the house was diagonally across the street from

An Affirmation of Faith

St. Titus. When I told Chaplain Earl Greenlaw at Great Lakes that the remodeling job had cost $10,000 he said it was the funniest thing he had heard in his life. It was five times the pay of a LTJG when I first came in, and five times the purchase price of our 7 bedroom home on Pekoe St.

Mr. and Mrs. Thompson hosted a pre-nuptial party for us on Friday night; Dr. and Mrs. Cooke hosted a breakfast the next morning. The Cooke's home was the show place on our side of the tracks. It contained the first king-sized bed I ever saw. So far as I know there had not been a wedding in our part of Durham with a White best man. George said he had not been in the company of so many intelligent people before. They were impressed with his genuineness as well. He did not look out of place because several of the bridesmaids and ushers were of White complexion. He and my sister-in-law were the only persons there without a southern drawl, and the two of them were the only blondes.

As a chaplain, I was gratified by the attendance at the wedding, standing room only, with people ringed around the church outside looking through the windows. As we came out of the church I noticed that Mr. C.C. Spaulding, president of the North Carolina Mutual, was one of those who could not get in. He was also president of the Mechanics and Farmers Bank.

Years earlier George had asked me how one could tell if a Black girl were pretty unless she looked like Lena Horne. I reminded him of this when we talked of coming to Durham. When Marion came in ready for the prenuptial party he said, "You are beautiful." At the reception, he saw other examples. All of the men in the wedding who were not in the Navy wore white dinner jackets but Papa, as we called my father-in-law; he wore white tie and tails. The wedding was recorded on wire, but the quality was poor. The organ was not functioning so a foot pedaled reed organ similar to the type chaplains used in the field and aboard ship was substituted. Marion could scarcely be heard. I did not transfer the recording to tape before I gave Goodwill my wire recorder.

We went to our house for supper. While waiting for the meal to be ready I wrote two letters to Great Lakes and to the Presbyterian Ministers Fund informing them of a change in beneficiary from my

An Affirmation of Faith

mother to my wife, then mailed the letters before starting our trip. The Presbyterian policy was for $1,000. I did not change the beneficiary on the N.C. Mutual policy for the same amount. Marion would receive the $10,000 Navy policy.

When my Dad asked where we would spend the first night I realized I had not thought of it. He made a reservation at the Arcade, a Black hotel in Raleigh, 26 miles away. Marion objected to the Arcade because we had many friends in Raleigh who might get wind of where we were and continue their pranks, which had already started with cans tied to the car, paper streamers, etc. We decided to go as far as Richmond, 150 miles away, and stop at Slaughter's. Two things I remember well about Slaughter's: we could hear the juke box in our room, which must have played "How High the Moon" by Les Paul and Mary Ford at least three times that night; and the waitress the next day spelled steak as "stake."

From Richmond, we went to Baltimore to stop over with my second cousin, Clarence, and his wife, Alice, who had moved there from Warren, Ohio. He had stopped social work and gone into real estate. She was out of the YWCA and into student center work at Morgan State College. From Baltimore we drove to Rochester, NY.

After visiting Niagara Falls, we decided to drive through Canada to Detroit, where Marion's sister lived. We stopped over in a Canadian motel that was so quiet and comfortable that we enjoyed the stay thoroughly. I still have a picture that I took with an automatic shutter release. I took the picture in dress khaki's and Marion was wearing her mink scarf.

Marion's sister, Vici, had reserved space for us at a Black hotel on John T. Street. It was as plush as the Canadian motel had been cozy. On counting the days of leave I had left, it became apparent that we could not make it back to Durham in time for me to get to Great Lakes for church at the brig on Sunday morning. We decided to drive as far as we could without my getting in trouble. At Akron, OH, the honeymoon ended when Marion put me on a train for Chicago. I was sorry the time had gone; but was deadly afraid of being late. We each had about 400 miles to go. It had been a great trip for me, but Marion had expected better planning, or maybe I should say some planning.

The next morning at the North Shore station I found that the Sunday schedule had far fewer trains to Great Lakes, so it was impossible for me to get to the brig on time. I called Chaplain William Edward Brooks, who had a later service at the chapel, explained the circumstances and asked him to take my service. He readily agreed, much to my relief. My fears were revived the next morning, however, when the master sergeant, Frank Pick, said Chaplain Brooks walked in with the words, "Put Parham on report, he is over the hill." Strangely enough, except for my visit to his office to thank him for taking the service I never heard anything about the incident from anyone.

It was different being married. One of the macho stewards greeted me publicly with "Now you have got your nose blowed," and he seemed to be a little bit sad over the thought. Of the three stewards named Johnson he was called "Big Johnson." The other two were called "Tug" and "M.S." The chaplains gave me a deep fat fryer at the next monthly get-together. The officers from the receiving station gave me a set of kitchen knives that we still use. I received the family allowance for married officers. Since I lived in the BOQ without charge, had no car and went out to eat very seldom I was able to save $2,000 my first year of marriage.

Mrs. C. Ruth Edwards, who sang at our wedding, had told me during her summer of graduate work she had written her husband daily. I resolved to write frequently and found it thrilling to address letters to Mrs. T. David Parham, Jr. Marion visited me at Great Lakes for the summer. We found a room in Lake Forest, IL with a childless couple that had accommodated Black officers at Great Lakes since such were first commissioned, and knew them all.

Lake Forest at that time was the suburban home site of Chicago millionaires like the Amours, the Swifts and General Woods of Sears and Roebuck. Our landlord specialized in dyeing shoes for society functions. He could shoot pheasants out of his bathroom window. The streets were laid out in curves, so traffic was slow. Dogs would lie in the street sunning; drivers drove around them. With a Lake Forest address, car insurance was only $50.00 per year.

Marion was well received by the Great Lakes chaplains. At our first visit to the Chapel by the Lake, Chaplain Hamilton, who was greeting departing worshippers on the chapel steps, went back into the chapel to get Mrs. Hamilton to show her the suit Marion was wearing. The Currys took to her because she was an Episcopalian. The Lampes were impressed that she was head of the art department at N.C. Central and was familiar with the art institutions in Chicago. Her biggest disappointment that summer was that she had worked so hard doing my khaki shirts only to find that the base laundry did them for $0.25.

CAPT Frank R. Hamilton was Ninth Naval District Chaplain and also Naval Training Center Chaplain. He had entered the Navy in the thirties, so he had experienced accelerated promotion during World War II. In fact, one of his peers, Chaplain Robert D. Workman, the first Chief of Chaplains to hold the rank of Rear Admiral, had been promoted to CDR and CAPT in the same year. Chaplain Hamilton was impeccable in dress. He brought a new cap cover to wear at inspections. Because of my interest in recording equipment, he had me to record conferences for him.

Because I was the only Black chaplain in the Navy, I received an inordinate amount of attention, first because there were so few Black officers at Great Lakes anyhow. I remember one warrant officer, two dentists and a doctor. One of the dentists, Dr. Rose, was my first roommate in the BOQ. Another, Dr. James, was a nephew of the Air Force's Chappie James who later made General. Years later John Calhoun, a red haired Black man from South Carolina who worked for the Nixon administration, told me that Sam Gravely would get his third star and be chosen as Chief of Staff of the Air Force. Watergate foiled the last prediction.

Chaplain John E. Johnson, the District and Center Chaplain where I did my first tour at Great Lakes in 1945, used to remind us that we had the greatest preaching opportunity in America. This time I found that we had the greatest evangelical opportunity in American in the matter of actually adding members to American churches. The architect of the recruiting operation was Chaplain Matthew A. Curry, an Episcopal chaplain who was known as the "Merchant of Venice" when he was on sea duty in the Mediterranean. His background was French but he spoke fluent Italian. In the chapel center in the basement of Building 1311 each recruit company came in for religious screening. Data records were filled out giving religious reference and level of religious involvement. Faith groups were separated out; Protestant, Catholic, Jewish, Orthodox, and others were interviewed by a chaplain representing the specific faith group. As a Presbyterian I interviewed those from Presbyterian and Reformed backgrounds. If we happened not to have a Congregationalist chaplain I took the Congregationalist recruits also.

When we found a recruit who had not been baptized, or had not been received into church membership, we offered that opportunity during the recruit training period. Instructions classes were held in the evenings, usually on Thursdays. Chaplain Arthur R. Anderson had a baptistery installed for immersion so use of the swimming pool was no longer necessary. At that time it was the second baptistery in the Navy, the other being at NTC San Diego in the chapel. Although Chaplain James Kelly, who later became Chief of Chaplains, had 40 baptisms per week before he was relieved by Chaplain Anderson, the best statistical record was held by Chaplain Curry who invited a Bishop in from Chicago to confirm 105 of those with Episcopal preference who had not been confirmed. I was able to bring 100 into full membership in the Presbyterian Church in a year's time.

In those days religion enjoyed a privileged position in the Navy. Church attendance was required during recruit training and at the Naval Academy. The Secretary of the Navy had issued an instruction on the "Protection of Moral Standards," the work of Chaplain John J. O'Connor, who later became Chief of Chaplains, still later Archbishop of New York.

The same Chaplain Kelly mentioned above implemented the Character Guidance Program to the extent that he was known as "Character Guidance Kelly." There was a series of flannel board presentations for recruit training, another for service schools, and others for fleet use. Films accompanied the flannel board kits and were of excellent quality. The one on alcohol abuse was produced by the Yale Institute of Alcohol Studies. It was a usual day for me to have five character guidance presentations in a day. American values such as citizenship and responsibility were emphasized in addition to the traditional moral values. As the years passed, the responsibility for implementation of character guidance was first shared with the line officers who showed interest, then made a line responsibility. Many chaplains felt that service personnel confused character guidance with religious worship or thought it to be a substitute.

As had Chaplain Hamilton before, Chaplain Curry had me to record the presentations given by other chaplains. He audited one of mine himself. He objected to some extra material I had brought into the sex presentation, pictures from a medical magazine of venereal disease in women I was using as a scare tactic. One chaplain was removed from his list of presenters of the sex subject because when a recruit asked him about masturbation his reply was, "Don't worry about it, everybody does it." Some of the recruits present complained to other chaplains about the comment.

Marion found Great Lakes interesting and was glad to be able to get into Chicago easily. The chaplains and wives were disappointed that she would return to work in September. My rationale was that I had no security as a reserve, so it was important for her to keep her position that she had held for ten years.

In those days a Black officer was a kind of folk hero for the enlisted Blacks and the Black community. There were many invitations to appear at all kinds of functions. My relationship to the stewards was somewhat of a cross between hero and a mascot. I spent many hours listening to their sea stories, and at times visited the nightspots they frequented.

It was a sad life for the stewards at Great Lakes. They seemed to have developed a "going on liberty splurge" attitude as a hangover from sea duty. They soon spent or gambled away their money on the first liberty after getting paid, leaving them 14 days of poverty until the next payday. When they reenlisted the bonus often went for a used car, which they often lost after several months due to maintenance costs and missed payments. Then they faced another four or six years without a car.

One day 13 of them wrote a letter to the Bureau of Naval Personnel requesting to be sent back to sea. The salutation in the latter was "Dear Bureau." Many of them were non-rated, either because of inability to pass the test for advancement or inability to stay out of trouble, consequently having been reduced in rate. One steward, who wore two hash marks, indicating over 8 years in service, had a jumper he wore on liberty with one hash mark and the insignia of a commissary man first class. In spite of the deference they paid me, somebody drank a bottle of my altar wine. When I complained to the chief it was replaced with a bottle of Petri.

During that period a nationally circulated magazine published an article entitled "The Floating Plantation," in which the Navy was accused of using the stewards as menials. When the NAACP and others made such strenuous objection to Blacks being recruited for this type of duty, Asiatic recruitment was stepped up, particularly in the Philippines. Therefore the Black population decreased as the Brown population increased, according to the article. I was informed that there was such a rush for the steward billets in the Philippines that the application list would take 25 years to be exhausted.

The problem essentially was that of self-esteem, stemming from the time that only stewards could be addressed as "Boy." At Great Lakes at this time there were a few remnants of the group of stewards who changed to that rate rather than face court martial for direct disobedience of orders after the ammunition ship blew up in Port Chicago. Out of fear, a number of men refused to go back to ammunition loading. The stewards compensated by buying big cars, partying, wearing a chip on the shoulder. Through the efforts of LCDR Dennis D. Nelson, whose father had been a steward, the special officer type uniforms stewards used to wear were discontinued; he kept urging that the rating be abolished, as it finally was. Until then, however, the rating was a continual source of embarrassment to all concerned, developing a paranoia in many who served therein.

I fell into a long-term friendly relationship with one of the cooks at the Naval Hospital, Julius Navy, and his wife, Sue. He used to get a kick out of calling for me at the office and leaving word for me to call. I would usually get the message, "Some clown called and wanted you to call Navy." We decided to buy a house in partnership, 611 N. Utica Street, Waukegan. It had five rooms up, five down. The house had cost us only $13,500. Julius would rent out my upper half and deposit the rent in my checking account. The name of the first tenant was Sullivan Skipper. We did our own painting until I got the "shakes" while painting the soffits under the second story roof. When I told Marion about the house she got excited about furnishing it.

Fearing that the furniture would cost more than the house, I bought a mobile home on the trailer lot next to Bldg. 1311, where my office was, so I was ready with a different type of housing when Marion came up the following summer.

The mobile home was a 33-footer, eight feet wide, a sizable unit in those days. It cost only $2,000. Chaplain Brooks lived in a similar type in the same trailer lot. The big excitement the summer we had the trailer was the visit of my in-laws, who were attending the National Medical Association convention at the Stevens Hotel in Chicago. They were pleasantly impressed by the convenience and neatness of the trailer.

The trailer also gave us the opportunity to entertain whatever chaplain might be having duty at Bldg. 1311, if he happened to be a friend of ours. This did not work for one chaplain who called and asked where one ate when standing the duty at 1311. I told him I did not know for sure, but assumed the cafeteria in the building would be the logical choice. When I thought about this later, I wondered if this Jewish Chaplain wondered if I did not like Jesus, so I never made a similar mistake.

The trailer court had a washhouse with washers and dryers. Marion listened to the *w*ives complain about being tired of the four walls and looking forward to the time they would have real houses. I discovered that if Marion had been given a choice, she would not have chosen trailer living. I was glad to get a buyer for it for $1800 in September. Years later in our quarters at Bainbridge Maryland, the master bedroom and the living room were each larger than that trailer. In addition there were eight bedrooms and five baths.

Before Marion left for work in Durham we had our first spat. I had cooked dinner, to begin with soup, which I had prepared by the appointed time. She had gone to visit the Currys, who had invited her to stay for dinner, and she did so without informing me. By the time she got home I had consumed both bowls of soup, each with a clove of garlic. That night she slept on the sofa.

By this time the police action in Korea was moving toward a stalemate. Orders came for me to the First Marine Division. When

An Affirmation of Faith

I proposed to Marion, I had promised that there would be no sea duty, but there was no thought of the Marines. I had heard that all of the Black Marine officers who had been commissioned during World War II had been released from active duty in 1946. I had also been told that General Vandergrift had said, "When I saw that globe and anchor on a Black man I knew our country was in trouble." I liked the fairness I knew at the brig but did not consider myself sufficiently gung ho to serve with them in combat. After puzzling over what might be going on, I learned that the orders were cancelled. I suspected that the Senior Chaplain at Great Lakes had taken a liking to Marion and did not want to see her widowed yet.

We were aware at Great Lakes of the large numbers of casualties when the police action began. One of the Red Cross Field Directors, a Mr. John Ballard, had been with the 24th Army Infantry in Japan, one of the first to be sent to Korea. Ballard and most of the 24th were Black. He came to Great Lakes instead of Korea. He told me that every letter he received told of more friends killed or wounded, so that it looked as though none would survive. Likely because of Ballards accounts, I did not ask anyone any questions about my cancelled orders.

The next month another set of orders came, Fleet Activities, Sasebo, Japan. That prospect was thrilling. Except for the few days in Canada during our honeymoon I had never been on foreign soil under foreign control. Although Chaplain Salisbury called it the pesthole of the orient, even that sounded intriguing. I had heard of Kagawa and had used his poetry in my sermons. I thought Marion could get a Sabbatical and join me there since she had been teaching ten years. I considered myself a fan of General Douglas MacArthur and admired the way the Japanese had kept his Rolls Royce in mint condition during their occupation of the Philippines.

At that time my brother was pastor of Faith Presbyterian Church in Oakland. I would be leaving from San Francisco. By not getting my shots at Great Lakes, I secured some visiting time there while taking shots. I asked to travel by sea, but was ordered to fly. A submarine Captain, a Line Lt, a Pratt Whitney engine and I were the cargo. When airborne, the pilot invited the submariner to test the difference between the feel of a plane and a sub. He found it interesting; I found it anxiety producing. The plane had two passenger seats. Being Junior (a staff officer), I settled in the web-type troop seating along the bulkhead, stretching out in about half of it. The CAPT saw this and did likewise, leaving the LT in his original seat. The LT did not order me out so I slept to Japan.

Japan

I was not prepared for the Japanese sights and sounds. Upon reaching the terminal I was puzzled by all the clatter, which I found to be the sound of wooden shoes on the concrete. When in Guam I had bought a kimono from the Black French merchant seaman, but it was drab in comparison to those being worn in Tokyo. I was wide eyed from the first day until I left over two years later. I had not expected the neon signs on the rooftops of the Tokyo office buildings, the largest being RCA.

In 1953 there was no landing strip at Sasebo. Mail and passengers came in by amphibious plane from Ittazuki Air Force Base, setting dock in Sasebo Harbor where a small boat ferried personnel and parcels to the pier. The plane was very noisy, seeming to take off and set down with difficulty. The transfer to the boat was without difficulty and the ride to the pier relatively smooth.

When we pulled alongside the pier I Saw a LCDR chaplain in khaki tropicals waiting for me. I climbed onto the pier with my two bags, dropped them and gave the smartest salute I could muster. Chaplain Vincent J. Lonergan picked up my two bags and said "Dr. James of Great Lakes has been waiting for you." The pier was adjacent to the Land's End Chapel, which was adjacent to the BOQ, both of them Quonset hut buildings. The personnel office was another Quonset hut diagonally across the street from the BOQ. So my check-in was complete in a matter of minutes. The chaplains had offices in a Quonset adjacent to the BOQ. The administration building was a two story concrete building, the only permanent structure on base.

The other attached chaplain was Frederick W. Brink, also LCDR, who had published a well-known book on marriage and had earned a Ph.D. He was internationally known for a booklet he wrote discouraging American-Japanese marriages, entitled *So You Want to Marry a Japanese Girl*. In Japan at that time 100 such weddings involving military personnel were taking place each week.

It did not take long to understand why this was happening. In many instances both officers and enlisted men lived with their girlfriends in the local community. It was considered normal for a man to report to Sasebo and inherit from the person he was relieving a job, a used car and a live-in girlfriend, if the man he was relieving had not married her during his tour. Many of the men had wives at home, making a complete transfer easier. For single men there was significant pressure applied toward marriage and many attractions to move in that direction. Some of the women were strikingly beautiful; others were quite intelligent and talented. Even more compelling was the way they had been programmed by the Japanese culture to treat the man as a king. I was invited to dinner in a fellow-officer's home. He told me that he had intended to leave his wife in Sasebo, but could not bring himself to do it; so had extended his tour to allow time for the marriage. When I arrived she took my coat, removed my shoes, seated us, cleaned his face with a washcloth and served the meal. After clearing the dishes from the table she came back with a comb, combed his hair, held both our coats, buttoned them up, and put on our shoes so we could leave for the theatre. He told me that he had promised she would not have to shave him when they got to the States. So when the cute little Sunday School teacher, who had gone to an American missionary college, told me she had talked it over with her mother and they wanted to make me comfortable because they knew that I missed my wife, I did not ask for details as one method of resisting temptation.

Later I was glad for this because one night she woke me up after midnight at the BOQ, incensed and confused because a sailor I had introduced to her propositioned her. The same young lady was again embarrassed because I asked the Navy Exchange Officer to give her a job so she could be off for Sunday School. At her first day on

An Affirmation of Faith

the job the other females wanted to know the identity of the officer-boyfriend who had gotten her the job.

Her church was the Kyodan Church (United Church of Christ) in the Hiramachi section of town, very near the Army BOQ. The name of the pastor was Inoue. He was apologetic over the fact that during 20 years as a missionary in Manchuria he had forgotten most of his English. The Hiramachi Church had previously been Methodist, but during the war the Japanese government had ordered all Protestant Churches to combine, perhaps the most effective church union movement ever. Congregations that refused lost their property. I was told that the Episcopalians lost their cathedral this way. Pastor Zenno, with whom I enjoyed conversing in German, served a former Presbyterian Church, near the railroad station. My first visit to this church was for a Wednesday evening prayer meeting. When I found that there were 200 people present, the explanation was that it was a joint service of thanksgiving for the recent visit of E. Stanley Jones, the famed Methodist missionary to India, as guest of all the Kyodan Churches.

Because he had been a missionary to India, Dr. John Hick Bowman at Pittsburgh Seminary had told us of Dr. Jones' remarkable work. I had read his *Abundant Living* and had been inspired by it. He was not impressive when he spoke in Pittsburgh because he was upset over the beginning of "our" war with Japan and because of the second century date he assigned to the Apostles' Creed, much too early in the opinion of that scholar. Twelve years later in Japan, I was impressed by their enthusiasm of his interpreter who mimicked his gestures, intonations, etc. I turned to my same Sunday school teacher and asked, "isn't that interpreter great?" Her reply was, "Yes, but I think he is Korean." He was larger than the average Japanese but she probably could tell by his accent.

So in the country where I felt like a human being for the first time in my life, racism was alive and well. I was told that when the South Koreans were offered the help of Japanese troops their attitude was that they would fight the Japanese instead of the North Koreans. It was somewhat of an honor in Korea not to understand Japanese because it meant one had been educated after the Japanese occupation. We heard of severe discrimination against Koreans in

Tokyo. At the E. Stanley Jones rally an Indian speaker congratulated the Japanese on needing an interpreter for English because it indicated the Japanese had never been British subjects.

The real thrill of the Jones meeting for me was that I was introduced to Kagawa by Pastor Inoue. I was flattered by the obvious pleasure Pastor Inoue took in making the introduction. Then I was even more impressed by the joy Kagawa demonstrated in the handshake. I had expected the usual bowing but he extended his hand, grasped mine firmly, then moved our hands from left to right several times as he smiled and told me how happy he was to meet me. Here was one of the best-known Christians in all the world. He had lived in the Tokyo slums where he contracted most of the prevalent diseases. I have been told by his host in Oakland that several public health officers were assigned to him during his visit to America to prevent his contaminating people. Early in his ministry one slum dweller who had heard that saying of Jesus, "That one should give to the asker one's inner coat", after having already given the outer one, asked this of Kagawa and received them. Many times I have recounted my meeting Kagawa. It is one of my most cherished blessings.

There were several Korean officers at our Fleet Activities Command in Sasebo. Other Koreans came into port on ships we had provided and continued to maintain with provisions to some extent. Some of the officers had finished the Koran Naval Academy, and then had gone to various schools at Great Lakes, where I met them. At Great Lakes they wore the rank of LTJG; when I saw them in Sasebo two years later they were mostly LCDRs and CDRs. They explained that the school billets at Great Lakes were for LTJGs, so they wore that rank until they graduated. I was sure the Korean Navy had the fastest promotions in the world.

These officers had the highest respect for the Japanese. I was at a local restaurant with LCDR Kim Kwang Ok, our Korean Liaison Officer, when I expressed curiosity over a piece of sculpture he explained as being a representation of a "woman's box." When I began to laugh he protested, "That not bad means, that not bad means," and went on to explain that many high-class Japanese had a picture of a couple in sexual intercourse sewn between the outer fabric and lining of a kimono.

It was my turn to be embarrassed when talking with Kim Kwang Ok one afternoon about vocational choices in the USA. Each profession he would mention prompted me to speculate on the amount of income one could expect. He asked me "Don't the American people know there is more to life than money, that there are such things as honor, respect and diligence?" I had been told by a Marine, that the best fighting man he had met was a Korean LtCOL whose pay was $15 a month. Nine years previously I was accused by Josephine Adams, a Red Cross Worker in Guam, of being secular in my values. Here it was again.

Chaplain Lonergan was soon relieved by Chaplain William J. Walsh, who was junior to Chaplain Brink. Chaplain Brink became the new senior chaplain. Chaplain Harold Bodle, a former missionary in the Philippines, was junior to me. I was sorry to see Chaplain Lonergan leave. He is perhaps the only chaplain for whom I have worked and I never heard a complaint from anybody in the command about him. If he heard someone curse he would say, "Careful, you are talking about my boss." At the weekly officers Saturday morning conference, at which the dirty joke was the usual fare, he told a clean one. When I tried to tell the Chief Staff Officer a clean one for the next meeting, he told me to tell it to myself.

Chaplain Brink offered me the choice of working in the chapel with him or with the approximately 90 ships in the harbor. I opted for the harbor ministry with a great deal of excitement. It involved visiting ships most of the day by boat, giving character guidance lectures on board and conducting worship on three of the ships each Sunday morning. I used the flannel graph presentations produced by "Character Guidance Kelly" and a set I designed for the Sasebo situation with pictures, slogans and key words painted by Marion. I took color pictures of these to send to the Chief of Chaplains. He wrote Chaplain Brink to include me in the new set he was writing for the Far East. The assignment of Chaplain Bodle was made to give Chaplain Brink more time to write.

Although the men had seen flannel board presentations in recruit training, they still seemed fascinated by the pictures staying in place on the flannel board and seemed to be waiting to see what was on the next picture. I enjoyed the process because I had new pictures that had been done by my wife that related to the local situation. One day I got an urgent message to bring the sex control presentation to an oil tanker. When I arrived and asked why the rush, I was told that they had just found that 75% of the enlisted men had venereal disease. The last time this had happened they got a growl from the type command asking what they had done about it. This time they were going to say they had brought a chaplain out to give a sex control presentation to the crew. This was why Chaplain Salisbury had called Sasebo the pesthole of the Orient. It was the practice to give penicillin tablets to those going on liberty. My assistant proudly saved his in a bottle. Some chaplains objected to this practice because it assumed that the men would be sexually active on liberty, even as they objected to wholesale passing out of condoms at liberty call. In an attempt to control the spread of venereal disease, word was passed to the prostitutes to have business cards printed in English and give one to each sailor as he left. If the sailor showed symptoms later he turned in the business card and the Navy medical team paid a visit to the skivvy house, card in hand so that the prostitute (called a business girl) could be treated. The medical team used a grey Navy carryall. As it came down the street the owners and business girls who happened to be outside at the time bowed as it passed. In my presentations I beat the drums for continence for religious, moral, health, psychological and financial reasons.

After six months in the country, Marion was able to get a sabbatical and join me. We rented the lower floor of a house that had been rented by one of the ships as its own party house for $50 a month with the provision that we pay for the installation of an American type toilet. When it was completed the landlady brought her little granddaughter over to use it. LT and Mrs. McMillan, Supply Corps, lived upstairs with daughter and dog. We changed the title on Marion's 1949 DeSoto to my name and had it shipped to Sasebo on my orders.

The living in Sasebo was easy in those days. For no expense two Navy couples could check out a carryall from special services and drive anywhere. The Army BOQ in the next block to our house served meals at field ration prices, $1.25 per day, except for the Sunday evening buffet for $2.00, a complete smorgasbord. A maid came in once a week for $2.79. Every Sunday afternoon a tugboat left the officers' landing for one of the small islands stocked with food and drink at a cost of $1.50 per person and towing a motor boat for surfboarding. Some played bridge all afternoon, others swam or sun bathed. If I was running late with my third service, I had my boat pull alongside the tug and then I hopped aboard, leaving my assistant to take the altar kit and organ back to the chapel with my vestment case.

Marion had published an article in *College Art Journal* on art facilities and resources at American universities and colleges. I encouraged her to do the same in Japan and accompanied her to help with picture taking and the language. We both took Japanese classes. We found that most professional people spoke either English or German because not many professional works had been translated into Japanese. We were impressed with the Japanese emphasis on art education. At one college the same size as N.C. Central, where Marion was the head of the art department, we found 27 art teachers.

When we walked into a sculpture class the teacher looked at me and exclaimed "A nose, a nose!" He asked that I sit for his class of about 30 students so they could do a bust. He promised to give me the best one. We have a slide of the 30 busts and the young sculptors. A year later Marion got a letter from the teacher stating, "I found your husband's head in a closet and will send it to you." We still have not received the head.

Marion and the other wives were upset over the prostitution situation. There were skivvy houses across the street from our house, behind it and around the corner on both sides of the street. Our bedroom was in the front of the house with a bricked in flower bed outside the windows. Sailors used to sit on the bricks of our flowerbed while waiting their turns at the skivvy house across the street. From our window we could see the business girls in negligees, smiling, waiting to be chosen by the next half-dozen sailors in line. The sliding door to the house remained open.

Marion thought I could have done more to combat the industry. She didn't like it when the business girls came running to me when

An Affirmation of Faith

I came home on May Day. They wanted to know where the sailors were. I explained that it was a Communist holiday and enlisted liberty had been cancelled for the fear someone would be hurt. A sailor was stabbed in Yokosuka the year before. She was only partially pleased when the young madam who acted as our landlady's interpreter told me that the business girls liked her because she said "konichi-wa" (good day) when she passed them on the street, whereas the other American wives did not.

The Hiramachi Church asked me to teach a Bible class in English which I did on Wednesday evenings. Marion went with me and prepared cocoa in cool weather and lemonade in warm weather to go with the cookies. We enjoyed this activity and were impressed by the seriousness of the students in learning Bible content as well as English. We found that there was no use in having class the week of the examination for admission to the next educational level because the students would be cramming every available minute. Without passing an examination one could not enter junior high or high school.

We spent a good deal of time shopping on "Black Market Alley," a single street in downtown Sasebo lined with small shops but having also a large department store. At the small shops there was a three tiered price arrangement. Ordinary Japanese got the best prices, business girls paid a little more, Americans paid more. It was customary for us to ask Japanese friends to buy for us when we knew exactly what we wanted. There was a small contingent of peanut sales persons, female pre-teens and early teens, who used to ply their trade every night, picking out sailors for special attention. I used to tell them peanuts were for monkeys so they all called me "stingy."

Marion decided we should do something for them so we invited them to come to our house one night after the shops closed and the traffic died down. We waited and led them home where Marion served the usual treats. One little peanut girl, as we called them, surprised us by jumping up and singing Sunday school songs with some tunes that were familiar to us. We had a delightful time. They had been going to some missionary Sunday school. After then they were always happy to see "Stingy" and his wife.

An Affirmation of Faith

One night they came up to us quite excited. One of them had become old enough, 14, to work in a bar. It just so happened that Dr. Macintosh, a Navy dentist, was with us. The kids led us to the bar and called the new barmaid out. She was in evening gown, well painted and quite proud of herself. Dr. Macintosh asked her to open her mouth. After he inspected her teeth he agreed that she was 14. Although we shared their joy over the promotion from the peanut route to the bar, it was also a sad time for me assuming that her next promotion would be business girl.

A rare opportunity came for me to make up for the lack of planning and the abrupt end of our honeymoon. The British had several troop carriers that made regular runs to Hong Kong and carried a few American passengers. We made the round trip, including a week's layover with a side flight to Bangkok. The sea trip cost about $50 for the two of us, including meals, tea twice a day and tips. The enlisted members of both crews were Indian, one Hindu the other Moslem. On our way down we had a British Army Chaplain also as a passenger. He wanted to find a filigree brooch in Hong Kong and get himself a pair of trousers. We wanted to buy practically everything that was not nailed down.

The third morning when we entered Hong Kong harbor the view from our porthole was breath taking. We had never seen a Chinese junk, but there was one near us in full sail, one of them red. Then we saw the sampans on which many people lived, whole families on such small boats, fishing, cooking, washing, sleeping, in very cramped circumstances. When we got ashore we found that the sampan dwellers were relatively fortunate since many homeless lived in packing crates and even cardboard boxes. We were told that there was more misery per square foot in Hong Kong than in any other place in the world. At the police station we saw a wall lined with pictures of unidentified people who had been fished out of the harbor. We were surrounded by beggars at every turn.

My solution to the beggar problem was to have a suit tailored of raw silk in Chinese "pajama" style, military collar, frog button, side splits on coat, and baggy trousers. Dressed in this rig we were hardly noticed at all. I also wore Chinese fabric shoes. Most of the tailor shops offered delivery the next day.

An Affirmation of Faith

Shopping bargains were almost unbelievable. Custom-made shoes were $3.00, cashmere jackets were $15, men's suits were $20, all made to order of fabrics and styles selected by the customer. We bought a five piece set of matched leather luggage for $10.00 and a quantity of jade which was mined in Colorado but set in Hong Kong at paste jewelry prices. In Bangkok I found a 15-carat Black sapphire for $3.00. Crocodile leather was selling for cowhide prices. Lavishly embroidered goods were cheaper than plain garments in the Navy Exchange in Japan.

We stayed in the Four Seas Hotel on the Kowloon (mainland) side of the city because Chaplain Bodle told us clergy got half price. He had used the hotel when he was a missionary in the Philippines. I noticed also, that there was a local congregation of Holiness people, who had services in that hotel. When I checked out I asked about the discount. The manager said it did not apply to me because I was in the Navy and was paid as much as anybody else. The only inconvenience we experienced at the hotel was the water shortage which required water hours. To get a bath at night one had to fill the bath that morning.

The side trip to Thailand was even more fascinating. We were able to get a tour guide for $15 a day which covered all transportation and admissions cost. He was as astute as he was intelligent. Discerning we were Protestants because we were married, he explained that the Thai form of Buddhism was the Protestant type without accretions, whereas the Mahayana type as we saw in Japan even allowed the priests to wear trousers instead of the saffron robe. In the temple of the Emerald Buddha he excused himself, prostrated and said a brief prayer, a demonstration of his own piety for my benefit, I suspected.

It did not seem likely that each of the big temples took 20 years to be built by 8,000 men or that the archer was stationed at the front of the royal barge to shoot out the eyes of anyone who dared look at the king. I knew that nobody was supposed to look down on the Japanese Emperor from a second story window but I could see no reason for a parade other than to be seen.

We were impressed by the amount of the gold used in the temples. At the temple of the Reclining Buddha, people were leaving gold leaf to complete the gilding of the statue. We were told that some of the temple statues of Buddha were really gilded corpses of monks who died in the crossed legged position of contemplation. Their bodies had been plastered over before gilding. They had died from complete rejection of the sensual world and its appetites, including conversation, food and water.

Marion was annoyed by the enormous supply of lizards that could be seen walking up the walls of the hotel and everywhere else. I had become accustomed to them in Guam, even enjoyed their singing after I found that the music was not from birds. She liked the Thai silk which was more expensive than we thought it would be.

We decided to go to the Chinese opera in downtown Bangkok. I had seen the building during our guided tour so was confident we could get there by streetcar. Because I did not know how to count Thai money I held out a handful of coins to the streetcar conductor so he could take what he needed.

It was not long before I realized that I should have seen the Chinese Opera House by now. Coca-Cola Signs did not help, so we got off the streetcar.

Then I saw a familiar sight, a man, European or American, wearing a moustache and carrying a bag emblazoned "Awake." When I began to ask him where the Chinese Opera was he exclaimed, "Oh, you are Americans." So he was glad to see us also. He called a motorized tricycle, so common in the orient in those days and likely made in Japan, told the driver where we wanted to go and paid him from our funds. He waved cheerily as we left. Many times since then I have told Jehovah's Witnesses calling at the house of the time I was really glad to see a Jehovah's Witness.

After all that trouble getting to the Chinese Opera House we found that the feature was "*Snow White*," Disney style. The costumes and sets lavish, the music was good and of course we understood what was going on. We were able to get to a Thai dance recital before we left, which we found intriguing. I found myself a little sensitive about the monkey masks and the monkey statuary all over Thailand but could find no reference to Blacks. In Hong Kong I had found a shoe polish advertised on billboards featuring a Rastus minstrel show character.

An Affirmation of Faith

At one of my English classes in Japan when I asked what they would like to sing someone suggested "Old Black Joe." Although this was my class at a high school and not at the Kyodan Church, I still felt no offense was intended. I am sure none was intended with the shoe polish. Foster's songs were popular in the United States when Japan was being opened to world commerce. Minstrel Shows were very popular in the United States until the 40's. I remember Silas Green from New Orleans coming to Durham when I was a teenager and the excitement we felt about the half-Chinese beauty with the show, Vera Wang, also a teenager. I was thrilled to meet her at the home of George Logan, a classmate whose dad owned the Black theatres.

I still have a shoeshine box with a footrest on top, like the one I outfitted in preparing to go to seminary. My mother, almost in tears, asked me not to take it with me as I had planned, promising to sacrifice and send money if I needed it. At the time I had not considered it degrading to shine the shoes of my classmates.

It is interesting how bits of American culture become adopted in the orient. One day we were walking on a Hong Kong sidewalk past a funeral in progress in a storefront. An English-speaking person, maybe even the undertaker, invited us in. There was a Buddhist Priest chanting prayers in one corner with a little group including the family around him. In another corner was a group of men smoking cigarettes. In a third corner there was a band playing a selection my dad used as a solo in church, "Flee as a Bird to your Mountain, Thou who Art Weary of Sin." There was a 36" x 44" portrait of the deceased to be carried in the funeral procession.

There were two disappointments during the Thailand trip. First, I had not realized until I got there that the next stop for the plane was Calcutta. I had so wanted to go to India for so many years but had not realized before I left Japan how close it would be. The second disappointment was in my failure to locate either of my two friends in the Royal Thai Navy. They had been students at Great Lakes, as had the Korean officers. When I took them to hear Duke Ellington I told Sue Navy I had taken two Siamese cats to the performance. She wondered what interest felines would have in Duke Ellington.

An Affirmation of Faith

LT Anult Hongsakul and his buddy, whose name I have forgotten (maybe the CNO by now), were not in Bangkok.

The second honeymoon still is a pleasant memory. I have not yet mounted the 15-carat sapphire; Marion hasn't worn the tiger belt and pocket book in many years.

On the return flight from Bangkok to Hong Kong the free tropical fruit juice, of which I drank too much because it was free, gave me the "runs." The cruise back to Japan was just as restful except that the steward was annoyed if we didn't let him in when he brought tea at 7:30 a.m. He was delighted when we mastered enough of the currency value to give him a tip of a half-crown.

Back in Japan the status remained quo and we resumed our exciting life. There was much preparation for Christmas by the ships and the station. Elsie Grenz of Colorado and Mabel Halvorsen from Canada had established a mission enterprise called "World Mission to Children." They took in half American children who were not wanted by their Japanese mothers. The fathers had been rotated back to the United States. The missionaries had taught the children to sing so they were in great demand for singing at religious services. The Catholic Chaplains in the area were doing things for the Catholic School on the hill. Japanese children were secured to come aboard the station for meals, parties and presents. There was a serious intention to involve the Japanese in the Christmas Holidays.

The Hiramachi Church, where I taught the Bible class, organized a caroling group of Americans and Japanese to make the round on Christmas Eve. They gave me my greatest disappointment of my tour. I was asleep when they got to our house. As I heard the strains of "Joy to the World" outside my window in words I could not understand, as I was half-awake, I thought I had died and gone to heaven. When they shouted "Merry Christmas," I knew it wasn't true. The disappointment almost ruined my Christmas. Many Years later when my cousin Clarence Parham died in Baltimore and a choir from Morgan State sang at his funeral, I told them the music was the second best I had ever heard. When they asked what the most beautiful had been I told them of the carolers outside our Sasebo bedroom window.

An Affirmation of Faith

Unfortunately, everything in Sasebo was not beautiful. On one of the LSTs I visited the junior officer of the deck upon being relieved remarked, "I think I'll go shoot myself." His relief replied, "Why don't you?" He did. When the bugler played taps at his funeral on the tank it was the most mournful music I ever heard as the sound echoed around that empty tank deck.

One Sunday morning two sailors decided to do some diving. The masks they picked up were for use in flight. Therefore as the water pressure built up the valves cut off the oxygen instead of releasing it as a mask for diving would have done. I got to the sick bay as the corpsmen were cutting their clothes off. I wrote a few lines later that day including, "There you lay the two of you so cold, so wet, so blue."

Ordinarily, the Japanese wives of sailors were faithful, but Osborne's wife liked a marine named Thibodeau. One evening Osborne slashed his wife and stabbed Thibodeau 18 times "until he stopped moving," he told me. Both men were Black. When I visited the wife in the hospital she asked about the marine. He was dead but I told her he wasn't doing so well. The nurses who worked on him were upset when they found in his medical record that he had syphilis.

Osborne, although a pal, was confined to the brig awaiting court martial. When his trial was held it was so apparent that his wife was trying to hang him that the court was quite lenient. He had read the Bible through twice while in confinement.

A CPO received a letter from his wife to the effect that she knew he was being unfaithful to her just like the rest of the servicemen in Sasebo. It upset him greatly and he unconsciously decided that since he had the name he had just as well have the game so the next time a bar girl sat on his lap so did he. Then remorse set in and he repented over and over, "She should not have written that letter." When they fished him out of the harbor he had the letter clenched in his fist.

We had one officer who arranged for a house in the community for his wife and hired a maid. When she arrived and was cooking breakfast one morning the maid said, "He doesn't like his eggs like that." The wife got permission to return to the United States. Our once a week maid was very beautiful, had a son, and thought she was married to Angel Illano until she tried to get an allotment. What she thought was a marriage license was a statement of paternity. Angel was in Hawaii, so the senior chaplain there was contacted. Chaplain Cuthriell had him to bring in a support allowance every month which was forwarded to Sasebo. Angel objected to this by announcing as he brought in his payment "Here is my contribution to Japanese prostitution." Later he and his wife came to Sasebo in hope of taking the son away with them but were denied custody.

A sick joke making the rounds was "Chaplain, do you save bad girls?" After the affirmative reply the punch line was "Then save me two for Saturday night." I thought of this when my favorite doctor came to me with his problem. He had two muses (from Japanese *musime*, "girl") who refused to live in the same apartment, so he was renting two apartments. I knew one of them because she came to play the organ in the chapel in a strange way. She had learned on an organ that needed to be supplied with wind by foot pedals. On the Hammond electronic she pumped the swell pedal as she played.

One day I got the word that the CO wanted to see me. When he seated me in his office he asked how I liked it in Sasebo. I told him that I was delighted with the assignment and had told the Chief of Chaplains that I would prefer to do my entire career there. He then pulled out a letter the chaplains had signed deploring the moral situation and suggesting that no servicemen under the age of 21 be assigned to the area. He then said "I assume that this was written by your buddy Brink, so I will deal with him." Captain Fitzwilliam then surprised me by saying in so many words that Sasebo was the last opportunity for pleasure the men had before going into the combat zone. It appeared to me that he felt it was his obligation to provide that opportunity. Presumably the memory of a recent sexual gratification would make a sailor happily die for his country whereas he would feel robbed without it. I take no small comfort in my signing the letter and not calling the CO's attention to the Christian principle involved and my commitment to it. I also wish I could say that this was the last time I failed to stand on principle before an authority figure.

Marion's one-year sabbatical ended, so she went back to Durham and her position at N.C. Central. I tried in vain to persuade her to

An Affirmation of Faith

return via Europe, which she still has not visited, so she could see the art treasures and complete what was to some extent a trip around the world. She said that she wanted to stay with me in Japan as long as she possibly could instead of leaving early to take in Europe. I did not appreciate that kind of reasoning then as I do now. When Chaplain Hamilton told me at Great Lakes after our marriage that I should treasure every opportunity to be together I looked at him as though he had a screw loose. He was surprised that Marion would be returning to Durham to teach after spending the summer at Great Lakes. My feeling was that as a reserve I could be released from active duty at any time so Marion needed to keep her job.

My second application for integration into the regular Navy in as many years was turned down while I was at Sasebo. The preference was for those below my rank of LCDR. I suspect also that the preference was for those who showed a little more maturity than I did at the time. Two incidents illustrate this.

While at Great Lakes I had taken the notion to revamp my Navy raincoat with the Black buttons arid belt with buckle and rank insignia on the shoulders into a lightweight bridge coat with gold buttons, half belt in the back and shoulder boards. When I wore it to work one morning Chaplain Curry, the senior recruit training chaplain told me that I could design my own uniforms when I became a vice Admiral, a rank no chaplain had ever held. I said that I could wear it in Sasebo, to which he agreed. The first (and last) day I wore it in Sasebo Chaplain Brink called me and said three people had called him asking what kind of coat I was wearing. Now all bridge coats are lightweight with zip in linings, but I doubt the Naval Uniform Board got the idea from me.

The profanity and vulgarity in Sasebo bothered me, so I designed a character guidance presentation on the subject. I began it with a quotation of the curse put on Baruch Spinoza by the Classis of Amsterdam and summed it up by saying, "In other words, God damn you." I called attention to the belief in Hebrew culture that blessings and curses were quite effective. Then I recounted how I translated for the Sunday school teacher what she heard one sailor call another and also interpreted it for her. The epithet was, "You God damned mother-fucking son of a bitch." Her response was a wide eyed, "Honto?" (really?). Then I assured the audience that the sailor really did not mean what he said but was just repeating what he had heard others say when angry.

Again Chaplain Brink called me, said he did not like the presentation, based on the reports he had heard immediately after it was over. Not only could I not quote such language but I could not have Marion reproduce it on the visual cards. So I put my tail between my legs again and retreated from what I considered a very drastically effective way of dealing with a problem. Again, I do not attribute the use of such language in the media today to my pioneering effort to discourage it.

For two years in succession I had been rejected for postgraduate school as well as regular Navy. A directive came out permitting LCDRs to agree to take a reduction in rank to get into the regular Navy. I applied immediately, reasoning that I would rather be a LT on the inside looking out than a LCDR on the out looking in. Then I applied again for postgraduate school. In what seemed to me to be record time I was accepted for postgraduate school for the following fiscal year. This led me to believe that I had been accepted for regular Navy also because I had not known of a reserve who had been selected for postgraduate school. It was then October and my tour was over.

Meanwhile at Iwakuni the Protestant Chaplain had gone home on emergency leave and it was not likely that he would return since he would have ended his tour" in a few months. I asked Chaplain J.A. Whitman, the force chaplain in Yokosuka, if I could fill in at Iwakuni until Chaplain Solomon's relief appeared. Permission was granted and I eagerly awaited the orders.

Sasebo had been a wonderful experience for me. There is a kind of camaraderie on overseas stations that does not exist on CONUS stations unless they are to some extent isolated. This led to an acceptance I had not experienced before except in the Black culture. At Sasebo I had it both on and off station. As housing officer, I had contacts with the Mayor and his wife and other influentials who owned rental property. As a tennis enthusiast I met Mr. Sakata, president of the Shinwa Bank, who played on our Navy court on occasion. Dr.

Low and I won the doubles in the tournament by my staying out of his way. He had played for Stanford.

I had resurrected my beginning piano lessons to play the organ on Sunday after my organist-assistant, a member of the American Guild of Organists, had been commandeered by Chaplain Brink for the chapel. I learned, note by note, "Jesus, Lover of my Soul," the easiest hymn in the book because three of the four lines in the hymns are identical, then "What a Friend We Have in Jesus," followed by "Nearer My God to Thee," the Gloria and the Doxology, then I was ready to play for a service.

By visiting three different ships each Sunday I could use those three hymns until we learned others. In time we had a repertoire of 22 hymns which would carry me for seven Sundays without repeating. It was difficult to read the music and the words at the same time so I memorized the words.

Sasebo was near Nagasaki, which we visited several times. The destruction caused by the atomic bomb was almost unbelievable. The prefecture which included Sasebo was headquartered at Nagasaki. We were invited to the governor's home there.

My first promotion to LCDR came at Sasebo. There were seven others on station who were promoted at the same time, so we decided to have a combined wetting down party. We rented the China Night nightclub for $200, $25 each, which has to be the most inexpensive wetting down party ever. I invited all the local pastors. I understood that the contract price included food and drink, but I had not known that the entertainers came with the package. Therefore I was quite embarrassed when the band began to play the usual strip number and the strippers came out and did their number. To me it was all strip and no tease, although I did appreciate the G-string one of them wore. It was decorated with a skull and cross-bones made of sequins. Marion later did a painting of her, which she refused to let me hang in my office.

She did another very interesting painting in Sasebo. When the PHILIPPINE SEA visited Sasebo Chaplain E. Richard Barnes organized sponsorship of the two children of Mrs. Nagao for American educations. A part of the agreement was that the ship would send Mrs. Nagao a monthly allowance for living expenses while her children were away. Chaplain Barnes sent the money to me; I changed it to Yen and took it to her. Marion was so enchanted by Mrs. Nagao's poise that she got permission to do a portrait.

At the end of my postgraduate year I was assigned to Camp Pendleton, 1st Marine Division, where Chaplain Barnes was the division chaplain. He was so thrilled when he saw the picture of Mrs. Nagao that Marion gave it to him. He called the *San Diego Union,* a reporter came out with a photographer and a feature article was published about the Nagao family and Chaplain Barnes, accompanied by a picture of the portrait, the artist and the benefactor. Later when the son became a judge and the daughter a social worker, an article appeared in a national magazine under the title, "How Do You Thank 20,000 Men?"

When Chaplain Barnes had the heart attack that separated him from the Navy, he called to say his big disappointment was that he was slated to be on the selection board considering me for CDR. I have since wondered if he would have made the difference so that I would have been selected that year instead of the following year.

Iwakuni at that time was a Naval Air Station, recently taken over from the Air Force, but largely populated by personnel of Marine Service Group 17. Air Force Sergeant Al Smith was still superintendent of the Sunday school, an Air Force wife played the organ and the ecclesiastical gear was Air Force property. I was interested that at social gatherings one could not tell the officers from the enlisted Air Force personnel. I reasoned it was because they were all on planes together and that rank pulling would be at least disruptive, at most a disaster. I remembered that the Air Force discontinued saluting then reinstated it for the benefit of officers of other service who would feel slighted if not saluted.

Then the Air Force personnel were transferred and the chapel equipment left also, including the organ. The Seabees motorized a foot pedaled organ for us, but it was too noisy. We were blessed to get a Hammond from a ship that had bought one, and altar gear from Yokosuka. My assistant, C. Richard Vernon, was a Marine PFC with quite a talent for administration. He is now a Ph.D. in civil service in the Norfolk area.

The chaplain and staff were in the school building. The auditorium was the chapel on Sundays. Sunday school used the classrooms. Dick Vernon and I had spacious offices available to us all week and a permanently assigned jeep.

I immediately became a conversation piece. One of the Marine wives told me that her 5-year-old son came home from Sunday school quite excitedly saying, "Mommy, you've got to come to church next Sunday. We have a darkie chaplain."

Rick was surprised and pleased with my sermon. I was delighted with my acceptance by all hands. It was my first air station duty. It seemed to me that the wives were unusually beautiful. The camaraderie was more intense than at Sasebo, likely because of the Marine majority.

The religious program received valuable assistance from the Watanabe family and other Japanese civilians. Dr. Watanabe had sent two of his daughters to Christian colleges. The daughter who attended the Catholic college played for Catholic Mass on station. The daughter who attended the Methodist College sang in the Protestant choir. The only boy in the family planned to be a doctor, the 17th generation of Watanabe physicians. Dr. Watanabe headed the Japanese VA hospital.

There was good rapport with the town of Iwakuni. The mayor's assistant was a graduate of the University of Nebraska, who delighted in calling himself a "cornhusker." There was only one orphanage in town, so the Christmas season was very busy with so many military groups desiring to entertain the orphans and give presents. In addition to NAS personnel and Marines there were CB's and a contingent of the New Zealand Air Force.

The New Zealanders were responsible for our getting the USO show from their country. It was a delightful program of music and dancing with the women in evening dresses and a quality of music and lyrics suitable for family attendance, although there were no New Zealand families on station, just Navy. Some Marines had dependents, whom they had brought over at their own expense and were not eligible for base housing. It was rumored that a Marine could be given a low mark in judgment on his fitness report for having his wife in Iwakuni. Many of the officers, being able to afford the expense with their flight pay, took this risk. One of them, who was in the habit of buzzing his house when ready to land so his wife could put dinner on the table, buzzed the gym during a basketball game. Everybody knew what was going on as she rose to go and the OOD left to make a report of the incident because he flew too low.

On another occasion we got a scare because a plane landed with wheels up. The pilot had been waved off at his first approach, so he retracted his wheels. He forgot to put them down again on his second approach, so he skidded down the runway, grinding off many thousands of dollars in metal in the process. The crash crew spread foam on the runway. There were no fires. Nobody was injured. Our tenor soloist was in the crew.

My most pleasant experience with a New Zealander came when a petty officer asked for confirmation instructions for the Church of England. His fiancée said she would not marry him until he got confirmed. I called the office of Bishop Yashiro of Yokohama, explained that I was married in the Episcopal Church and was quite familiar with the doctrine and the *Book of Common Prayer*. Permission was granted, so we began with a study of the Thirty-Nine Articles. The candidate was later confirmed by the bishop and returned to New Zealand to be married and live happily ever after. In 1956, when I was studying at the Menninger Foundation in Topeka, Kansas, Bishop Yashiro visited Grace Cathedral. I was able to meet him and remind him of the New Zealand petty officer.

There were two unique tourist attractions available to us at Iwakuni. The most important was nearby Hiroshima, with the same kind of atomic damage as Nagasaki. The second was the Kintai Bridge, a graceful arch over the river constructed of wood supposedly without any metal. The usual bridge in a Japanese garden looks like the Kintai.

Iwakuni was my first Navy experience with a family chapel program. At Great Lakes, Hawaii and Guam the congregations were almost exclusively male congregations. At Charleston I was allowed to preach only in the brig or the stewards' barracks. At Sasebo my ministry was with the ships in the harbor. It was stimulating to hear female voices in the choir, to see children in Sunday school. Nevertheless, because Marion had gone back to her job I did begin to long for a return to CONUS. On one Sunday morning I remarked that I was going to meet Chaplain Petre's plane (he was to be my relief), slap him on the back and say, "Tag Bud, you are it," then board the plane myself. I really did give him a longer turnover period. When I got to Great Lakes and found that I was to get per diem for the time at Iwakuni I began to wonder what my rush was.

My third tour at Great Lakes was shorter than the other two, intended to occupy me until time for matriculation at the Menninger Foundation in clinical marriage counseling, 5 July. I had chosen this training instead of a year at Harvard.

My mother-in-law felt that I made a mistake because of Harvard's greater prestige. I considered my option as being on the cutting edge of things to come. Menninger was the largest psychiatric training center in the world, producing 25% of the nation's psychiatrists. The Menninger brothers, Karl and William, were to psychiatry what the Mayo brothers were to medicine. The staff at Menninger read like an international Who's Who in psychiatry. My first order of business was to read every book the Menninger's had written before I left for Topeka.

My orders for integration into the regular Navy arrived. So I bought rank insignia for LT to replace those for LCDR, saving the old ones for future use. I had been told that at least I would retire at the highest rank held and that a regular LCDR could remain on active duty for 20 years without being promoted. The day I attained regular status was of tremendous importance to me. It meant that I had a guaranteed income for life. Now Marion could leave her job. She did plan to go to Kansas with me. I deeply regret that this kind of option is no longer available to officers in the Navy. Although such a provision did allow some officers to stay who were not productive I think the moral factor of permanent job security far outweighed the amount of dead wood the Navy carried. I met only one such person, a LCDR in the Supply Corps who did not get up until noon. Even so, he maintained that he did his work and the ship did not require more of his time. Unfortunately for good order and discipline, his parting shot always was, "So let them write me a bad fitness report."

At the present time many younger officers rightfully feel insecure from a career perspective. Promotions to LTJG are no longer automatic. Promotions to LT are no longer 95% of the zone and those to LCDR are not at 85%. Especially is promotion difficult for minorities if several of them are in the same zone. Last year, of four females up for promotion to LCDR in the Chaplain Corps, the two Whites were selected, the two Blacks were not. This was a 50% selection opportunity. In 1951 the entire zone going from CDR to CAPT in the line made it. Although much attention is being given now to the difficulty of recruiting Black officers because of the promotion hazards I suspect job security is more important than many will admit. It implies a desire to be retained even when mediocre. For minorities it is more of an insurance provision that discrimination might be prevented from ending a useful career.

It seemed to me that during this short tour Great Lakes was but a shadow of its former greatness. I missed most of all the intensive push to get recruits involved in religious instruction leading to baptism or church membership, as in "the old days" with Chaplains Kelly, Curry and Anderson. I did a lot of talking about how things used to be and wrote up a description of how the plan worked and passed it up the chain. I suspect that my suggestions sounded like criticism of current procedures. I then sent the memorandum to the senior chaplains of all the recruit training centers and the Chief of Chaplains. When a new Chief of Chaplains took office I sent a copy to him. It was my feeling that a unique opportunity for evangelism was being missed.

The prospect of moving to Topeka and setting up housekeeping for the first time was exciting after four years of marriage. Marion still had her 1949 DeSoto which had been backed into by a British lorry in Sasebo and repaired by the British garage. I had a 1946 Dodge I bought at a distress sale for $100. Marion did not want to take either to Kansas, saying we would look like *Tobacco Road* if we took both. Marion's sister's husband, Grover McCants, knew several Chrysler dealers in Detroit so we decided to shop there with his help. When we found a new Chrysler Newport that we liked for $3,000 the trade in offered was so low that we kept the Desoto until I returned to Great Lakes and had the opportunity to drive to Chicago where I gave it to Chicago Presbytery. Presbytery used it in the summer camp program.

Grover McCants knew the Chrysler dealers because he bought vans for his Grover's Delivery Service. He had a franchise for delivering bags that did not arrive with passengers at Detroit airports. He also owned a Chrysler Imperial, Chrysler 300 convertible, Cadillac Eldorado and Lincoln Continental. I never knew of anyone in a large city who had this kind of lucrative monopoly. Other firms were continually attempting to replace him unsuccessfully as long as he lived.

Topeka, KA

In Topeka we found a rental two-bedroom house near Forbes Air Force Base after a brief stay at the home of Mr. and Mrs. John Quinn. The Quinn's daughter was a nursing assistant at Menninger, who saw to it that we met the Black residents in the psychiatry program, Dr. Baker and Dr. Bateman. Dr. Bateman turned out to be the former Mildred Mitchell, daughter of Dr. and Mrs. S.Q. Mitchell. I had met the Mitchells 20 years earlier in Charlotte at Johnson C. Smith University during a youth conference. I saw the family again when Dr. Mitchell came to First African Presbyterian Church, Philadelphia where he doubled the membership. Mildred attended the Medical College for Women there. She has since been Chairperson of psychiatry at two medical schools and head of the Mental Health Department of the State of West Virginia.

Our class was the first all chaplain group to matriculate at Menninger. There was one army chaplain, LtCOL Edward J. Saunders of the Catholic Archdiocese of Chicago and two other Navy chaplains, LCDR George A. Rossback of the Catholic Archdiocese of New York and LCDR Ralph W. Below, Southern Baptist. Our supervisor was Dr. Robert G. Foster, a lay (non-MD) psychoanalyst and Dean Johnson who had just completed *Counseling in the Counselor*, assisted Dr. Foster. Our consulting psychiatrist was Dr. Clark Case, also a psychoanalyst curriculum.

Although we had our own curriculum we were allowed to audit any of the courses for the psychiatric residents. Our courses were taught by Dr. Foster, Dean Johnson, Mrs. Luella Foster (Dr. Bob's wife) and other invited members of the staff. I've attended case conferences and done counseling at Menninger, the Topeka Counseling Center and Forbes Air Force Base. Our favorite teacher to audit was Dr. Rudolph Ekstein, because of his uncanny ability to anticipate the process in therapy sessions of his residents. He also put us in touch with a lay analyst group in Toledo, Ohio composed of clergymen.

I had previously been impressed by my uncle's accounts of Hitler's oratory. He used to listen to Hitler via radio at 2 a.m. Dr. Ekstein told of one evening he went to hear Hitler speak. After not appearing until 0100 hours, he appeared on stage with a whip in his hand and explained that he had been flogging enemies of the state. A man seated next to Dr. Ekstein stood up in his seat and screamed, "Heil Hitler." The crowd took up the chant and continued it for such a long time that Hitler never got to speak at all.

The Menninger brothers were known as Dr. Karl and Dr. Will. Dr. Will was a former Brigadier General as head of the Army Psychiatric Service. He spent most of his time in development and in speaking before state legislatures to encourage the adoption of the Kansas model of mental health care. Under the guidance of the Menninger's, mental health care was no longer only custodial but was returning useful citizens to productive lives in society. Dr. Karl did a lot of teaching, writing for publications, therapy and public speaking as well. We prized his reading notes. We hardly ever missed his informal talk sessions at which questions could be asked and issues raised.

My primary problem as a trainee in counseling was to keep from slipping over the line between counseling and therapy. Dean Johnson was exasperated with me at times. It appeared to me that the psychiatrists were protective of their turf. This made the clergy somewhat defensive about their role and on occasion critical of and hostile to psychiatrists. After all, Freud had called religion the "Opiate of the People," and Menninger was strictly Freudian in philosophy although Dr. Karl was a faithful member of First Presbyterian Church and still taught his mother's Sunday School class. He also was very chummy with Chaplain Tom Klink of Topeka State Hospital and sponsored annually the Gallahue Symposium on Religion and Psychiatry. It was at this symposium that I heard Dr. Karl Stern of Canada and Bishop James Pike of San Francisco.

An Affirmation of Faith

My only disagreement theologically with Dr. Karl was on the matter of human freedom. He said that he could find none anywhere. When he added Freudian psychosexual development to hereditary influences and environmental determinants without even mentioning divine predestination he felt we were completely programmed (although he did not use that word). I feel that even when options are beyond our control we have the freedom of volition, motive and attitude.

Dr. Foster found Marion a job as art teacher at the Boys Industrial School in Topeka. It was a state reformatory strongly influenced by the Menningers. Therefore we spoke the same language, attended the same functions and cultivated the same friends. In our car pool to Menninger was Dr. William Grier, who had known Marion's sister Vici at the University of Michigan. Years later with Dr. Price Cobbs he wrote the very popular *Black Rage*. When I saw him in Los Angeles, where he was then living, I told him he had omitted the religious dimension in his book. He said that was a job for me but the next year he published a sequel dealing with Black religion. Sometimes I felt that I learned as much in the car pool as I did in class.

My major disagreement with Dr. Grier was over the near inevitability of divorce. In *Black Rage* he stated that he did not know any reputable psychiatrist who had not been divorced. Since psychiatrists have more therapy than anyone else it implies that divorce is an enlightened choice. Possibly because of his own divorce Dr. Karl would not take anyone in therapy unless the spouse was in therapy also, in an effort to allow the spouses to cope with personality changes in each other. In any event I am thankful that Marion and I had similar exposures to psychiatry.

We were still praying nightly the prayer for children taken from the wedding service from the Episcopal Prayer Book. Marion had been checked by specialists in New York and Japan; I had been checked out in Japan. At Forbes Air Force Base Marion found a doctor who had the answer; stress and anxiety had been causing her to secrete some chemical that destroyed sperm cells. The psychiatric community at Topeka lowered piety and stress levels to the point that conception was possible before we left for my next assignment, Fifth Marines, First Marine Division, Camp Pendleton, Calif.

Topeka had been a good experience. It had gotten me in on the ground floor of the Chaplain Corps new interest in marriage counseling. For several years after our class other chaplains would be coming to Menninger, but we were the first. In Topeka we met the father of Major General Frank Peterson, USMC, the first Black pilot to be commissioned in the Marine Corps. We saw the famous murals of John Brown in the capitol and heard the local Blacks in the barbershop talking about "Free Kansas." Here was the site of the Brown vs. Board of Education suit that integrated education by law and in practice to some extent. In Topeka Charles F. Parham inaugurated the modern Pentecostal movement. At Menninger I was given a part time job as reader of the papers of the residents for English errors, which allowed me to consider myself a member of the Menninger staff. I worked for Dr. Karl's wife, Jeanetta, the librarian.

This had been our first experience of housekeeping, in a house rather than a mobile home. Having been reduced in rank to enter the regular Navy, and with Marion having resigned as head of the art department at N.C. Central, we economized. We bought mattress and springs for the bedroom, put the springs on an adjustable frame on rollers. Marion used a barrel set upright as a dressing table. We still have the springs and frame. We bought two chairs from the telephone company at $2.00 each; now I wish we had bought six because the two are still in use. Mrs. Quinn loaned us a card table. For $125 we bought a sectional sofa for the living room, now in the family room having been upholstered twice, and added a lacquered cocktail table we bought from Japan for $25. Then we found a dinette set in wood for $79 that is still in use.

We were glad for these economies because I got a letter from the pay office at Great Lakes to the effect that I would not draw any pay until further notice because my pay had continued at the old rate after I was reduced in rank. Fortunately, I had followed my custom of drawing a "dead horse" with my transfer orders. One at that time could draw two months pay in advance, to be taken out of one's pay in six months with no interest charge. I usually did this and deposited the money in my savings and loan account to draw interest as long as I could afford to leave it there. With the transfer to Great Lakes from Japan, Topeka from Great Lakes and Camp Pendleton from Topeka I drew three dead horses in 18 months.

We left Topeka for leave in Durham. We invited Marion's parents to make the drive to California with us; Mama and Papa we called them, with the accent on the last syllable in both cases. The Chrysler was only a year old so we set out for a comfortable drive of about 450 miles per day stopping four nights. Our only problem came in Lebanon, TN where in a rainstorm I entered a downtown hotel in uniform and engaged rooms. When I brought the rest of my party in the Black bellhop told us there had been a mistake that we would not be allowed to stay. Papa asked if he knew where we could stay. He happily took us to a very comfortable rooming house owned and operated by pleasant Black people. Papa was so pleased with the accommodations and the hot breakfast with biscuits the next morning that he left a $20 tip.

The rest of our nights were spent in motels without incident. In Santa Rosa, New Mexico, Papa used some of his Spanish. On St. Vincent's Island, British West India where he was born, the primers were in three languages, English, French and Spanish. He still remembered stories from his primer in the three languages as I remember the first page of my primer: "Baby Ray has a dog; the dog is little. Baby Ray loves his little dog; the little dog loves Baby Ray." The next page began, "Baby Ray has two cunning kitty cats." But I do not remember what Baby Ray had three and four of, etc.

The Chrysler, as most cars of the time, was not air conditioned, so driving across the desert was uncomfortable until we were so enthralled by the scenery of the Painted Desert and the mountains that we nearly forgot the heat. This was the first of 13 cross-country drives we made before receiving east coast orders eight years later.

First Marine Division, Camp Pendleton, CA

We were not prepared for our abrupt arrival at Camp Pendleton. By following the map we were on the right highway, but we had not supposed the highway ran directly into the guard gate. We expected an access road or a turnoff to the base. When I saw we were about to enter the gate and I was wearing shorts I got out of the car on the side of the road to don some trousers. The guard raised his telescope to see what was going on. When we pulled alongside he smiled although he tried not to do it as he gave us directions to the headquarters of the Fifth Marine Regiment, which was nearer the main gate than the back gate we had entered from Fallbrook.

When I checked in I found that the Hostess House was full, so we went to a Spanish type motel in Oceanside, the nearest city to the main gate. It was a new experience for me to find that the speed limit on base was 55 and that the base was 30 miles long. One could live in Wire Mountain Housing and drive 25 miles to work at Camp San Onofre. We enjoyed the few days in Oceanside until room was available at the Hostess House. Papa was reluctant to leave but honored my desire to save on expenses. When we checked with the housing office the next day to see how long a wait we had the Sgt. said, "How about tomorrow?"

We were assigned a two-bedroom house in the DeLuz area on Wonsan Drive at Wonju Circle, completely adequate for our needs. It was just 4 miles from work, within two miles of the hospital so that I could stand hospital duty by telephone at home. I estimated that I could drive from home to the emergency room quicker than a chaplain could walk from the duty room.

Our household effects had arrived and so were delivered. Mama and Papa helped us unpack the Japanese souvenirs, including our collection of Hakata Dolls. The figure of the old man in the hot tub looked enough like Papa that one might suspect he had been the model. I thought when Mama dropped it she was shocked by the likeness, but she denied this. After two days of unpacking I thought we were about to enjoy an extended visit. We went to Tijuana, were invited by Chaplain Hedges Capers to visit him in LaJolla. He had the Seventh Marines at Camp Pulgas (fleas) just up the road from my Camp Margarita. The problem was that he did not realize that when he said "LaHoya" I would not know it would be spelled LaJolla, so we couldn't find him.

Hedges was interested in the Menninger training, so he asked my advice about being sure to be ordered there. I needed his advice about being a Marine Chaplain. My CO sent me a printed program from a Christmas Service in Hedges chapel with a note expressing a wish that we could do likewise. He had a choir and the most effective junior chaplain I ever saw, Stan Linzey (Assembly of God). Stan had ten children, drove a Cadillac limousine he bought from a mortician, because it held more passengers than a station wagon. He walked with the troops on hikes but had his field organ and hymnbooks in his jeep. At rest stops he would take the organ off set it up, pass out hymnbooks and lead the Marines in a songfest. Stan was a former enlisted Navy musician. He favored me years later by asking me to write a forward for his book, Pentecost in the Pentagon.

Hedges did get to Menninger, began a personal psychoanalysis and later moved into Clinical Pastoral Education and Transactional Analysis. He moved to a larger house in LaJolla where he could hold seminars in the renovated garage. He sold this house for a million dollars after he retired. One day he called me quite excitedly saying, "Dave, you've just got to meet my new daughter-in-law, she's a Negress." Donna and Hedges, Jr. had been singing in a San Diego nightclub. They decided that since they were going to stay up all night together they might as well get married. Their first record was "All the Beautiful Colors."

Following Hedges example we did have a Christmas Candlelight Service. General Bare and Mrs. Bare attended it. Mrs. Bare held our daughter Evangeline so Marion could go to the Communion rail.

Colonel Rothwell, my CO, sent regrets because that evening was always a family affair for them. Colonel Codispotti tapped one of his junior officers to recruit and train a choir. We appeared on San Diego TV with Colonel Lyle Stephenson, the XO of the Fifth Marines. The Lord provided two super star junior chaplains George Paulsons, Greek Orthodox who dedicated our first Greek Orthodox Chapel at Pendleton, possibly in the Marine Corps or even the Navy. The first Sunday he preached at the Protestant Service the assistants put his sermon manuscript on the bulletin board with the heading, "The Best Sermon in the World." The other was Walter B. (for Beauregard he told people) Feagins, Southern Baptist. He had just come from destroyer duty where Edward R. Murrow had done a documentary on his work for CBS called *"Christmas in the Formosa Straits."* Walt had a copy he shared with us. It was my first time to watch someone direct the band left-handed.

Walt had evangelical fervor and soon set about instructing Marines for baptism in the Pacific Ocean. He and George assisted me with plans that culminated in the setting up of a Butler Hut chapel instead of the Quonset Hut that we found when we came. It proved to be the only chapel I ever built during my naval career. Mrs. Bare cut the ribbon at the dedication and the former Chief of Chaplains, Stan Salisbury, preached the sermon.

Being with the Fifth Marines was a heady experience. The Fifth as well as the Sixth Marines on the east coast were permitted to wear a French decoration, a *forguerre*, which we called a "pogey" rope. If it had been gold instead of green and red someone might have supposed the wearer to be the general's aide. I wore it on my Navy as well as my Marine uniforms. I bought Marine utilities, greens and whites, but was told that Navy personnel could not wear Marine dress blues nor mess dress. It became my policy to participate in every Marine activity although I drank tomato juice at the cocktail parties. I justified my support of the club by the example of Jesus in making wine out of water for the wedding feast at Cana. Chaplain Stuart Robinson of the First Marines could not conscien-

An Affirmation of Faith

tiously pay club dues so he had to write a letter to the general to this effect, after which he was barred from the club even as a guest. This meant that we could have no functions at the club for chaplains if we wanted him there. Stu was brilliant. He had been an assistant to Dr. Clarence Edward MacCartney of the First Presbyterian Church of Pittsburgh before entering the Navy. I wondered years later if his attitude toward the club hurt his career.

Captain John Metas was a company commander who epitomized the gung ho attitude. When we had a surprise field exercise sprung on us, he strapped on his pearl handled .45 and kissed his wife goodbye. He also headed the rifle range. When he asked me to fire the range with the troops I was delighted. Everyone was surprised when I fired 231 with the M71. Expert score was 220. John called the public information office to take pictures and do a story. Then somebody decided that the Russians might interpret this as an intention to violate the terms of the Geneva Convention by which chaplains are non-combatants.

I had heard the story of a chaplain in combat who saw one of the enemy sneaking up on the bunker he had left to go to the latrine. Realizing that his buddies would be killed if the soldier threw his grenade the chaplain made hamburger out of him with his .45. Then he had to be returned stateside in a straight jacket. I felt that by becoming an expert I could hit an enemy in both legs rather than his head.

John's reason for having me fire the range was that he wanted to tell the troops, "If that old man can do it, you can do it." I was 36 at the time. In the Marine Corps anyone who fired expert after the age of 35 was entitled to wear the medal for the rest of his life which I continue to do. Others have to re-qualify annually. For the same reason he had me do calisthenics with the troops, including one armed push-ups. I had been doing pushups since I sent for a Charles Atlas course in 1932 but never with one arm.

So with my Marine uniforms "pogey" rope and expert rifle medal I felt fully accepted, even a minor celebrity. I issued an order that everybody who worked for me had to fire expert. To assist the process I gave my shooting jacket, my shooting glove, loaned my leather rifle sling and my shooting glasses to the chapel. Captain

Metas sent me Don Tambornino, as Don's reward for doing 100 pushups, to be one of my assistants. My senior assistant, Sgt Dick Jones, son of a Methodist preacher and now a detective in Seattle, qualified expert on the rifle, pistol and BAR (Browning automatic rifle).

When Colonel "Buck" Schmuck took over in the Fifth he announced plans for a 100 mile hike to San Diego and back. We heard that he had been promoted to Lt. Col when he was 27 and was as gung ho as Captain Metas. The chaplains then had been transferred from the regiment to the various battalions in a move to make the battalions the preeminent fighting units. I went to Lt. Col Loy's First Battalion. He was a lawyer who commuted daily from Balboa Island, somewhat of a millionaire colony. Dr. Beauchamp, an ex-Navy dentist owner of eight California dental clinics, married to the sister of the Union Pacific Railroad president, lived there in a palatial home once owned by reserve Chaplain C. Pardee Erdman, who drove a Rolls and picked up the tab for the chaplains banquet at which Ronald Reagan was the speaker.

We began doing practice hikes, 15 miles or so, since we would have 4 days to finish the 100. At the regimental meeting someone said it would not be practical to expect the Navy types, doctors, dentists, chaplains, to try the hike. Colonel Loy told me he then said, "I have one Navy chaplain who will walk as far as anybody." I enjoyed this vote of confidence.

We planned to walk 25 miles a day, starting at daylight, keeping on the back road and ending the trek in the early afternoon. The usual rate for walking with a light marching pack was 2½ miles an hour. I soon found that it was better to be in front of the column because those at the end had to slow down when going downhill as the front of the column climbed the next hill, then had to speed up climbing uphill to keep up with the column going downhill on the other side. I also found that it was easier on the feet to walk on the shoulder of the road, in the grass or in the dirt. The Geneva Convention rules assisted also in that I carried neither rifle nor pistol, added weight on a hike.

Food service units accompanied us with trucks, immersion burners for washing the mess trays, portable stoves, and plenty of

An Affirmation of Faith

food and water. Also with us was "Reckless," a horse used as ammunition carrier in Korea, now the mascot for the Fifth. I was a mite disappointed that Colonel Schmuck did not ride the horse. We had one battalion CO who developed bloody, painful feet because he had just come to us from a communications job. His chaplain and I went to Colonel Schmuck and requested that he be excused from the rest of the hike. Colonel Schmuck said, "I think he should walk until he drops." We lost a chaplain the first day because of shin splints.

Colonel Schmuck denied my second request also. On the third day we had covered so much ground that it seemed to me to be a shame to not continue and arrive home a day early. He did not want to change the schedule. So we breezed in easily the fourth day, awaited by families, the generals, the press and some of the dropouts. Morale was high around the chapel as in the rest of the camp. In later years other regiments duplicated the exercise.

I mentioned that Mrs. Bare had held Evangeline for Marion to go to Communion on Christmas Eve, but had not told of Evangeline's arrival. Because of the staggered church services on Sunday I was able to preach at two chapels and also to sing in the Ranch House Chapel Choir with Marion. On Thursday September 13, 1956 we decided to pay a call on Lt. Colonel and Mrs. Lyle Stephenson in Wire Mountain before going to choir practice. We enjoyed the visit, ate the cheese and peanuts liberally since we had not had dinner and left in time to make it to choir practice. We practiced a duet, "My Faith Looks Up to Thee," for soprano and tenor to sing the next Sunday.

Marion had eminent symptoms before midnight, called the hospital and was advised to come in. We went over, she was examined, and it was decided that she would stay for observation. I returned home and to bed. At 0300 hours, the doorbell rang. There stood Chaplain Don LeMaster in his pajamas with right hand extended. "Congratulations," he said; "you have a little girl."

I had wanted four boys because of my closeness to the Fleming brothers but agreed that we should also have a girl. My sister had a girl before she had her four boys so it seemed we were following her pattern. I went back to the hospital to find mother and baby in good condition even though the baby was two months early and weighed a little less than 5 pounds. We decided that the baby was in a hurry to get to California as 1500 people a day were back then or that the cheese and peanuts triggered the early arrival. In my family my older sister was named for her aunts and mother, we named our first for this same sister and Marion's younger sister who died while in her college years. We never got to sing that duet at the Ranch House Chapel.

Finally at home, Evangeline was given meticulous care. I cleaned out the car every time she was to ride in it. We likely had the cleanest car at Pendleton because we took her everywhere we went. As a preemie, she had to be fed every two hours around the clock. I assumed the watch at midnight and kept it until I had to go to work. She wet 30 minutes after each feeding. It was cause for celebration when she drank two full ounces. We were so happy that our prayer for children had been answered in the affirmative. It was then discontinued.

Two things were distinctive about our new arrival: she had scarcely any hair (I told her we were going to use a thumb tack or Scotch tape to attach a ribbon) and her complexion was fair, so much so that a Marine wife neighbor wanted to know from Marion, whether I had accepted her as mine, somewhat to Marion's disgust. If she had asked me, I would have told her about my other sister and my grandmother of the same complexion. Fortunately, for this neighbor's peace of mind the California sunshine tanned Evangeline into conformity.

With the Fifth Marines at that time Blacks were in scarce supply. There was one Black Marine officer who drove a gull-wing Mercedes, one Black doctor, two Black gunnery sergeants and a scattering of Blacks in the lower enlisted ratings. As usual, I was the only Black chaplain and the senior Black in the area. Our doctor was Bobby Higgins, son of the AME Bishop of South Carolina. He turned 25 just before the 100-mile hike and was looking forward to the drop in his automobile insurance premium. When we visited his home, we found that his wife belonged to a Baptist Church in upstate New York where my classmate Rev. Doyle John Thomas of the Loyal Baptist Church, Danville, preached a revival every year. We also visited a Dr. Organ, who was spending his brief tour in the Navy at Pendleton. Years later I saw him in Omaha during a recruiting tour.

Two of the battalion CO's were avid supporters of the chapel program. One day Lt. Colonel Gildo S. Codispotti asked me how we were doing. I told him things were going very well but chapel attendance could be better. His reply was "How many does the chapel hold?" I told him 200. "We'll fill up the damn place," he said. So he had the word passed to fill up the chapel, volunteered a junior officer to recruit and direct a choir and came himself to read the Scripture. He was a picturesque person, of burly stature with busy eyebrows like those of John L. Lewis of the United Mineworkers Union. I notice such eyebrows because my dad had them. I invited him to make an inspection of the chapel during the time I had my TV on for the World Series. My last communication from his family was a Christmas card from Hawaii with the family decked out in aloha shirts, mumus and grass skirts. Several were wearing festive straw hats.

Our other Marine angel was Lt. Colonel John Nicolas McLaughlin of Savannah. He was just as ardent Catholic as his wife Marilee was Protestant. She called me one night because the chaplain she said was the best preacher in the Navy had just been killed by a fall on his aircraft carrier. Colonel McLaughlin had used "Cornbread" as his call sign in Korea where he had been held prisoner. He told me one day that his interrogator told him they were tired of getting no information from him so they were going to kill him. The Korean had an American .45 and there was a round in the chamber. He put it to the Colonel's head and squeezed the trigger. It did not fire, and after that they let him alone.

At a battalion party at their house, I presented him a commission as a Kentucky Colonel. One of the junior officers began to sing "Oh, I wish I was in the land of," but instead of "cotton" he sang "taters, cotton-mouths and alligators." He got several instant invitations to leave on the first from the Colonel's lady, all in jest.

Our closest friends in DeLuz housing were Chaplain and Mrs. Kenneth Paul Zeller and Dr. Emerson and Mrs. Deidre Graham, the latter family Black. Ken and Lorraine Zeller had a daughter Cindy who thought the current Belafonte hit was about her. Deidre

An Affirmation of Faith

Graham was a nurse so we leaned on her quite heavily. Lorraine was an accomplished organist. Ken and Lorraine were also favorites of Division Chaplain E. Richard Barnes to whom Marion gave the painting of Mrs. Nakao mentioned previously. Ken had prior service in the Supply Corps. I usually stood in awe of those who had such experiences assuming that it gave them rapport with their former comrades as well as additional useful skills.

It was comforting for all of us to rely upon each other as one or two of the husbands left for a field problem or exercise of some sort. Even if all the Division husbands left, Don LeMaster would still be at the hospital and the wives would have each other.

After a while, the field problems began to look alike, the friendly forces would chase the aggressors over the same hills. Often the last day of the exercise would find us at the same campsite as a previous exercise. I usually slept at the battalion aid station under the Donabedian tent. It may have been the forerunner of the pop up trailer tent. It was designed by Dr. Donabedian, one of several doctors who preferred Marine duty and saw much of it.

The unexpected did happen. One night we were left in a field all night without any gear when the helicopter sent to pick us up could not see us because of the fog. On another exercise in which the aggressors were to land via helicopters, Colonel Schmuck discovered their landing site by sifting papers from trash cans and strung simulated wires on simulated telephone poles that downed all the simulated helicopters. Each year a rumor went around that the Division exercise would be held in Cuba instead of at Pendleton. One morning in the chapel I said, "I guess it's about time to start that Cuba rumor again." That afternoon an excited Marine came in with "Chaplain, guess what I just heard." Killjoy that I am, I told him I originated the rumor.

The real mover among the Division chaplains was Dick Barnes' assistant, Art Dominy, American Baptist. He would breeze through the barracks on Sunday afternoons, inviting Marines to the evening service at the Base Chapel. He organized the weekend religious retreats, assigning the preachers, song leaders, etc., taking the final service himself. He was active in the Officers Christian Fellowship. He had the Haven of Rest Quartet to sing at one of the evening services I attended. A senior reserve Chaplain doing two weeks active duty called him a "fireball."

There were a couple of discouraging features of the life at Pendleton. The first was the problem of one of the privates. One of his friends in another outfit came to his home to visit his wife during our field exercises. My suggestion was to get a transfer for one of the men. I was told that the Marine Corps holds men individually responsible for their family affairs.

The other situation I did not verify, but I was told that there was a key club in the trailer court. Every Friday night the men put their keys in a hat and then drew keys to see where they would spend the night. One fellow was quite upset because he drew his own key. Another chaplain was assigned to the trailer area. I really didn't want to be the one to blow the whistle on the wife swapping. We had no such rumors in our regiment.

Our next exciting event came some months later when the Fifth was picked to see a demonstration explosion of an atomic bomb. I promised the regimental CO that he would have a chaplain for the exercise. As the time neared, the chaplains found reasons they could not make the trip. I was reluctant because Marion was pregnant again, but I had given my word. We decided to make a trip to Durban before the exercise began and I left Marion there while I went on the exercise. A neighbor had a Studebaker that he wanted driven to the east coast so we volunteered to drop it off for him. En-route we ran into heavy rain through Arkansas and Missouri. For one stretch, the highway was covered with so much water that I had to drive with my head out the window so I could see the white line in the center of the highway. We passed houses with water well over the foundations, nearly up to floor level. Providentially we did complete the trip.

I had never been to Las Vegas. When I saw that the Ink Spots were in town I went to the club looking for James Holmes, who had been in our choir at Great Lakes in 1945, only to find that he was in another Ink Spots group. Jack Benny was in town with Mary Livingston. The hotel was interested in inviting the Marines to two shows, one for Whites, one for Blacks. LtCOL Stephenson told the manager that there was only one color in the Marine Corps, green,

An Affirmation of Faith

and if we could not go together, we could not go at all. I wondered if Jack Benny knew about this exchange. We all attended the show and enjoyed it. BGEN Teirji asked me the next week how it went. He had already been told that Jack had said "damn," which was not allowed on radio or TV in those days.

On this exercise I learned to be careful in talking to Generals. One of our men had been hit on the lake by a motor boat. The screw had cut his shoulder, so he was in sickbay where I saw him. As I was on my way back, the same General called to me and asked if all were going well. I said "Except for the private who was hit by the motorboat." He turned to his legal officer and told him to investigate the incident. That evening we were in the regimental office when someone wanted to know if the General's legal officer might still be around. I picked up that he was around because the General had him investigating the boating incident. LCOL Stephenson wanted to know how the General knew about it. When I said I had told him, he rushed out of the office, saying the General would wonder why he had not told him that he was conducting his own investigation. Many times later, I heard the complaint from superiors, "Why was I not informed?" I can't remember these words having been directed at me.

To help us keep in shape, a 15-mile hike was set for the middle of one day when the temperature was about 110. I was surprised at how little it was necessary to perspire. The explanation was that it was dry heat. We wore air utilities with shirts on and the usual boots and carried light marching packs.

The atomic explosion was the most spectacular thing I have ever seen. We were lined up in the desert near a tower which held loud speakers. We were commanded to turn our backs to the explosion area. Soon after the explosion we were hit by a shock wave that felt like someone slapping one on the back of the head with an open palm. We were then ordered to turn around to see the mushroom cloud shooting skyward at what seemed incredible speed. Another shock wave was coming, raising a cloud of dust about six inches high that was racing toward us like a flock of roadrunners. The Marines shouted all kinds of exclamations, profane, vulgar and religious as we all watched in near disbelief. We were certainly convinced that there could be no escape or defense against atomic power within range. It was a sobering experience that we had all seen on TV, but the real thing was not the same.

Another reason that I remember this exercise is that I met Capt Frank Peterson, USMC, the Marine Corps' first Black pilot. I had met his father in Topeka where he ran an electronics business. Frank, who drove a red Thunderbird, really took to the Marine Corps. Years later, I attended his promotion ceremony to Brigadier General, another first.

The final reason I remember this exercise in that one night I got the word that our second daughter had been born dead, but Marion was doing fine. Emergency leave was arranged for me, and a sedan was sent to take me to my flight. Nearly in tears, I told the driver why I was going. He replied that he had experienced this three times and thus dried up my tears instantly.

Marion had decided to come back to Pendleton to be there when I arrived. She had stopped by Detroit to see her sister Vici. They had gone to a circus or a fair with Vici's boys. When Marion got back to Oceanside, she could not find anyone to help with her luggage. When all this is added to the cross-country trip in the little Studebaker through the flood, the loss of the baby at five months is not difficult to explain. In addition, Evangeline was in diapers still and needed to be picked up often.

Don LeMaster was a Godsend for us. He was a skilled counselor, highly respected by the psychiatrists and psychologists. California law required a burial for all babies of five months and older. Don did the funeral service for us. We named her Sarah Marion, with the first name after Marion's sister, Evangeline. We ordered a small gravestone and later visited the site. Occasionally I see the deed to the grave among my important papers. For years, I used to share this experience with those who were going through it until I learned from Henri Nouwen that one should not do this, but concentrate on the other's pain.

Because there are many people who have never read Henri Nouwen, we were amazed at the number of friends who told of their own like experiences. One Colonel's wife had gone through it five times. She sent an Azalea plant. We certainly appreciated those who shared their pain with us. Nevertheless, I found the truth in the Nouwen procedure many years later at Portsmouth Naval Hospital. Rev. Junius Mason of St. James Episcopal Church came regularly to the hospital to offer Episcopal Communion and to visit Episcopal patients, as did several other clergy from the area. I noticed, however, that he was the only one I approached for his address, so a contribution could be sent to his church. On each occasion, I asked the patient if Father Mason had told of his extended almost terminal, hospitalization and found that he had not mentioned a word of it. Obviously, he had been concerned primarily with their problems, for which they were quite grateful.

Marion and I grieved together, thankful that we still had Evangeline and for the support of friends. Marion came back to normal sooner than I expected, for which I was very thankful to God. I felt that I had a deeper appreciation of the meaning of the death of a child that would make me a better chaplain. At least I would no longer feel guilty in ministering to others since I had not escaped the experience myself.

For several years, even before our wedding, Papa had endured a growth on his forehead. He assisted Dr. Swift in removing it, only to have it return. Because of other symptoms, he entered Lincoln Hospital in Durham, where he had been chief of surgery, to find that he had several tumors, which proved to be malignant. Marion went home and when his condition worsened, I took emergency leave, the only 30-day leave I ever had. Vincent, Marion's brother came from Long Island, where he was head of thoracic surgery, to watch the exploratory surgery. He agreed with the local surgeons that the cancer had metastasized, leaving no remedy. Papa came home for a few days but had to return. The family decided that someone should be with him at all times so I volunteered to spend the nights as long as my leave lasted.

Since I was a little boy I had retained a certain amount of fear of Papa. I remember a tearful incident when I was to receive some kind of inoculation. I asked if I could do it myself but was relieved of the syringe when I started pushing the plunger without inserting the needle. Papa said, "You are wasting my vaccine."

An Affirmation of Faith

When I was 15 years old, I stepped on an upturned nail in a board that penetrated my foot so deeply that I had to take my shoe off to get the nail out of my foot. I went to his office. He used forceps to clean the wound with gauze dipped in iodine then gave me a tetanus shot. When he told me my bill was $2, I expressed surprise. He said, "Everybody who sits in that chair pays $2" So I gave him the $2, for which I could have bought 20 loaves of bread or ten quarts of milk or ten gallons of kerosene. Beef stew and rice in a restaurant then cost 15 cents. A favorite $0.15 lunch for laborers then was a loaf of bread, a can of pork and beans and a quart of buttermilk. Using unsliced bread, the procedure was to ram a hand down the end of the loaf, pour the pork and beans in the hole and eat the result like an ice cream cone.

When I graduated with honors from seminary Papa told me he never thought I would make it. When we went on our honeymoon, Papa gave Marion $200.00 in case she needed it to get back home. Sitting with him night after night, listening to him talk about his experiences in childhood on St. Vincent's Island, his coming to America, his hotel work to finance his education, his unique experience as the only doctor in Aurora N.C., when the White doctors were drafted for World War I, and the influenza epidemic allowed me to understand him as I had not been able to do before. I learned to love him in a way I had not experienced with my own father. Of all those I knew who have died I miss him most.

When my leave was about to expire I told Papa I had to get back to Pendleton but would see him again in June; it was then March. He said vigorously with a smile, "You won't see me in June!" I smiled, too, as we shook hands and said. "Well, all right." Marion returned to Pendleton with me. Two weeks later we got a call from Vincent's wife, Marguerite, saying Papa had taken a turn for the worse. We left for Durham again but not in time to see Papa alive. So I attended my second funeral at St. Titus Church. Only he and Evangeline rest in the family plot. He was buried with the honor befitting the Senior Warden of the church with additional gravesite rites by the Masons. Mama is still escorted to the annual Masonic banquet in memory of the deceased after 20 years have passed.

Mama remained in Durham working as head of the Mount Vernon Baptist Church's Day Care Center. I found that her income was too large for me to claim her as a dependent, although we wished for her to become a member of our household. She decided to take a YWCA tour of Europe and enjoyed it thoroughly. Papa had shown me a copy of his Will, leaving everything to her as a life estate with the three children as contingent beneficiaries. I liked this plan so well I followed it myself.

It was time for me to leave Pendleton. My next duty was to be with COMPHIBRON 1, home ported in San Diego. Jim Kelly had been the Amphibious Force Chaplain. When he asked if I would like that kind of duty I jumped at it because at Pendleton we had ridden amphibious ships on exercises. I thought there would be many carryovers and that I would likely be host to many of my old buddies. The Fifth had a drum and bugle corps led by Sgt. Tanzie Johnson who was with us in Sasebo. He knew that my favorite selection in their repertoire was "The Old Oaken Bucket." Therefore on my last morning with the Fifth at colors the drum and bugle corps played my song. I left with much regret because I felt that at Pendleton I really found myself as a chaplain and the first Black one to have Marine duty.

COMPHIBRON 1, San Diego, CA

When I reported to COMPHIBRON 1, I was the first Black chaplain to go to sea. The stewards were particularly excited to have me on the flagship USS HENRICO. It was a converted merchant ship in rather poor condition. When it got over ten knots at sea it shook, rattled and rolled. Some wise guys said it was held together by the paint and the cockroaches holding hands. I was assigned the troop commander's stateroom, which had its own bathroom and no roommate. The stewards were proud of this also and possibly had a hand in arranging it. The only problem was that when the ship listed to port an unpleasant odor came from the commode. The stewards poured pine oil in it at such times.

There were 18 ships in the squadron, 10 "heavies," as we called them, and 8 LSTs. To help me, I had two chaplains. The Catholic Chaplain, John Newton, usually rode one of the heavies, while the other Protestant Chaplain Paul Reiss took care of the LSTs. He was later relieved by Ron Roberson. Jack Newton was extremely personable. He was a dead ringer for Phil Silvers. On a former tour when his ship visited Saudi Arabia, he was advised not to substitute the cross on his collar for a silver bar because he would be taken for a Jew regardless of his apparel.

Paul Reiss was a study in perpetual motion. Ben said that when he finished three days of orientation prior to relieving Paul, he had to take a day off to rest. The three of us covered all the ships rather well, keeping CO's and lay leaders informed as to our whereabouts. I found an additional resource for Protestant Sunday Services. In San Diego there was a group called the Floating Christian Endeavor, headed by Mr. Frank Biscak. He had some storage space in a Navy building and listed services via his home telephone. Each Monday I would call him with a list of the 12 ships of the 18 that would not be having Protestant Services on the following Sunday. Ron and I would take three each. Frank would schedule volunteer evangelistic teams on as many ships as he had teams for that Sunday. Their services were in the evenings because the team members went to their own churches on Sunday mornings.

From time to time, I would attend those evening services, particularly on the HENRICO. I found the teams to vary greatly in talent and skill. Some came with guitars and accomplished vocalists, others with neither. One Sunday night I was disturbed when one volunteer used the altar for a hat rack. The next day when I called Frank about it he said he could understand my feelings, having been a Catholic himself, but that he had to take whomever the Lord sent.

I heard some years later that an amphibious force senior chaplain had terminated the use of the Floating Christian Endeavor. There was at that time some opposition to evangelical movements. Some chaplains complained about the Navigators. I was glad when the Navigators became not only appreciated but also highly prized.

Marion and I decided to visit the commanding officers and executive officers of the ships on Wednesday afternoons. With the ten heavy ships, that took 20 weeks, by which time there were some changes. We enjoyed these official calls. We met these same people at official functions as well as at the clubs. I felt more comfortable when riding their ships. When we went to Hong Kong, the plan was to have each ship spend a few days, possibly five, in the harbor. I was able to transfer from the ship departing to the ship arriving. The natives got so used to seeing me that they wondered if I had plans not to leave at all.

The extended residence in Hong Kong Harbor was beneficial in two ways. One ship I was riding had a picnic. One of the officers had his wife and parents in town so they were invited to the picnic. One of them left a wallet in the taxicab. The driver came back to return it when he discovered it because he had seen me at the picnic and thought I would recognize him. The other benefit was personal. As I shopped for furniture, I stored it on whatever ship I was aboard.

An Affirmation of Faith

Then when we got to San Diego, I got a pickup truck and went from ship to ship collecting my furniture. This furniture still constitutes a large segment of our household effects.

Most of the furniture was made by George Zee, a graduate of Princeton Seminary who had too many relatives to support as a minister, so he went into merchandising in Shanghai. When the Communists were coming, he escaped to Hong Kong. He had a policy that if any of his furniture split he would replace it if sent a picture of it. None of mine ever split. Zee was at Princeton with Chaplain Brink, my senior at Sasebo.

In those days Kew Hoo would make a pair of shoes measured to your feet for $3; Dynasty dresses could be bought for $20, and suits tailored for $30. One of the Admirals got a suit of blues tailored at James S. Lee's of black material. When the tailor told me this, I had some done also, including a mess dress outfit. As the years passed, blue-blues disappeared. Cashmere sport jackets were the rage then and could be bought for as little as $15 ready-made in a blend such as the one I still wear. We went broke saving money. I bought ten Dynasty dresses for Marion, intending to give her one on each gift occasion, Christmas, Valentine's and birthday, therefore having enough for three years.

Two of the ships were my favorites, the THOMASTON, LSD and the BEXAR, APA 237. THOMASTON was the only ship with four-section liberty, where a man stood duty one night out of four; the rest had three section liberty. Other ships did not like to be on the same pier with THOMASTON to hear their PA announcement that liberty would commence for three sections. One day I noticed an announcement on the bulletin board of the THOMASTON that due to a visit by an Admiral they would wear uniform of the day "with shoes." The well deck was used sometimes as a volleyball court. Somebody told me that one could follow the trail of the ship by the volleyballs that had been knocked over the sides of the well deck.

On other occasions, the well dock was flooded to make a swimming pool. Both sports depended on there being no boats in the well dock, which was designed so boats could come into the flooded well dock on their own power, and then be transported at high speed over long distances with the water pumped out of the well dock. At the destination, the dock could be flooded so the boats could leave under their own power. So an LSTD was a floating high-speed dry dock. The well dock was lined and floored with timbers, so there was much less steel dock space to chip and paint than on ships of comparable size. This also contributed to morale. It was a pleasure to ride a happy ship.

THOMASTON also supplied most of the members of my choir. It was my practice to take the choir to sing in local churches of the ports we visited. At Okinawa, we did the first Navy TV show ever, featuring our commander, CAPT Charles E. King, and the choir. We also sang at the Naha Baptist Church. The pastor, Rev. Bellinger, liked to preach revivals and invited us to accompany him. In Hong Kong, we invited a Chinese Baptist choir to sing on board. In the Philippines, we sang at the Methodist Church in Olongapo. In the local and/or native churches, we found an enthusiastic welcome. For them it was such a change to meet sailors with Christian values, and it was a welcome change for us not to be propositioned as we often were on the streets.

My other favorite ship was commanded by CAPT Draper L. Kaufman, the son of a vice Admiral. His steward Corsi had worked for his father. CAPT Kaufman came to church and sat on the front row with a large well-worn Bible on his lap. When he sat down, he would smile broadly. How welcome can a chaplain feel? He told me that every time he went to Washington he looked up a Catholic Chaplain, John O'Connor, who was only a LT but full of good ideas, some of which he shared with me. John later became Chief of Chaplains, then Archbishop of New York. CAPT Kaufman later became Vice Admiral, holding the same command at Sangley Point once held by his father.

Later when Admiral Kaufman became CO, NTC, Great Lakes, he took seriously the suggestions of one of the chaplains that the Navy should do something about alcohol abuse as well as the drug abuse that was getting so much attention. He contacted the Chief of Naval Personnel and the extensive alcohol rehabilitation program was the result. Admiral Kaufman was also responsible for the UDT forces in the U.S. Navy, patterned after the English Navy in which he served after graduating from Annapolis and temporarily working

An Affirmation of Faith

as an ambulance driver in the Spanish Civil War. Only half of his graduating class at Annapolis got commissioned because we were in the throes of the depression. His eyes caused him to be non-selected. I listened to him with rapt attention and was privileged to visit him in his office at Sangley Point

Ron Roberson was detached, relieved by Roy Bevan, one of the most gung ho chaplains I ever met. His hair was cut in flat top style on top, long at the sides. His sons wore the same style. He was an eloquent speaker with a flair for the dramatic. His wife, Lucille, was right in there pitching with him. All of our ships participated in a landing exercise in Borneo in which one contingent of troops were Gurkas from an English regiment in India. They did not wear steel helmets because the helmets made noise when brushed by tree branches. I watched a group of them land on the beach one day in camouflage; in 30 seconds they were invisible.

A Black member of the Thomaston choir, a native wearing a sort of turban, and I, all of us walking down the beach wearing khaki shorts and no shoes, met Roy and one of the officers in uniform walking from the opposite direction. As we passed we exchanged "Hellos". Roy told me later that when they got out of earshot his friend wanted to know "How did those guys learn English?" We did find Borneo quite interesting.

Years later, while serving at the Portsmouth Naval Hospital, I met a Marine Major who was reputed to be the most decorated Marine. He hung his beribboned and bemedaled shirt over his hospital bed. A corpsman saw it and said I never saw so many decorations before. He answered, "That's because there ain't that many anywhere else." He told me that he had spent time in India and had become a legitimate Gurka.

The real high point of our Westpac deployment was our visit to Thailand. I had hoped to see the two Thai officers I had entertained at Great Lakes in 1945 but they were not available. We got a soccer team together to play the team of the Royal Thai Navy. The King and Queen Sirikit attended the game and were seated not far from us in the stadium. I found the queen to be so beautiful that I missed a good bit of the game. Our team was no match for the Thais. I saw several groups of Thai youth standing in circles on the streets keeping a woven bamboo ball in the air with the use of heads, shoulders, elbows and feet. One might say soccer is as native to them as baseball to us.

The star of our team was the Henrico executive officer, CDR Wagner, playing the goalie position. He made many diving saves. He was a native of Rochester, NY the home of Cab Calloway. His daughter Wendy was somewhat of a celebrity, doing some of the stunts in "Surfside Six." We had first seen her aboard the Henrico when she joined a dependents' cruise with hair below hip length and bare feet. Then when Marilyn Monroe was on location at Coronado, where the Wagner home was located, she strolled by the set and was asked to take a screen test. She was wearing a black bathing suit. I watched Marilyn from the small boat pier through binoculars but was not properly impressed, having seen Wendy at close range.

CDR Wagner was a hard charger; he was nicknamed "Blackjack." When we deployed our landing craft in a simulated amphibious landing, he shouted commands from the bridge using a megaphone. After each such exercise, which we called a One-Alpha, he was so hoarse he could hardly talk.

After our return from deployment, the COMPHIBRON flag shifted to our newest ship, the Paul Revere. It made the Henrico seem small potatoes. Again, I was assigned the troop commander's stateroom, which to my delight had an attached conference room with a stationary round table. The whole ship was larger and faster, stood higher in the water, and was without the shake rattle and roll. Only on Sunday mornings was the Henrico preferable to the Paul Revere, because in order to get to the worship area on the Paul Revere, one had to go through the TV lounge to an adjoining lounge. Many men never completed the journey, either because of interest in what happened to be on TV at the time or because they did not want the others already watching TV in the lounge to know that they were going to church. There were no such hazards en-route to church on the Henrico.

Another chaplain, one of the Catholic Kellys, had a complaint against the Paul Revere. He was coming to offer Mass from another ship. When he found there was no gangway down, he climbed up a Jacob's ladder (a rope ladder with wooden rungs). By the time he

An Affirmation of Faith

got to the quarterdeck, his blues were quite dusty. The OOD asked what happened to him. His reply was, "I always look this way, but either the Paul Revere is unbelievably disorganized or cares nothing for religion, and it had better not be the latter." Ron Roberson used to call the ship the Paul Reverse.

Nevertheless, I liked the ship and enjoyed my stay, in spite of the way Rev. George Walker Smith's visit on board was interrupted. We were talking in my conference room when a sailor shouted as he ran by the door, "A man just got stabbed on the mess deck." George bolted from his seat saying, "I'm gone." I found that two sailors were arguing. One, who held a steak knife (the kind ordinarily called a butcher knife except by butchers), said, "I ought to run you through with this knife." The other replied, "You give me that knife and I'll run you through with it." The first handed him the knife only to find that it was no bluff. Our doctor went with the wounded man to the hospital but he died en-route. The other man went to the brig where I tried to offer him some comfort.

George never visited me again, although he accepted my offer to return to his Golden Hills United Presbyterian Church in San Diego as his old gray haired assistant after my retirement. Unfortunately, I had to disappoint George because of the inflationary spiral in real estate in California in the intervening years. A house that was selling for $17,000 at that time was selling for $217,000 when I retired.

There was quite a bit of satisfaction for me to be a PHIBRON senior chaplain engaged in amphibious landings. As I had expected, the opportunity came to play host to my former regimental XO, Colonel Van Evera. When he came aboard, I shifted to another ship so he could have my palatial quarters. It was also quite pleasurable to hear the order "Land the landing force" over the 1MC system at daybreak, and then turn over and go back to sleep while the Marines scrambled for the small boats, as I had done when I was with the 5th Marines. It was great fun to greet former comrades and colleagues. They and the enlisted Marines were so happy to see a familiar face.

PHIBRON duty was not all fun and games, however. Somebody pulled the plug on the THOMASTON, and it shipped a good deal of water before the mistake could be rectified. The CO of one of the ships did not get back to his ship in time to be relieved, so the change of command was affected without him. The BEXAR had a fire; some men were swept overboard in a storm, and ENS Stanus, the Protestant Lay Leader, died in an attempt to affect a rescue. Orders came for the XO, CDR Grazda, to relieve the CO, CAPT Ross. CDR Grazda told me it was the hardest thing he ever had to do in his whole life. After an investigation, CAPT Ross was absolved of any blame and was ordered to the command of an east coast PHIBRON. During the days of the investigation, I tried to be supportive of the CO and XO, reminding them of how meticulous they were in having the word passed frequently to stay off the weather decks during turbulent weather when I had been aboard.

The new CO, CAPT Wesche, felt that CDR Grazda should have been partially to blame for the tragedy; CAPT Ross came to his defense. Years later, when I was alighting from a Pentagon bus at the Navy Annex, CDR Grazda was waiting to board the same bus. I spoke as I passed him, but he appeared not to see me at all. I had the feeling that the sight of me mobilized all of the stress and trauma of his BEXAR experience, but on the other hand, he could have been preoccupied with something else. I am soft-spoken and may not have been heard above the noise of the traffic.

On CAPT Wesche's first Sunday aboard his impact was obvious. Not only was he at church, but so were three times as many men as one would expect. As I arrived, I asked the new Protestant Lay Leader what was going on. He was non-committal. One sailor told me he saw the CO on Friday and was told, "I'll see you at church on Sunday." The first scheduled service was Catholic Mass so the sailor went, although he was Protestant, looking for the CO. Not finding him, he came to the Protestant Service where he was much relieved to see him.

CAPT Wesche came to the retreat I scheduled for the heavy ships. He also came to the retreat Roy held for the LST's. Frankly, such all out support made me a little nervous. He gave me the impression that to conjecture about command permission for anything religious was a pure waste of time and energy because any request would be granted.

It was also during my PHIBRON tour that I was first nonselected for promotion. Of the ten of us in the promotion zone for commander, three were selected: Adam Schutz, Joseph Snellbaker and Keene Hedges Capers. To make matters worse, I could not compare myself favorably to even one of them. I remember reading the list over several times, looking for my name even as I had at the University of Chicago when I flunked the German reading exam. I remember saying to CDR Joe Perry, our new XO, "It's not so bad being a has-been." He fired back, "You are not a has-been," with such an authoritative tone of voice that I believed him. So I promised myself that I would be the sharpest passed over LCDR in the entire Navy.

Then I wrote Chaplain Kermit Cassiday, who had been similarly non-selected when we were at Camp Pendleton, and then selected the next year. I asked for a set of "how to" instructions for the eleven months before the next board. I followed his suggestions, added to them and for years afterward sent a "care package" to my friends who suffered a similar fate.

My first need had already been met, good rapport with the CO. Our commodore, (an unofficial title given to a squadron commander) CAPT C.E. King, was already kindly disposed and had told the fleet chaplain that I was the best chaplain he ever had. This came about because I had sent a message for him to all the squadron ships requesting aid for flood victims in Nagoya, Japan. He got a message back from his type commander referencing my message as the first one received after our squadron entered his zone and congratulating him on his demonstrated intention to be cooperative in task force concerns. The commodore called me up to his stateroom, showed me the message and thanked me for making him look good. I have already mentioned how I featured him on the first Navy TV show to be aired in Okinawa.

Then I wrote the commodore a long memorandum intended to inform him of the various activities and projects I had going on the various ships of the squadron, assuming that he was too busy to be cognizant of them all. The next time I looked at my fitness report file I found the entire listing included just as I had prepared it.

Blessed with a thin physique, it did not take much doing to be ready for inspection every day with immaculate uniforms, glistening shoes and sparkling gold braid. On the ship, laundry and haircuts were free so I used both resources well. I tried to be neater than anyone else on board.

When we got back to San Diego, I was invited by the force chaplain, CAPT Harry C. Wood, to man his office during his leave. In doing so, I received a fitness report from VADM John Sylvester that further assisted the cause. At a party at the club, retired Chief of Chaplains Staunton W. Salisbury was present. I introduced my commodore to him. Much to my surprise, Chaplain Salisbury said to my commodore, "Your Chaplain got passed over for promotion. You write him a good fitness report."

The commodore replied weakly "They only picked three, and if you take a Protestant, Catholic and Jew there isn't much of a chance." That was fast thinking so I never told the commodore the three picked were all Protestants.

On our annual trip to North Carolina, I saw to it that I visited the office of the Chief of Chaplains in Washington. I had learned over the years that such visits are highly appreciated, particularly from those who have been at sea. I also touched base with the Presbyterian Department of Chaplains to whom I continued to feed a stream of photographs of my activities. The publication *Frontlines* often carried my material. Irene, the wife of Chaplain Al Ekkens, told me that any time she did not see my picture in *Frontlines* she wondered what was wrong.

Marion became pregnant again after a second pregnancy aborted, so we resolved to be more careful, no long drives across country, no heavy lifting, no strenuous sightseeing trips. This time she was able to get past the seventh month before delivery on Friday the 13th of February 1959. We agreed on the names "Mae," after her grandmother and my aunt, and "Marian," after her mom. When Mae got older, I told her she was fortunate to be born on the 13th because if it had been a day earlier we would have named her Abraham, after Lincoln.

She also weighed less than five pounds, but was alert and hungry. However, because Marion needed post operative care she was boarded in until Marion was discharged. She differed from Evangeline in several aspects; she had a full head of curly black hair, was of darker complexion, and she was small boned. Marion suggested that we offer special daily prayers for her and we did. Nightly we visited the neo-natal unit. Usually a fat jolly nurse would hold her up behind the glass partition so we could see her. We had the impression she was in good hands.

When she passed the five-pound mark and could come home, we started the old routine of a bottle every two hours and a diaper change 30 minutes after feeding, with my assuming the watch at midnight. Again, there was great joy when she took two full ounces of milk.

My brother Ward had baptized Evangeline, but he had by then moved to my old Butler Memorial Presbyterian Church in Youngstown, Ohio. Therefore, we asked the former Chief of Chaplains, Stan Salisbury, to baptize Mae. The event took place in the chapel of White Sands in LaJolla, a former hotel that had become a Presbyterian retirement home. It was there that we met Mrs. Sealy of the mattress family and where I found out to my disappointment that the Abilone steak I ordered was seafood.

At the time, we were living in government quarters in National City called Bayview. We could stand in our front yard and see the squadron ships in the harbor. This was apartment type housing with the units arranged in quadrangles. Because most of the husbands were sea going, a strong camaraderie developed among the wives, which were shared by the husbands when their ships were in port. LCDR Barney O'Rourke was a highly prized administrative officer on one of the ships because he had been in the yeoman or personnel man rating as an enlisted man. His wife Nita was somewhat of the leader of our quadrangle wives group.

Our closest friends were the Tippins and the Groces, later the Ingalls also. Glenn Tippin was a Navy dentist, Jean was a florist, and Tommy Groces was a line officer in another squadron. Betty had five small children. The Tippins and us shared the same babysitter, Mrs. Ivy, whose daughter was married to a Guamanian chief petty officer. The Groces were Black. We assumed Mrs. Ivy was White until she told us one day that her grandfather was one of the founders of the African Methodist Episcopal Zion Church. I do not remember any other Black officer family in Bayview nor in our squadron. I thought

An Affirmation of Faith

one of the squadron supply officers was Black until I saw that he wore a Georgia Tech ring.

The PHIBRON did not get another Westpac deployment before I left the squadron, but the periodic landing exercises were interesting. One of them took us to Seattle, Washington where we embarked Army units from Fort Lewis. Somehow, a large percentage of the Black soldiers had German wives. To me it seemed odd to see a Black soldier who did not have one. A close friend from college days, Colonel Claude Young of the Medical Service Corps, who had lived at my grandmother's house while he attended Fayetteville State had just left Fort Lewis with his German wife.

On one exercise, an engineering breakdown had the ship I was riding at the time incapacitated in San Diego waters for five days while a needed part was flown in by the manufacturer. It was some part that should not have broken in the first place and the CO blamed the XO. The CO told the XO that he wanted him to take leave when we got into port to await his transfer orders, and if the orders had not arrived at the end of his ten day leave, he should take ten more. The XO was helping me rig for church one Sunday morning when I remarked, "This cross certainly is heavy." He replied, "Crosses always are." His career was of course ruined. I groaned with him, not understanding how he was blamed rather than the chief engineer. I was told that the XO had the ship running at an excessive speed for the ship's condition.

Two Black officers that I would see later were in the area at that time, Samuel L. Graveley, who would become the first Black Admiral, and Alvin Tucker, XO of one of the service force ships. My time as the only Black chaplain ended with the appointment of Carroll Chambliss, whose son Chris would become first baseman for the Yankees, and Thomas Hayswood McPhatter, who was ordered to San Diego while we were at Bayview.

Mac bought a house in Emerald Hills, San Diego, the same development in which the Mayor lived. There was a storm of protest and much notoriety in the local media. It may not have been intentional block busting on the part of the realtor, and it certainly was not Mac's intention. He was as tired as I was of being shown houses in Valencia Park no matter who the real estate agent might be. The

An Affirmation of Faith

Emerald Hills houses were larger, nicer and newer. Another former Chief of Chaplains was District Chaplain at the time, Edward V. Harp. He supported Mac wholeheartedly. When I asked Mac why he did not sell the house at a profit, which he had opportunity to do, he replied that he would be selling his birthright. He still lives in Emerald Hills.

Mac was a Presbyterian, also from Lumberton, a different type of North Carolina community because of its Indian history. North Carolina law required separate but equal schools. Indians were not allowed in the White schools; they refused to go to the Black schools. Therefore, a separate Indian system was set up in Lumberton extending through college. This was the community from which the Indian had come to Durham to scalp the man who impregnated his sister and deserted her. It was there that the Indians shot up the Ku Klux Klan parade. Lumberton was one of many sites in the South where Presbyterians established schools for Blacks before there was any public education for Indians. Mac's middle name, Hayswood, is for Dr. Hayswood, the head of Redstone Academy, the Presbyterian school in Lumberton, comparable to Mary Potter School in Oxford and Henderson Institute in Henderson.

Mac had been an enlisted Marine, trained at Montfort Point, the Black training camp at Camp LeJeune. He has served as president of the Montfort Point Association. I consider him a true pioneer.

Some Navy chaplains are strongly attracted to the Marines; I am one of them. My preference for my next duty assignment was another tour of Marine duty, not only because of my Marine bias but because a Marine major wore scrambled eggs with his dress uniform. So even as a passed over LCDR, I would be in the command officer category, whereas I would have to be a CDR in the Navy to have equal prestige.

MCRD San Diego, CA

Again the detailer in the Chief of Chaplains Office nominated me for Marine orders, this time to Marine Corps Recruit Depot in San Diego, which meant I would not have to move and could continue in sunny California. I was assigned to regimental headquarters under Chaplain J.W. Paul. He was the grandfather type, par excellence. When my clerk wrote a letter to the Chief of Naval Operations without using the chain of command, he was put on report by a CNO letter to the Commanding General. I heard Chaplain Paul plead with the legal officer for leniency, "Now don't hurt him too badly, Hub. He didn't mean any harm. He didn't hurt anybody. He's a good boy."

Gary Mundon was a "good boy." His wife had recently received a rather large inheritance. Except for buying a new car, they retained their humility. One day Gary saw me typing a letter. He said, "Chaplain I am your clerk. I should be typing that letter, right?" I agreed, but explained that I thought I could have it finished by the time I explained what I wanted to him. Then for the first and only time I heard these words from a clerk, yeoman or secretary "Chaplain, I feel like I am working for the Lord when I do your work, and that's what I want to do." Hub did take pity on Gary, much to our relief.

In those days church attendance was still mandatory in recruit training, a practice, which I was convinced, was right. I had not heard of Ervin Goffman's concept of the total institution at that time, but I experienced it at MCRD. Every facet of life was prescribed; rising, dress, grooming, classes, drill, exercise, sports, meals, retiring, with next to no choice and certainly no freedom for

An Affirmation of Faith

the whole recruit training period of two months. The only non-prescribed interludes came when nothing important needed to be done. To say church attendance is optional is to pronounce it unimportant. The cause to which I had dedicated my life and my reason for being in the Navy in the first place, I felt was very important. An example of how meticulous the direction was came in the chow hall when the men were lined up at attention behind the mess benches while their food trays waited on the tables. The first command was given, seats, followed by grace, when everyone bowed silently, and then the command to eat.

The Protestant Service in the base theatre was to me an inspiring ritual. The recruits were marched into the theatre and seated. The drill instructors came with them. Then the officers gathered in the balcony. Out front, the regimental commander and perhaps a battalion commander or so would wait on the steps facing the parade field. At five minutes before time for service, a blue Mercedes came down the road beside the grinder, bringing the Commanding General, Victor H. (Brute) Krulak, to church. When he arrived in the balcony, John Ross had the choir to sing the introit. John was a civilian choir director on salary and was quite talented.

The chaplains took turns preaching in the theatre, which gave us a month or more to prepare a sermon. In my opinion, the quality was outstanding and the response quite gratifying. I remember one Sunday when Chaplain Roger Crabtree asked, "Do you really want to be free?" The recruits thundered, "Yes Sir." "Then get with God's program for your life," he replied, adding "In God's will is perfect freedom." I had thought Chaplain Crabtree was asking a rhetorical question.

My sermon approach leaned heavily on Dr. Norman Vincent Peale's positive thinking. I preached in my Marine uniform with the expert rifleman badge worn with pride. I recounted stories of fantastic achievements by recruits in spite of poor beginnings and my hundred-mile hike with the Fifth Marines at an advanced age. It was particularly gratifying to me to receive two letters from General Krulak to the effect that he was sure that some recruits who might have been dropped would likely succeed because of hearing my sermons. I asked the Depot Chaplain, CAPT Emil Redman, what I should do with the first letter. His advice was to frame it. My commanding officer, LtCOL Frank R. Wilkinson, suggested that I send it to the Chaplain Division, along with any such letters, press releases etc., for possible consideration by the selection board.

I did see another of General Krulak's letters framed in the den of a 1st Lt., who had knocked off his Smoky Bear hat with his sword while passing in review. The letter read "Twenty-five years ago on the same parade field I knocked off my hat in the same way. I seem to have survived."

Chaplain Roy Baxter, whom we knew at Pendleton, was also at MCRD at the Weapons Training Battalion. As he had at Pendleton, he said again that his CO was one of the finest Christian gentlemen he had ever met. I felt the same way about General Krulak and Colonel Wilkinson. On the Sundays that I preached, I invited Colonel Wilkinson to say a few words before my sermon. He always advised the recruits to get acquainted with the Lord while in boot camp, so that when they called on Him in combat they would not call on Him as a stranger. Many of the recruits took this advice seriously. I tried to arrange religious instructions for the unchurched, to conclude in baptism or confirmation by the date of graduation. The goal was to graduate a Marine totally equipped for duty anywhere, militarily, physically, mentally and spiritually.

One recruit shared my vision completely. When we were setting the date for his baptism, he asked if he could bring his buddy to be baptized also. When I asked "What about his instructions," the recruit said he had taught him everything he had learned. I accepted this and baptized the two on graduation day. After the ceremony, I asked the recruit I instructed about his plans for leave and was delighted to hear him say that he was going to get his mother baptized.

That year I was invited to speak at the General Assembly of the Presbyterian Church in Buffalo's Kleinhans Auditorium as a part of the report of the Department of Chaplains. While I was out on a sightseeing tour with Dr. Loren Woods, who had left the Navy and was working for the Bell system, the time for the report was moved up. When we arrived the head of the department, Chaplain Harry C. Wood, was waiting on the steps with a copy of my speech. It would

An Affirmation of Faith

have been read if I had not arrived when I did. He ushered me to the podium as the Moderator and the whole Assembly breathed a sigh of relief, here he is. I could have read nursery rhymes, so high was the expectation, but the story of the recruit rushing home to get his mother baptized occasioned a standing ovation. Incidents like this assure me of the presence of guardian angels who rescue us in the nick of time.

Being in Buffalo also allowed me the time to contact my relatives there that my brother had discovered when he came there to work for Union Carbide during the summer after his junior year in college. The family name was Burtt; their mother was the daughter of my paternal grandfather's brother Bob, then deceased. Justine and her husband had adopted a German war orphan girl who spoke no English. When I met her two years later, at the age of eight, she spoke no German.

Graduation day at MCRD was a festive occasion. General Krulak usually spoke at the graduation ceremony in the theatre. He told the recruits they must have faith in God, in their country, in themselves and in their Marine Corps buddies. Six years later at Quonset Point, Rhode Island, a Seabee invited me to a graduation in his battalion. I promised to be there if I could arrange transportation to nearby Davisville since my car was in for repair. I did catch a ride over and was welcomed at the gymnasium door by the CO and invited to sit on the speakers' platform. I could see the surprise on the face of the Chief who had extended the first invitation. My surprise came when the CO said to the audience "We always have a speaker at these affairs, and today our speaker is Chaplain Parham." It was General Krulak's speech to the rescue with the change from Marine Corps buddies to Seabee buddies. Then the Chief's mouth dropped open. When the ceremony was over, I hastened to explain how it happened. The guardian angels rode again.

Only one graduation had a tinge of sadness. Colonel Merril Day, the Chief of Staff, was to make the speech; a gunnery sergeant was to put his introduction on the podium for the use of the Capt. who was to make the introduction. In the excitement of the occasion, he still had the sheet in his hand at the back of the theatre when the Capt. rose to make the introduction. He held it up as he hung his head in shame. It reminded me of the small red flag they wave on the rifle range from the target area when someone misses the whole target. They call the flag "Maggie's Drawers." The Capt. made a valiant effort, but I heard one officer remark after the ceremony, "That was the strangest introduction I ever heard."

John Ross, the choir director, drove a little N.S.U. Prinz, a German import similar to but smaller then a Renault Dauphine. Recruits used to delight in picking up the car with him in it and setting it on the sidewalk. When he and his wife had their first child, they wanted a larger model and settled on a Chevrolet but were told they would be allowed only $450 on a trade-in, and the car was only four years old. I offered him the amount in cash, which he accepted that day. The recruits dubbed it the "white jeep," and would pass the information from one battalion area to the next that the white jeep was en-route. It was large enough to seat four, but small enough for me to wipe the inside of the rear window while sitting in the driver's seat. The two cylinder four-cycle engine in the rear got 40 miles on a gallon but would barely go 45 mph on the freeway, the legal minimum. There I had to keep watch for police and floor it when I saw one behind me.

Twice I was hit in traffic. The first time, a Pontiac rammed me in the rear as I pulled away when the light changed. The driver ran up and said, "Man, I thought you were gone," maybe thinking it was a sports car. The next time I was making a left turn and was hit by a woman who did not see me at first when the car ahead of me turned. She bent my fender slightly. After rushing to my window to see if I was hurt, she returned to her car and came back with a huge pair of pliers with which she straightened the fender. Often I would be told, "I surely wouldn't want to be hit in that car by a big truck." My stock reply was, "I would hate to be hit in anything by a big truck, but I have one advantage if I see one coming I can climb a tree." Actually, the trucks were helpful in their slipstream; it was easy to maintain my speed going uphill. Only one trucker slowed down when he saw what I was doing.

A valuable assist to the effort of the chaplains to facilitate the mental health of recruits during the stress of recruit training was the arrival of Chaplain Leonard W. Dodson, who had two earned

An Affirmation of Faith

doctorates, in theology and in psychology. I called on him often, and one day, when I considered the recruit so depressed that I did not want him out of my sight, Len agreed to come over. As I was about to introduce them Len barked at the seated recruit, "On your feet, you are in the presence of a Naval Officer." This dried his tears and interrupted his whining. When he in calmer voice said, "Chaplain I just can't make it," Len fired back "How do you know you can't make it?" At that point, I left, convinced the recruit was in good hands.

Len's CO, LCOL Simpson, told me one day that he had no idea how useful a chaplain could be until Len was assigned to his battalion. He said that he was having difficulty getting a pet project approved on the regimental level until Len got it approved by General Krulak, with whom he was having dinner that night. When I asked Capt. Jack Ingalls what he thought of Len, he said, "He would make a good battalion commander." When I asked about LtCOL Simpson, he said, "He would make a good chaplain." When he retired, LtCOL Simpson did enroll in an Episcopal seminary, and I began clearing anything of importance to the Depot with Len.

Jack Ingalls and I used to car pool together, so it was distressing for me when he was not selected for Major. I asked him if there was any skill or talent he had that would make him exceptional. He was an expert with the sabre. Therefore, I suggested that he organize a sabre team and get some publicity on it, which he did, including a very nice article with pictures in the *Navy Times*. I also talked with Len and with the General's aide. With prayer and the guardian angels, he was selected the next time around. Jack's dad was the largest tie manufacturer in Brooklyn so I received a dozen silk ties that I still use. I gave him a cap frame with scrambled eggs that I had not worn because Navy chaplains were not allowed to wear the Marine dress uniform.

MCRD also had its moments of disappointment. As had been my experience at Pendleton, one of the sharpest Marines proved to be less than honest. He broke into a coke machine to finance a date with a woman Marine. Another, in a fit of rage, set a fire in a Sgt.'s car and to the dossal behind the altar in the chapel. After calming

An Affirmation of Faith

down he resolved to make restitution. Several recruits were bruised and the excuse given was that they had fallen over locker boxes.

There were some shotgun weddings in which the bride was below 16 and had to get permission of the court. An old gray deputy sheriff gave one couple the finest words of encouragement I ever heard on the general subject of how, in spite of their ages, they could act as responsible adults in their commitment to each other.

One recruit whose fiancée was coming from the Midwest asked me to take him to meet her train. I admired him because of his willingness to attempt practically anything. He had never been swimming, but he jumped from the high platform loaded with combat gear and swam out of the pool. He was being considered for the Marine Recons. When the passengers came off the train he asked if he had told me his fiancée was Caucasian (he was Black).

He had not explained that they decided deliberately on the pregnancy as a way of getting permission for their marriage. Since it was the afternoon of his graduation we invited them to spend their honeymoon with us. We kept in touch through the years, until their son dropped dead after a football game in which he played at the local high school.

Not long after Jack Ingalls' selection came the news of mine. I was called to the General's office where I waited for my congratulations with another chaplain who was waiting for his words of sympathy for not being selected. He told me he had submitted an appeal, through the chain of command, to the Chief of Chaplains office in which there was an endorsement by his CO to the effect that any Bureau Chief who would refuse the humanitarian transfer he had requested was not fit to be a Bureau Chief. I thought he was a fine chaplain in so many ways, particularly in his physical conditioning. We jogged and exercised in the afternoons. When he did his push-ups he pushed from a 45-degree angle by putting his feet on a sewer manhole three feet above ground level. He had applied for paratroop training at Fort Benning but had been rejected. He thought that as a Catholic if he made joint application with a Protestant they would accept us both. I agreed, but was most relieved when the second rejection arrived.

An Affirmation of Faith

When I was in Hawaii an eleven-year-old, jumping with his parents, was killed when his chute did not open. The parents jumped again the next Sunday.

Only once did I ever wear a parachute. I was hitchhiking from NAS Olathe, Kansas in a C-119. The pilot said, "I want you to hear this bell, because the next time you hear it you had better jump because we are gone." When Davey was a teenager I told him that as long as he lived at home there would be no parachutes, no hang gliders and no motorcycles. He wanted to know what was wrong with parachutes. I told him that they did not open sometimes.

My promotion ceremony took place in the General's office. General Krulak pinned the silver leaf on the right shoulder of my Marine greens; Marion did the other side. I felt that I had arrived. When I was at Pendleton, Chaplain Eric Arendt, the base chaplain, had remarked that if I ever made commander I could consider myself as having succeeded. I had heartily agreed. So I bought another scrambled eggs cap and really felt like sleeping in it. That summer, when we made the annual pilgrimage east, I went to the Chaplains Division to thank everybody I could find for such an act of kindness.

The trip that year was made by train. The military rate round trip to Washington, D.C. for the four of us was $150. We paid a few dollars for reclining seats on the glass-domed coach and bought meal tickets for the train that gave us substantial savings. Marion's brother, Dr. J.W.V. Cordice Jr., and his wife, Marguerite, came down from Long Island to meet us at the station in Washington. We ate lunch there, sang the grace, "God is great and God is good...," before eating. Then the kids piped up, that was not loud enough, sing it again. This time the other lunchers looked over, bemused, while we felt self-conscious.

The trip was wonderful, interesting and very restful for me, as I slept most of the way. For Marion, it was taxing because the rest room was two cars back and the girls took turns needing to go.

On the return trip we stopped over in Washington, PA where I had a preaching engagement. The pastor of the church was Alan Dale Sowers, with whom I had worked at a Presbyterian Senior High Camp at Bethany College, Bethany, West Virginia. On the campus was the home of Alexander Campbell, founder of the Disciples of

Christ. Dale was a gifted baritone, who maintained with a friend a New York apartment for use during the opera season and rented it out the rest of the year. Also as a guest of the church that Sunday, he had a Japanese Christian whose views of life in Japan differed somewhat from mine. I realized later how brazen it was of me to consider myself an expert on Japan when she had lived there all her life.

My last assignment at MCRD was to replace Roy Baxter at the Weapons Training Battalion at Camp Matthews, the present site of the University of California, San Diego. Roy had instituted the practice of having a Prayer Service the evening before qualification day, at which he passed out cards containing the Rifleman's Prayer by Chaplain Walter Mahler. Then the next morning he came to the range at daybreak and led the men in the prayer before firing began. It was of prime importance for a recruit to qualify with the M-1, at least at the 190-marksman level. Sharpshooter 210 or expert 220 would be even better. Rumors went around that somebody had fired a "possible" perfect score of 250 which meant a bulls eye with every shot from the standing, sitting, kneeling and prone positions. I was happy to tell all who asked that my score was 231. I also added to the program therapy groups for non-qualifiers as of the first week. We were always elated when those from these groups qualified also.

On qualification day we hiked back to MCRD, 7 miles, including a sizable hill we called a mountain. Since it was Saturday children were out of school. Two of them about 11 years old, accompanied by a dog, used to climb the mountain with us, amusing themselves by harassing those who were finding the climb difficult. One Saturday, a recruit, who had lost some front teeth and much of the stamina he should have had, was apparently about to drop out. I took his rifle, and a buddy on each side grabbed him in the belt to pull him up the hill. Then he asked, "What is a good song to sing at a time like this?" I replied, "Onward Christian Soldiers" and led them in it. I can still hear him singing with his teeth missing as we made it over the hill. After he graduated, he became a sermon illustration.

Just as the housing in Bayview was ideal when I was with PHIBRON 1, the new Capehart housing at Pacific Beach would be ideal for MCRD, so I applied for it, as did Jack Ingalls, Roy Baxter and others. We moved into a new four-bedroom house with central air conditioning, fireplace, attached garage and view of the bay. It was on a hill, so I could park the Prinz facing downhill and be sure of getting started every morning. There was no longer a need for car-pooling since we were much closer. Wives in one-car families could easily drop husbands off. Marion's sister, Mrs. Victoria McCants, and her two sons, Vincent and Robbie, came to visit. The boys were then in their early teens.

We took them to Tijuana where the boys bought fireworks and other tourist merchandise. The boys were impressed by uniforms, especially fatigues, rifles, guns, parades and the Prinz. An unusual honoree at one parade was Chaplain Len Dodson. Instead of a sword he carried his Bible, "the sword of the Spirit." He returned salutes by hand, since he had no sword. He was the only LT to be so honored while I was at MCRD and the only chaplain. Years later, when Chaplain John O'Connor was a Commander, he was so honored at Quantico. The chaplains from MCRD San Diego were included on the duty roster for funerals at the Veterans Administration cemetery Fort Rosecrans on Point Loma. I did not relish this prospect because while I was at Pendleton a Black chaplain, Worth Barber, had locked horns with the district chaplain, Ray Hohenstein, about his assignment to Black funerals only. Ray told me he was concerned with giving maximum comfort to families and was quite surprised when Worth said that he would rather a White chaplain serve a Black family as he did the Whites on his duty day rather than to dispatch a Black chaplain for that one family. My cowardly reply to Ray was that it was hard for a young person to be patient sometimes. I agreed to talk to Worth about it when Ray arranged a time, which he did not do, possibly because the matter had been referred to the Chief of Chaplains in Washington.

When Ray and Worth could not agree, Worth wrote a confidential letter to his endorsing agent, Dr. Jernigan in Washington. Dr. Jernigan took the letter and placed it on the desk of the Chief of Chaplains who in turn wrote Ray for an appropriate reply to Dr. Jernigan. Ray then asked Worth to help him prepare the reply which I could not imagine as satisfactory to Dr. Jernigan.

Dr. Jernigan had visited Manana Barracks when I was stationed there. We assembled 241 all hands in the theatre to hear him. He asked the audience, "Who brought you over here?" The men answered, "God". Then he asked, "And who is going to take you back home?" The same answer returned with conviction. Dr. Jernigan was a patriot and he loved the Navy. As I remember it, he was around 70 years of age then and had to have all of his teeth extracted before the Navy would approve his trip. He had seen the segregated 40s, and was not willing to see the same pattern in the late 50s.

In my opinion, two unfortunate consequences followed. First, Chaplain Worth left active duty when his obligated time ended. I do not know if he continued in the reserves. In the second place, Chaplain Ray Hohenstein was not retained at the next screening for Captains to remain on active duty. His career had been distinguished. He was the only chaplain under attack at Pearl Harbor who was on the Missouri when the Japanese signed the unconditional surrender. When Chaplain Thornton Millar retired as Rear Admiral, Ray was the one chaplain he specifically requested to be on hand.

I suspect that Ray went to his death believing that at least I understood him and that Worth assumed I had sold out to the racists. Possibly if I had heard of the flap before Worth wrote the letter to Dr. Jernigan, I could have convinced Ray that the American myth about the easier access of Blacks to God would have given the White bereaved families more comfort than a White chaplain could have.

Therefore I was much relieved to find that there was no problem of a racial nature about the funeral duty roster. Still this duty could be depressing. The wind came up the hill from the bay, quite chilling when it was raining and the ground was muddy. I was cold even in my bridge coat. One day I had nine funerals, some back to back. For most of them, only the undertaker came, bringing the body in a panel truck, taking the flag away with him. I often wondered what happened to it. The burial detail told tales of chaplains not showing up. A crematorium employee brought in a small box on which the rent was overdue, dropped it on the counter in the office saying, "Baked goods."

An Affirmation of Faith

In a lighter vein, one of the watchmen told me that he was able to catch enough rabbits on the grounds to take care of his daily lunches. He was eating a rabbit sandwich with relish as he said this, which occasioned no envy at all in me. General Krulak on occasion had the Depot officer in his quarters for a reception.

There I had *pate de foi gras* for the first time, and also for the first time saw some Japanese grass that did not grow tall enough to be mowed. One 2nd Lt always enjoyed these occasions because he said the General was the only person on the Depot shorter than he. Another officer was embarrassed because when he told the General his name the General said, "You insult me when you do that, I know everybody on the Depot."

I was feeling particularly light-hearted when the general said to me, "You don't drink. I have a son in seminary and he drinks. Why don't you drink?" I told him it was because my great grandfather was poisoned by his wife in a drink of whiskey, leaving my grandmother, her brother and sister orphans. Grandmother never prayed, but she did ask the Lord to run whiskey out the land and command wars to cease. He wanted to know what kind of poison she used. I said I suspected rat poison because he was a rat. My great grandmother was his live-in girlfriend. In South Carolina in those days there was no divorce, a circumstance true until the 40s. There were no interracial marriages either.

There were so many people at MCRD who were conversation pieces. There was the Sgt who had saved General Krulak's life by dropping a sniper perched in the tree. Don Wilson and Stan Ellsholz were recruited for the MCRD tennis team. Don went to the quarter-finals at Wimbledon. Chaplain Jack Graham and a dentist played doubles with Wilson and Ellsholz, the fastest tennis I ever watched in person. Chaplain Dick Heil won a PGA tournament, but the title was taken from him when they found he did not belong to the PGA. Chaplain Bob McComas won the senior tennis title, but he could not go to the All-Marine because he was Navy. Chaplain Ted Hanawalt had come into the Navy from First Presbyterian Church, Louisville at a significant drop in income. Chaplain Bob Bigler had been a guard at San Quentin.

Chaplain E. Richard Barnes was at that time retired because of his heart attack, but kept himself busy in the state legislature and as a proponent of the current anti-communist crusade spearheaded by Dr. Swartz of Australia, whose book *You Can Trust the Communists (to be communist)*, was in paper-back. I attended the rallies in San Diego and led the audience in the singing of "God Bless America" at one of them.

Chaplain Cecil Threadgill had been an enlisted Marine. He kept his enlisted dress blues hanging in his office. He would not accept failure of any recruit from Texas.

USS VALLEY FORGE (LPH-8)

The last time I had asked for a specific sea tour it was at the invitation of Chaplain Kelly who was Force Chaplain of Amphibious Forces, Pacific. In talking with Chaplain Francis L. Garrett about this choice he said that I should ask for a carrier. Therefore while at MCRD I did request a carrier and the detailer and the guardian angel came through again in a surprising way. My orders were to the USS VALLEY FORGE LPH 8, a helicopter carrier used to land Marines that had formerly been a carrier of fixed wing aircraft, modified to accommodate helicopters.

Although it involved a move, it was a short one up to Long Beach and would again throw me in with some of my old buddies from Pendleton as well as MCRD days. The ship was also under PHIBPAC so I would be with old Navy friends as well. When the nomination for orders arrived the ship was in WESTPAC and the time was November. Therefore, I got on the phone to Washington and suggested that I go out and ride the ship back. The answer was, "We thought you would think of that, to do your Christmas shopping. The answer is no!" So my vision of having a whole aircraft carrier to transport my loot back home instead of parceling it out over several squadron ships blew up. Nevertheless, I had tried.

VALLEY FORGE was scheduled for a yard period in Bremerton, Washington after the deployment, so we decided to look for a modest house in Long Beach since I would be in Bremerton much of the time and Marion would likely spend some time in Durham.

With the help of a Black agent, we found a 2-bedroom stucco on Hill Street with a banana tree in front and a lemon tree in the back yard. It also had a full basement which the agent called a bomb shelter. The owner was reluctant to rent it, preferring to sell, but did accept my offer of two years rent in advance, $2400. Our closest neighbors were a Japanese family with two boys the same ages as our girls and a third boy born around the same time as our son, Thomas David Parham III. We used the same alley to get to our garages.

When my orders came, there was no rumor of any kind of a farewell party so Marion and I decided to give our own. We invited every chaplain and wife that we knew, so the Pacific Beach house was bulging. We left with many fond memories.

When we moved I drove the Prinz with the parakeet cage in the back seat. Marion drove the Chrysler, accompanied by the girls. Because of the full basement we were able to get all our gear into the smaller house. It was so small that with a 25 feet cord on the telephone in the hall we could talk from any room in the house. In later years Marion referred to the house as a hovel. I enjoyed it as much as I had enjoyed the trailer at Great Lakes.

I relieved a Chaplain Ben Barrett who was a reserve, one of the finest chaplains I ever met. He felt that the reserves were not treated fairly in the matter of promotions. He felt also that if they were good enough to be used during war, they should also be promoted in times of peace. There was a prevalent opinion that a reserve would have been integrated into the regular Navy if sufficiently qualified or committed, but I do not know how widely this opinion was held. I felt it was sufficiently strong that it was worth it to lose a rank to get into the regulars as I did.

Ben had done something for the VALLEY that I have not seen anywhere else. On the hanger deck there was what they called the Shrine Area. Attached to the bulkhead, but with sufficient space between it and the bulkhead to store a piano, pulpit, lectern two altar rails all on rollers, was a folding triptych made of anodized aluminum.

Each panel was 15 ft. long and 7 ft. tall. There was stained glass in the top third of each panel. The center panel had a back lighted Jesus in the Garden of Gethsemane. A fourth panel was raised by a pulley to form a partial roof for the whole assembly. The furniture

An Affirmation of Faith

was white enamel; the kneelers were cushioned in black vinyl. Ben had paid $4,000 to get the display constructed. Just above the triptych on the bulkhead was the projection booth for movies, where there was space for a Hammond organ. When we were in port the wife of a storekeeper, Ellen, was organist or my 8-year-old second cousin, Marion Holloway.

Several years later I visited the ship only to find that the shrine area was gone and nobody knew what had happened to it. I assume that in the height of combat in Vietnam somebody decided that the 45 feet of deck space could not be spared for a religious center or that a vehicle smashed it beyond repair. It could have been argued that no other ship had a similar installation.

Ben had also outfitted a chapel on the 0-3 level, called "The Upper Room Chapel." It had 13 body contoured plastic chairs, so even Judas was included. It was handy for Bible classes, noon devotions and daily Rosary services. It was a pleasure to welcome chaplains aboard for exercises and to watch them drool over our unusual facilities.

In addition to this situation as I found it, CDR Elliott, the damage control officer, decided that there should be a kind of reception room for visitors during in-port periods. He also decided that the chaplain would be the logical one to welcome such visitors. Therefore, he took a large space, about 45 feet long, where the aircraft maintenance metal shop had been when fixed wing aircraft was on board. He outfitted it with an asphalt tile deck and walnut paneling on the bulkhead. My assistant had his desk at the entrance. My private office was at the far end with the overhead painted black to minimize the impact of the many pipes. This space was large enough for daily Catholic Mass and services on special days. It was good for weddings. Davey was baptized there by our former Chief of Chaplains, Stan Salisbury. I enjoyed telling people about my 40 feet walnut paneled office.

The VALLEY had many conversation points. In the flight deck there was a commemorative plaque in a section removed from the FRANKLIN, on which Chaplain O'Callihan became the first Navy chaplain to receive the Medal of Honor. We had the silver service from the PENNSYLVANIA, since it was out of commission. We carried the nickname "Happy Valley." In the wardroom, we sang to the tune of Mickey Mouse, "V-A-L–L-E-Y — F-O-R-G-E."

I had some anxiety about relieving Ben because I thought he would be so missed by all hands that I would suffer by comparison. I remember how I got along famously in PHIBRON-1 because the chaplain I relieved was not beloved by the crew. I found that Ben had left such a reservoir of good will that I had only to add to it. On the "Happy Valley" this was not hard to do.

The same situation pertained to the commanding officers. The former CAPT Jackson was often mentioned in endearing terms. When we got to Pearl Harbor, where he was stationed, we invited him to our smoker. CAPT Fidel was just as beloved. One night when we were in Subic Bay a Black PO2 had returned from liberty very drunk. He swung a Karate chop at the OOD, missing him but knocking his hat off. I saw the incident. When he came up for Captain's Mast, CAPT Fidel began by saying,"(name), I am not going to bust you, and that was all anybody heard except the murmur of relief that went over all of us standing there. CAPT Fidel could have asked anybody there for anything he could have imagined, and it would have been freely given. We had been told that no LPH CO had ever been selected for Admiral. We hoped CAPT Fidel would be the first. We were disappointed when he retired unselected.

In addition to the on-board services I furnished transportation to the Saturday night Youth for Christ rallies in Long Beach. Jerry Klippert was the facilitator. At one of the rallies, Ethel Waters sang her theme song and the title of her book, *"His Eye is on the Sparrow,"* and some other numbers. She walked with difficulty, steadying herself as she moved past the piano to the mike. In listing her ailments she said, "You name it, I've got it." When she died later, Billy Graham, whom she called her son, came to preach her funeral; President Nixon sent a telegram. She had a marvelous facility for communicating her love.

When I heard that the "Princeton" Chaplain, Hank Austin, who played the violin, had a popcorn machine, I requested the same privilege as a means of providing money for the various charities by selling the corn during the hanger deck movies. The men told me that the Chief Master at Arms was so much easier to get along with if he had a bag of popcorn during the movies. There was some regulation somewhere that sales should be handled by supply or special services, in which case the proceeds could not be donated. I remember the decision voiced by CDR Ed Vereen that there were only two reasons to disregard regulations: morals and charity, and my proposal was covered by both of them. Therefore the very next charity appeal got a check from the popcorn fund.

As it turned out, we did not go to Bremerton for overhaul because our availability was changed to the Naval Shipyard, Long Beach. This meant that we had taken a house too small for the expected entertaining and had paid two years rent. Fortunately the deployments and exercises did keep us out of port quite a bit, and most of the social life centered around the officers' club at the Naval Station. During this period Marion's cousin, Dr. Joseph Boyd of Toledo, decided to move to Los Angeles for a residency in Psychiatry on a $10,000 per annum tax free scholarship. He and his wife, Inez, were practically adopted by the VALLEY FORGE wardroom. They attended so many of our functions that people asked for an explanation when they were not present.

Another cousin, Christine Wyatt, whose husband and son were attorneys, enjoyed the Happy Valley hospitality. The wardroom food was excellent, as it was economical. The families of officers who were on duty often were on board for the evening meal. The Wyatt's lived in Los Angeles in a suburb called Viewpoint. They had a 180-degree view of the ocean until Ray Charles built a two-story house across the street from them. Ben Wyatt Jr. missed winning a seat in Congress by 400 votes.

For the third successive year, VALLEY FORGE found itself in Hawaii for Easter. So I was excited about the whole thing, particularly when I heard from a chaplain at NAS Barbers Point that he was having a female chorus from the University of California in concert on Sunday night and that they would be available for our morning service. The shrine area never looked more beautiful, with the 35 or 40 singers in pastel green and pink dresses. No chaplain ever had less difficulty finding junior officers to escort the singers for a tour of the ship after the service and then brunch in the wardroom.

An Affirmation of Faith

The Special Services officer at the Naval Station told me that he had been trying to get a Hawaiian dance group from the Church College of the Pacific to perform on station. Their manager had refused, saying that he would rather perform on one of the ships. Guess who volunteered his ship in nothing flat? As I introduced the group I said "Your friendly chaplain presents," and out they came in bare feet, grass skirts, leis, musical instruments, to the delight of all hands. One of them hung a carved wooden lai around my neck. I was disposed of it by Marion when we returned. The manager visited the ship after we returned to Long Beach when the group was in CONUS for a tour.

On my previous sea tour I had written Marion daily and sent frequent pictures and tapes. This time I added movies. At the end of each reel I would hold the camera at arm's length pointed at myself and wave goodbye. Marion used to show the films to the wives in Long Beach. When I met our new CO's wife for the first time, after we returned to Long Beach, she said, "I feel like I ought to do like this" (she waved as I did in the films).

My picture taking got me in trouble one beautiful Sunday. I was returning from service on another ship in a helicopter, when I decided it would be interesting to film our landing on the flight deck. The crew chief was holding me by the belt and I was holding to the top of the doorframe with my left hand as I leaned out. All was going well until I saw the XO in my viewfinder, standing on the flight deck with his hands on his hips. As I sheepishly alighted he said, "I hope your family enjoys those pictures that you risked your life to take." I should have apologized and explained that the crew chief had me by the belt and I was holding the frame but I didn't. I still tend to freeze in a crisis.

I gave the XO, CDR Millar, another reason for considering me a lame brain. We were about to end our deployment, so in the Chaplain's Corner of the ship's newspaper I wrote an exhortation to continence as the way to avoid venereal disease. I remarked that we had shipmates praying every night that their symptoms would clear up before we got back to Long Beach. One of the officers came to the XO and told him he would not send the paper home because his wife would suspect he was one of those praying. The XO ordered the whole issue destroyed, called me in and told me I had embarrassed the command and to go up and tell the CO what I had done. Again I was speechless but obeyed the order. The only thing I ever heard about the incident was a letter I got from a civilian pastor in the Midwest enjoining me to keep up the good work. Obviously one issue at least was smuggled off the ship.

Our XO was a bona fide hero. He dove from the flight deck of an earlier carrier to rescue someone, and his back still gave him trouble, so he often went to sickbay. One day we were talking about VD and he speculated that the crew thought VD was his problem. I admitted that I had heard such, but did not have the presence of mind to say that I always tried to set the record straight.

We had other problems on the Happy Valley. One day during the yard period a shipmate fell from the flight deck to the bottom of the dry dock. We assumed that he tripped or stumbled as he was on his way down to the hanger deck. He had tried to hold to the guy wire, which had cut into his hand, which was closed around the congealed blood. He had planned to be a missionary. The woman who preached at his funeral had one of his jackets over the back of a chair near the pulpit. She dwelt on the urgency of getting someone else to wear the jacket of the deceased as a missionary.

We lost another shipmate during the yard period through an administrative discharge. He admitted to homosexual relationships with the yard workers, describing himself as a whore. He was somewhat concerned about his future career and thought perhaps he would do well to settle in the San Francisco area.

In spite of the dust and dirt of the yard period, we continued to have the usual religious program, in spite of the reduced attendance. Due to a liberal leave policy, many of the crew went on liberty and others in various training programs at service schools. I think it helped to bring religion to bear in a situation often conducive to depression, boredom and frustration. The old saying, "A sailor belongs on a ship and the ship belongs at sea," designates a yard period as an anomaly for the sailor; it is even more so for senior officers and particularly the CO. In those days a CO might have only one year in command, and if most or all of this time had to be in a yard, he could question whether he was destined for flag rank.

It was during this time that some of the shipyard workers invited me to go to a prayer breakfast hosted by Demos Shakarian, founder of the Full Gospel Businessmen's International. The site was Clifton's Cafeteria in Los Angeles. I had heard of this restaurant from the seven Black Red Cross field workers in Guam in 1946. It had caged birds singing, inspirational booklets, "Food for Thought," for distribution, and an announced policy that one could pay the suggested price for the food, more as a charitable gift to the hungry the restaurant fed, or as much less as one's dissatisfaction indicated, even nothing at all. Demos asked those attending, plus his radio audience, to pray for the safety of the VALLEY during our imminent deployment. I had the joy of returning to a breakfast at Clifton's eight months later to report that we had not lost a single life. I was much impressed with Demos, who at that time was the largest dairy farmer in America, and with his organization of committed Christian businessmen. They were decidedly pro-military and remain so. Every one of his conventions that I have known of had a military breakfast with a senior military speaker, usually a flag officer.

To talk of deployment to some people was like waving a red flag at a bull; they did not want any part of it. I was kept busy with those who were trying to find a way to get off the ship before deployment date. All kinds of hardship transfers were requested, some of them valid. One of our shipmates the day before deployment declared himself a homosexual and was duly detached.

For those of us who remained the situation was exciting. We embarked a squadron of Marines with helicopters. The CO, Colonel Ross, was squadron commander of the year. We also had a battalion aboard, expecting that we might get orders to land Marines in Vietnam. It was a pleasure to welcome a chaplain serving with Marines from time to time during the whole deployment. Often we had a Catholic chaplain who could offer Masses on board and also on other nearby ships. At one time during the deployment I set up a schedule of 21 religious services over one weekend, utilizing all the chaplains in the task force. One chaplain requested omission from the list, except for his own ship, so I assigned him to another ship with a landing pad, so he would not have to be let down by the horse collar, as we called it.

An Affirmation of Faith

On the way through Pearl this time I decided to support the sunrise service to be held Easter Sunday at Camp Smith, Fleet Marine Force headquarters, so I arranged for a bus to take us over. It rained all day Saturday and early Sunday morning. At 15 minutes before time for the service the rain stopped, so we could gather at the outdoor location. I spoke to Bob McComas, the force chaplain, as we were leaving, remarking that he looked sleepy. He said he had prayed all night long and the early morning hours with no sleep at all. When we boarded the bus, the rain began, so nobody got wet. I thanked God for stopping the rain for Bob.

Helicopter pilots have to be a special breed. I have never seen anyone so completely exhausted as a helicopter pilot after several hours of operational flying. I had heard that it was difficult to get the Vietnamese troops to disembark after reaching the specified destination. The pilots told stories of having to drag them out with their gear and live chickens. To pilot a helicopter with the bicycle grips, pedals, etc., reminds me of the childhood game of scratching your head, rubbing your stomach and patting your feet at the same time.

In addition some kind of turbulence can occur when landing. Twice during the deployment we lost a helicopter that flopped over the side from the same location on the flight deck. In both instances the pilot got out in time. An attempt to retrieve a helicopter from salt water would be futile because of the rapid rate of corrosion. We had to hose down helicopters that had been subjected to salt spray. So the magnesium from which helicopters are constructed is not only very highly flammable but subject to instant corrosion by salt water.

One problem I was never able to get solved was the segregated recreation areas in Japan, Okinawa and the Philippines. My solution was to close them all, but my pleas fell on deaf ears because of the complicated situations involving political, social and economic factors.

In Japan, near the Naval Station at Yokosuka was the "Alley." There was an understanding that it was for Blacks only. It contained the bars, souvenir shops, restaurants and other entertainment spots that one found on the other streets in the same section. In Okinawa, the comparable location was Koza or "Four Corners." In Olongapo, Philippines it was "The Jungle."

The owners of the establishments considered this arrangement good for business. Some fights were certainly eliminated that would have derived from racial incidents. I never heard anyone say so, but I suspect that there were White sailors who would not care to use a prostitute who would service Blacks also. It was also understood that Black officers would not frequent the segregated areas. One Black officer told me that he had to flee for his life when someone recognized him in Four Corners. It was quite dangerous for any White to be seen there, except in uniform and in a shore patrol vehicle.

My problem, in addition to the moral one, was that the men would go on liberty to such places after all day in an integrated work situation, and while there reinforce whatever prejudicial attitudes they had. When they got back to the ships they had chips on their shoulders and were ready to fight. One night when the liberty boats were delayed and the men from several ships were waiting on the pier at Olongapo, a racial fight erupted. When word of it got back to the Valley, a contingent of shore patrolmen was hastily organized, armed with short lengths of pipe and sent to the pier by boat. The men on the pier were herded into their respective boats as fast as possible, finally leaving nobody to fight.

Providentially, nobody was killed or seriously injured, likely because of the absence of firearms among the men. It did provide excitement for an otherwise boring evening. When one of my assistants we called "Big Moose" came up the gangway spattered with blood, the OOD asked, "Moose, were you in that fight?" His smiling rejoinder was, "What fight?" We were blessed with much less violence than the other carriers. Their fights made the news back in the states. I felt a climate of opinion aboard that since the other carriers had riots we should have one too. One night when I was asleep some of the crew tried to get one started. They were armed with tie-down chains (used to secure the helicopters on the hanger deck). A PO1 Holmes got their attention and ordered them to desist. He was able to exert such a commanding presence that the men quieted down. The ship awarded him a commendation for his timely intervention.

Discontent continued, however. One night after I had retired, I answered a knock at my stateroom door to find five Black non-rated sailors who wanted to talk. I invited them in, seated them and then asked what they had in mind. I was not prepared for the reply which came from the spokesman. They had checked with the Blacks in the embarked Marine battalion and had planned to take over the ship. Then with great pride, one spoke the unbelievable words, "And we want you to be the commanding officer."

As carefully as I could, with concerted effort not to deflate them too rapidly, I explained that I was a not capable of commanding the ship because the Naval Academy was not admitting Blacks when I went to college, nor was the Navy commissioning Black officers by the time I finished seminary. They started this the very year I finished seminary, when I had already prepared for another profession. Therefore, I knew nothing about navigation and could not even tell them where we were at the time. Then I wondered what we would do when we ran out of food or fuel; we were helpless without the Navy support system.

They found it hard to believe that I was not qualified to command the ship but took my word for it. Since there was no other Black senior officer aboard, the takeover plan had no chance of success. So five disappointed, misguided, men trailed out of my stateroom. It was a sad experience for me. It reminded me of the time in Youngstown when Rev. Harry Brown Gibson had said to me, "Dave, our people have a long way to go, and they ain't going to make it either." After years of resisting his notion that night I was about to agree with him.

On the other hand the proposal was so ridiculous and such an impossibility to achieve that I considered it not worthy of reporting to anyone. Nevertheless, I used the incident often in speaking to Black audiences and had it included in the Navy publication, *The Pioneers*. Also, *The Pioneers* included a brief account of the careers of Chaplain J. Russell Brown, the first Black chaplain, and myself. The five would be insurgents unfortunately felt the need to act out anyhow in several incidents ashore for which they were put on report. The XO investigated each incident and the person involved, painstakingly and without consulting me at any point. They were all transferred off the VALLEY. We heard that several of them were court-martialed. Racial tension was not the only problem the Jungle brought us. There was a very high incidence of venereal disease on board because of the Jungle and the other entertainment areas as well. Infected men had to fall in at restricted muster every day. When the infection appeared they were given a check-in sheet, on which I was one of the signators. I always asked two questions: "First time?" and after an affirmative answer, "Last time?" This question gave an enormous amount of relief to the man in question. I suspect some of them expected a Hell-fire and damnation sermon. I often quoted F. Stanley Jones to the effect that we do not break God's laws, as we suppose, but are broken upon them. The laws stand. Then I would be certain that they understood that God's forgiveness (through Christ for Christians) was most readily available. I was actually distressed by those who had non-specific urethritis, which did not respond to antibiotics and was considered incurable. Although there might be periods of remission, they were told the symptoms could reappear. I do not remember anyone asking for anointing for healing in such an instance. I never suggested it a sin of omission on my part, possibly caused by unconscious anger at their disregard of moral and Naval law.

From my first visit to Hong Kong, I was fascinated by the Mercedes diesel taxis. On a previous deployment I ordered a diesel station wagon but got my money back when it was not delivered before the next year's models came out. The delay was caused by the backlog of orders and the fact that the station wagon bodies were put on at a different factory after the chassis had been assembled. This time I ordered the four-door sedan to be delivered in New York. The total cost, including duty and taxes, was about $3200. The last new motor, transmission etc., two years ago cost twice that amount. In Long Beach, I gave the 1955 Chrysler Newport and the 1960 NSU Prinz to a Presbyterian Church. They were both in service the next year. We flew to New York, picked up the diesel in the snow and drove to Durham two weeks later. So our girls were in 4 schools each that year: Long Beach, Long Island, Durham and Quonset Point.

We were in and out of areas within striking distance of Vietnam. We expected any time to be given the command, "Land the landing force", but it never came. The closest I got to any action at all during this period was to have a service one Sunday aboard a destroyer that had been involved in an incident with two Vietnamese boats a few days previously. I was met at the quarterdeck by the CO, who told me his name was Jester. He wore shorts and loafers. The crew was fairly brimming with excitement. Church attendance was unusually large.

My allotted two years had gone by, but I did not want to leave. When I thought of asking for an extension, I decided that it just would not be fair to someone else who would have the same fulfillment I had found. When my relief was named I knew I had made the right decision. He was Joe Davis, LCDR, who would be relieving a CDR. I prepared an extensive turnover file with pictures of many activities. When he came aboard, I took him all over and introduced him around. I was motivated to do my best for him because he had recently lost an 18-year-old daughter in an automobile accident.

When I had completed the kind of turnover I would have wanted, Joe's response deflated me when he said as kindly as he could, "Dave, I appreciate what you tried to do. But I have learned that it is better for me to do a few things and to do them well, rather than to spread myself all over the place, the way you do." Then I could see his silver leaves flying away and regretted that I had not extended. I had never sat on a selection board for promotion because those who had been non-selected at any time were not invited to do so. Nevertheless, I was convinced that promotion was based on "What do ye more than others?" The Valley certainly offered the locus of an innovative and multifaceted ministry. Years later when the policy was changed and I served on selection boards, I saw the wisdom of Joe's stance and that "This one thing I do" can also be a successful promotion strategy.

We had been in California eight years; the girls were now in elementary school. At the school Evangeline attended, there was a ten-minute outdoor recess every hour. It seemed to me that there was not the emphasis on academics I had experienced. A new superintendent of public instruction for California, Max Rafferty, had mounted a campaign to reemphasize the three R's, and was meeting strong opposition from educators. The use of pot, LSD, etc. was expanding. When someone suggested that the border to Mexico at Tijuana be closed, the reply was given that more drugs could be bought on the playground at Grossmont High School than in Tijuana. I felt that the fun in the sun philosophy was OK for retired people but not for children. My dad's health had failed, and my mother, in her upper 70s had placed him in a nursing home. So again, the detailer and the guardian angel provided exactly what I wanted.

Several considerations were behind my first preference for my next duty, a Naval Air Station on the East Coast. Except for a brief temporary duty assignment at Naval Air Station, Iwakuni, Japan, this was my first experience with the brown shoe Navy, as they called the flying components then, as distinguished from the seagoing Black shoe Navy. Air officers did wear brown shoes and aviation greens similar to Marine greens. As had been the case with Marines, I was quite impressed by the airmen, their professionalism, their dash, their interest in the religious programs

The Amphibious Force Chaplain at the time was Harold McNeill, who had come to Coronado from Quonset Point. He had me to come to San Diego for two reasons: to give me a complete briefing on Quonset Point and to direct a sensitivity training seminar that would heavily involve a chaplain he noticed acting out inappropriately. I entered into both activities with great relish. I could hardly wait to get to Quonset. I was delighted with the process of the seminar.

Part IV.
Walking Confidently into New Experiences

Quonset Point, RI

Since Harold told me that my quarters would be on the golf course, I thought it would be politically expedient to take up the game. Because I had failed selection to Commander the first time, I assumed I would likewise fail selection to Captain. But if I played golf with the Admiral and the CO, I might make it the second time around. Harold also told me that Rod Harrison, whom I would relieve, had been a professional basketball player. I found, however, that Rod did not appreciate this kind of advance press, and he was miffed that Harold had (he thought) pictured him with a basketball in one hand and a dog leash in the other, not Rod's ideal image of a chaplain.

Rod was tall, crew cut and handsome. The dog, Oliver, was unusual. As we were about to leave the house for dinner at the club, Rod said, "Its cold outside Oliver; go get your sweater." Oliver tore upstairs and came down with the sweater in his mouth. Just as "Casey" Casady had been the life of the wardroom on the Henrico, Rod was the life of the Admiral's staff. Two commanders from the staff sang in the choir, Carl Dalland and Bob Severn. The Admiral, McGruder Tuttle, had responsibility for antisubmarine warfare. The local newspaper carried a feature article on him titled, "The Best Advice I Ever Received." He was told while single, "Marry a girl whom you meet in church with her parents." He had followed this advice. He still remained an avid churchman.

The other chaplains were George T. Boyd, Southern Baptist, Pius F. Keating, Catholic, and Earnest A. Dollar, Wesleyan Methodist. George's wife, Mary, was organist and choir director. Ernie's wife,

Norma, was the mainstay of the Sunday school. Pius carried his name on his license tags, told people he was the Pope's brother, and imported his own organist-choir director from Providence. We all had very adequate offices in the same building with Navy Relief, which I served as Vice-President under the Admiral. Lucy Roberts Harold was still the executive secretary. There were still two nurses with a Plymouth sedan for the use of each in visiting newborns and some of the ill.

The Dixie Kiefer Chapel was named for a former CO who was killed en-route to an Army/Navy football game. It was that typical white frame colonial structure outside, but inside was a balcony and a four-sided revolving altar located between a large and a small chapel. Therefore, two services could be going on at the same time, or consecutively, in either chapel with almost no time required to change the altar setting. I found chapel attendance to be phenomenal.

My delight at Quonset was the Junior Choir of 30 voices that sang twice a month. They processed according to height, so my daughter, Mae, and one of the Schultz's girls, Debbie, led the procession. They wore blue robes with white square Puritan collars. Two officers' wives, Mrs. Smith and Mrs. Benford, served as choir mothers.

It bothered me that our 1100 hour service was not very convenient for golfers. In talking to the CO, CAPT Scarpino, about my problem, he promised me that he would attend a service at 0800 hours if he could tee off at 0830 hours. We then inaugurated the golfers' service, which was convenient for Sunday school teachers who did not want to stay for the later service, for those working the 2300-0700 hour shift, and for those going sailing in summer or skiing in winter.

We lived in Quarters J, which I told people stood for Jesus. The CO's quarters were at the head of the circle, from which his wife sent a steward one day with a box of black kittens to ask how many we wanted. We took one, keeping him until we were transferred, to the delight of the children.

As soon as the weather permitted, I did get out on the golf course with the clubs by McGregor that I had bought at a sale on the Valley, playing with a foursome which included a supply officer. I teed up at my turn and took a vicious swing at the bottom of which I heard a thud. As I followed through and scanned the sky for the ball I heard a voice saying, "Swing again." I had completely missed the ball.

My game improved very slowly. It bothered me that the balls were expensive and could be so easily lost at a water hazard. It bothered me that there was so little exercise involved except for the walking. My brother-in-law raved about the ability of the game to relieve his tensions and anxieties, but I did not admit having any tensions and anxieties. In playing a Scotch foursome with the CO and his wife, I was embarrassed by being the low scorer.

Finally, a kind act of providence put me out of my misery. I was selected for Captain, and I forthwith gave my golf clubs to the Navy Relief thrift shop. It was a most serendipitous moment, completely unexpected not only by me but also many of my friends. When one called to say how surprised he was, I replied that I was more than surprised, shocked. James Farmer told the press that it was a prime example of tokenism. When I got a copy of the list and saw that Chaplain Art Dominy was not selected I cried. He had been such a capable assistant division chaplain at Camp Pendleton.

Perhaps the best way to describe my feelings, other than to use the words of gratitude, would be the words of the song, "Any way you want to bless me, Lord, I'll be satisfied." From the list of members of the board, I realized that I knew them all and highly respected them. I knew they would be getting some guff from some quarters, so I was determined to justify their confidence in me.

The news came to me via a telephone call from Chaplain Frederick W. Brink, who had been my senior chaplain at Sasebo. My response to him was, "Are you sure?" I should have known better than to ask this because no chaplain would take the chance of giving out false information of this magnitude and certainly not Chaplain Brink, who was an administrative genius. He called during a breakfast I was hosting for the Providence Chapter of the Full Gospel Businessmen's Fellowship International on a Saturday morning. This group is known for praising the Lord, and there was an additional reason for praise that morning.

Soon after arriving at Quonset I heard about a brown baggers' prayer group that met at noon, like the one at Long Beach that led

An Affirmation of Faith

me to Demos Shakarian's prayer breakfast at Clifton's Restaurant. Rev. Robert Gooding, pastor of the Appanaug Pentecostal Church nearby, invited me to meet with them. He was employed by the Naval Repair Facility on the base with 5000 employees. It was the largest employer in Rhode Island. Rev. Gooding said he was impressed when he saw me at the Oral Roberts Crusade in Providence.

From associations with members of the brown bag prayer group, I was invited to the Providence meetings of Full Gospel Business Men's Fellowship International and then to a regional convention in New York City. Before an evening session at the convention, Rev. Gooding, Harris Halverson and Carlin Nash were praying with me for my baptism in the Holy Spirit. I saw a vision of Jesus on the cross, with blood and water flowing from his side in a veritable torrent. I was protected behind that cross from Satan, who was unsuccessfully trying to reach me through that torrent of water and blood. I laughed for joy as I saw Satan bowled over, head over heels to the foot of Calvary. I thought of the lines of the hymn, "Floods of joy o'er my soul like the sea billows roll, since Jesus came into my heart." Until then it had seemed strange to me to hear Christians speak of not being able to verbally express their joy and praise to God. In that experience, I found I could be speechless and yet express praise in apparently meaningless sounds.

This charismatic experience moved my level of religious experience from one of belief to that of knowledge that my many, many sins were and still are forgiven. On my morning runs, I relived that experience as a conclusion to my daily prayers. Meanwhile, the selection and subsequent promotion generated a surprising amount of publicity in the media. The associated press sent a reporter to Quarters for an interview and pictures. I heard from friends across the country. There was some discussion as to whether I was the second Black Captain, as I thought, or the first. The official Navy position, as told to me, is that Captain Robert Smalls, the Charleston, SC harbor pilot who stole the PLANTER from the Confederate Navy and delivered it to the Union flotilla, was not given an instant commission with the rank of Captain, but was later listed as Captain, U. S. Navy, Retired. I consider myself the second Captain because that is the way I first heard it and because of my esteem for his family.

Quonset Point was nearly as much of a family type community as Sasebo had been. The station was unusually self-contained to be in CONUS. Our little hospital also serviced the Davisville Seabees adjacent to us. Admiral Tuttle suggested that I join the Rotary Club in nearby East Greenwich, so I rode to meetings with him. VX-6, the squadron that serviced the South Pole was based at Quonset so we supported the dependents during deployment as well as the dependents of the ESSEX, "The Oldest and the Boldest," and the LAKE CHAMPLAIN, "The Straightest and the Greatest." Both were straight deck instead of canted deck carriers as the VALLEY FORGE had been before its conversion to an LPH.

Being a small state, there was a closer relationship with state government than usually seen. Senator John Chafee was governor then. He used to come out to Quonset when VX-6 departed for or returned from deployment. One day I got all excited because the governor's office had called. I found that the governor's secretary wanted to invite me to hear David Wilkerson, author of *The Cross and the Switchblade* at a Methodist Church in nearby Barrington.

With two carriers and their air groups, there were 16 changes of command every year, most of them in the spring. Therefore the Admiral and I had several in a week, two in one day. I could have made his speeches; he could have offered my prayers. As a member of the Admiral's staff, I got tapped for inspections of chaplains on other ships engaged in anti-submarine warfare, the specific assignment of Commander Fleet Air Quonset. As vice-president of Navy Relief, I needed to visit the branch activity in Brunswick, Maine.

Quonset was the nearest landing spot for VIP's headed for Newport. When the son of General Krulak was in indoctrination school for the Chaplain Corps at Newport, the General was invited to speak at the War College. Marion and I went to meet his plane because Mrs. Krulak was to be on board. It was a happy hugging reunion. As we expected, the plane landed at the precise moment specified, the way it had in the Philippines when I met his flight. He was still using the same C-130 with "Pacific Commander" painted on the side.

President Lyndon Johnson visited Quonset briefly. Our station photographer took a picture of him shaking hands with my sister-in-

An Affirmation of Faith

law as she stood beside my mother-in-law. I had 11 X 14 enlargements made, sent them to Bill Moyers and asked him to run them through the President's signature machine, which he did.

Quonset was the first CONUS stop for the planes from Iceland. Personnel came down on leave; the chaplain came to do Christmas shopping. The blue and gold submarine teams embarked at Quonset for Holy Loch. I never visited either place. The USA had an agreement with Iceland not to send Blacks there. When my promotion came through I decided on a brunch as a wetting down party. It was held at the club after church. The club gave us filet mignon for $1.50 per plate. The second time such a brunch was scheduled it was for the Barrington College Choir. Unfortunately, NAS Norfolk was snowed in that morning and a planeload of sailors from Puerto Rico landed at Quonset. Pea coats were rounded up and the galley gave the men our steaks. The choir had hamburgers.

Mrs. Eleanor Searle Whitney, the divorced wife of Harry Paine Whitney of Newport, was much in demand as a speaker and singer among evangelicals and charismatic. I heard her give her testimony at a charismatic rally in Providence, after having been introduced by Harold Bredeson, a pillar of the charismatic movement. She agreed to come to Quonset. We were excited because of her Newport connections. The mansion everyone wanted to visit there, "The Breakers," belonged to her mother-in-law.

So she attracted a large congregation the evening she spoke and sang. Marion and I hosted a reception for her at Quarters J afterward, which 75 mostly officers and wives attended. I watched Mrs. Whitney do a lot of personal evangelism at the reception. She even got the Admiral to promise to start a Bible class in his quarters.

Another guest that I invited drew a large Sunday congregation, Bishop Higgins of the Episcopal Church. At my request, he did the junior sermon also. He told the children of the various distinctive types of clothing worn in his native England by various tradesman, then dwelt on the proper clothing for the Christian, how one should be clothed in righteousness peace, etc.

Annually the Navy Relief campaign for funds featured an air show. One performer in the comedy collection of old planes was known as the "Flying Professor." He would mount the cockpit with

An Affirmation of Faith

a book titled in very large print, *How to Fly*. A reserve commander, he always came to the golfer's service in uniform. When he was later killed in a stunt somewhere else, we were all saddened by the news. We also were spared accidents with the "Blue Angels," who performed every year.

As was the case at my other assignments, all was not sweetness and light. One day a teenaged dependent came to inform me that her friend had run away from home and was hiding out in the chapel where she had been feeding her. There was a severe mother-daughter conflict. The mother had told the daughter that she had a face like a mule's ass. The runaway, after a time, consented to return One Friday evening I got a call at quarters that really rocked me. The caller said she had a newborn baby, which she did not want, nor did her husband now deployed want it. She was therefore trying to decide whether to kill the baby or herself. I asked her if she had to do either before Monday morning; she said she could wait that long. So I told her to bring me the baby on Monday morning and that I would be at my office at eight o'clock. I explained that the Navy Relief and Red Cross were closed for the weekend but would be open then also. Much to my relief, she did come in with the baby. I called a friend, whom I knew was waiting for an adoption to come through, and invited her to get some practice in the meantime. She came right over.

Then I began to realize how the Lord takes care of babies and fools. I had no guarantee the mother would keep her promise. I had visions of her jumping off a bridge or throwing the baby off that Friday night, leaving me to regret it the rest of my life. I should have gotten her address and telephone and told her to wait right there until I arrived to pick the baby up.

On occasion we lost a plane. During one unhappy week, I had seven funerals. I always marveled at the attitude of the surviving pilots that the dead ones had made mistakes they would not make. This allowed them to fly the same or the next day in full confidence of their ability.

The memory of the Bennington disaster was still fresh at Quonset. One of the catapults had exploded with the loss of lives and many injuries. One of the dead was Harold Wright, a steward and husband of the former Marguerite Mitcham, whom we knew at Great Lakes and then saw much of in Topeka, Kansas while studying at Menninger's.

Automobile accidents were far too frequent. I remember going to tell a wife of the death of her husband within the hour. She stared in disbelief, saying that he had just gone to pick up some beer. She accompanied us back to the hospital where he was still on the examining table without a visible mark on him. After caressing him for a while, she was convinced of his death.

My next-door neighbor, CAPT Bob Metzger, developed a circulatory problem, which necessitated the amputation of a leg. The ship's physician said smoking was the cause.

We also lost Admiral Bullard to a heart attack. Mrs. Bullard said he had gone to sea so often that this time it seemed as if he had just gone to sea again.

It appeared to me that it was extremely difficult for an aviator to get past the rank of CDR. One problem seemed to be the lack of experience as a commanding officer. A pilot could hope to be operations office of a squadron, then XO, finally CO of another squadron. The next step, air group commander, was very difficult because of the size of the available field. In the so-called Black shoe Navy, one might have commanded several ships in a comparable period of time, starting as CO of a mine sweep as a LT. We had many passed over commanders. One of them, CDR X Holmes, and aircraft maintenance officers put up a reserved parking sign at the club, "Passed Over Commanders." He was told to take it down. Some of these men were able to find jobs in the aircraft industry' others became pilots for commercial airlines. We were always sorry to lose them.

The Dixie Kiefer Chapel was always a joy for me. The music was exceptional. At one time there had been money to pay choir members. When I arrived, Helen Bennett was the only remaining singer of the paid group who continued as a volunteer. I have never heard anyone else sing my favorite of her solos, "God Hath Been Merciful." I thought it strange that the console of the organ was behind a screen. Then I met Priscilla Baslow, the former organist, who was so beautiful she might have been considered a distraction. I think she was single also. As the procession of beautiful organist

An Affirmation of Faith

continued, Mary Boyd, Maxine Van Norden and Margaret Smith, it was well that the screen remained.

Then there were the pleasant surprises. One Monday morning we had to get special permission of the CO to send a check to the American Bible Society in the amount of $800. The rules of the Chapel Fund allowed no check to be written for more than $200.00 without the CO's permission. One of the pilots had given a check for $700.00 in a special collection for the Bible Society.

One evening during a confirmation class, I said that our belief in salvation stipulates that anyone who trusts Jesus as Lord and Savior is forgiven all sins and is entitled at death to entrance into Heaven. One cute little teenager exclaimed, "Really?" One got the idea that for her it was too good to be true. My reply was "Absolutely!" She seemed to experience genuine relief, so much so that I wondered on what basis Satan had been tormenting her. Yet I rejoiced with her because my experience had been similar.

Rhode Island was America's most Catholic state, so we had many Catholics who asked for Quonset or Quonset home-ported ships to be near home. The Saturday evening Mass was often standing room only. I attended a Confirmation at which Bishop Kelly announced to those being confirmed, "I am now going to give you the Holy Spirit. It will not be necessary, therefore, for you to go anywhere and tarry to receive the Holy Spirit." When I met him after the Confirmation I remarked that it sounded as though he had charismatics in mind. He admitted this. I learned that there was a strong charismatic Catholic group in Providence that had taken over a run-down parish and revitalized it, particularly the school.

Providence College, owned by the Dominicans, was the scene of a significant event for me. The President, Father Haas, invited me to meet a delegation of European Orthodox bishops, then in charge of some of the churches mentioned in the New Testament. I was particularly thrilled to meet the Bishop of Philadelphia. I was also invited to the dedication of a new Orthodox Church in Providence. It was on the estate of a wealthy man who had a turntable in the multi-car garage, which allowed a car to be turned around to face outward so one would not have to back out of the garage. It was there that I met Archbishop Iakovos, Archbishop of the Greek Orthodox Archdiocese of North and South America.

An event that I attended involved both the Catholics and the Orthodox. At the Catholic Cathedral, there was a celebration of the lifting of the mutual excommunications of these two churches that took place in the eleventh century. My primary contact with the Orthodox was Father Theodore Baglaneas, who had relatives working for the Kennedys at Hyannis Port. He wanted to come into the Navy as a chaplain, but he could not get the permission of his bishop. I still have an icon of Mary and Jesus that he gave me.

The Catholic organist, Mrs. Boisvert, arranged for a Catholic choir in Providence to join with our choir in singing the "Seven Last Words" of Jesus from the cross. Since the Catholics already knew the music in Latin, we decided to learn it in Latin, so were able to sing it on Maundy Thursday in our chapel. In return we learned more Latin music for the Benediction of the Blessed Sacrament, which we sang in their church. Signs over the confessionals in the church were in French.

One very interesting activity was Marion's and my involvement with the classes at indoctrination for chaplain's school in Newport. Each class came to Quonset for helicopter familiarization. It was assumed that they would have needed to go from ship to ship via helicopter, using a sling that we called the horse collar. On a specified day each member of the class would be lifted from the landing pad and then returned to it. Following the exercise, we had them come to Quarters J for ham biscuits and spiced apple cider tea, a concoction served hot, containing also pineapple juice.

We would sit around telling sea stories, answering questions and hearing what the students were most concerned about at the time. Since I had been in for over 20 years, there were many questions. I particularly remember the joshing taken by a chaplain who had asked for active duty so he could go to Vietnam, Vincent Cappadono. When he posthumously received the Congressional Medal of Honor we could say we remembered him "when." For the rest of my time on active duty I was running into those chaplains who had visited Quarters J.

An Affirmation of Faith

Because of my experience at Menninger, I was invited from time to time to teach a class at Newport. I really felt as though I belonged on the staff, although I never asked for duty there. Chaplain Kelly came up for a graduation while he was Chief of Chaplains traveling commercial, so we picked him up at the Providence airport. The next day he wanted to leave before his scheduled flight, so he asked me to see if Admiral Massey would send him down or if one of the squadrons might have something going. Admiral Massey's plane was promised for another flight and no squadron had anything going to Washington.

When I reported this to Chaplain Kelly, he was keenly disappointed and I was acutely embarrassed. Then providentially VX-6, called a C-130, was going to take some gear to Admiral Bakutis, so Chaplain Kelly got his ride and I owed a big debt of gratitude to VX-6.

In addition to the changes of command, all the squadrons had mass nights, banquets, and other occasions at which a chaplain could be called upon for prayer. I remember one banquet VX-6 had, at which I offered the invocations, when the CO turned to me privately and asked if I would say a few words since there was no banquet speaker. I gladly agreed. It was an opportunity to reciprocate for the ride for Chaplain Kelly.

I was intrigued by the mission of VX-6 to support the South Pole forces. I liked the C-130 they flew. They could land on snow and ice or on a carrier deck. Their safety record was superb. It was not hard to collect a few pertinent thoughts. I told of one of the squadron petty officers I had in counseling who so often mentioned a shipmate of his that I wondered why. He said it was because they were walking along one day at the South Pole and he fell in a crevasse. This friend caught him on his way down and pulled him out, indubitably saving his life.

One of the most pleasant experiences at Quonset was living in officers' circle. The Admirals had quarters elsewhere, but the rest of the most senior officers lived on the Circle, with the chapel across the street from the entrance and the club a block away from the only other exit. A path led to the area where the chaplain Navy Relief Sunday School building was. It was a converted barracks that accommodated us very well. When they were in season, I picked an apple from a tree in our back yard and could eat it by the time I got to the office. One day somebody asked me what I had against doctors.

Fast friendships were formed there. The Browns, our next-door neighbors, invited us to Pensacola years later to participate in their repetition of their marriage ceremony after 35 years. The Hennars and Metzgers got with us when we moved to Washington. I found one CO, CAPT Scarpino, in San Diego, and another, CAPT Hardakar, in Washington. The cat from Mrs. Scarpino was named D.C. after the Disney Darned Cat.

There was another housing area for officers, attached mostly to fleet units, called Dog patch. It bore no resemblance to the town of the same name in the Al Capp cartoon.

Marion and I both registered at the University of Rhode Island for evening classes. In one class in Juvenile Delinquency, the assignment was to determine the incidence of juvenile delinquency in the census tract in which we lived during the previous year. We found there was not a single case of juvenile delinquency in our tract, which included Quonset housing. For years afterward, I cited this fact to argue that the military presence fostered good citizenship and a law-abiding atmosphere.

Quonset was my only assignment at which church attendance increased in the summer months. There were summer homes adjacent to Quonset housing that were occupied by the owners after school closed. Our chapel was very convenient for them. We expected to see them every summer, only to lose them every fall. I used to call Quonset the poor man's Newport. In addition to the cooler temperature which was so valuable in the days before air conditioning, many people spent a lot of time in water sports.

There was one other senior Black officer, CDR John Anderson, a dentist who had bought his own house near the base. His wife, Toni, was the daughter of Dr. Vernon Johns, President of Lynchburg Seminary. Dr. Johns had given the baccalaureate address at my college graduation. Johns was a member of Abyssinia Baptist Church in New York, pastored at that time by Congressman Adam Clayton

An Affirmation of Faith

Powell. There were a few Black pilots and navigators in the squadrons that I have seen since in airline jobs.

Somehow it seems that our family was racially isolated as a general rule, which may be responsible for the minimal involvement in Black affairs during the impressionable years of the children. My younger daughter to this day has never had a date with an African American, never attended any kind of Black school and has a husband of French extraction. Until I left active duty we never had a Black next-door neighbor. There were Blacks in all of my ships and chapels, but in small percentages. I am listed as White on several of my annual physicals. I remember one day in counseling when the counselee said, "You know how it is, you are free, White and 21." I agreed with him, a little amused but happy that rapport had been established. I was not making a conscious effort to blend into the woodwork, and realized that I had not when a White seaman, who had been attacked because of his Black girlfriend, came in to complain about "those White cats."

I was also gratified when one of my junior chaplains came in disturbed; he had requested that his tour be shortened because I was the senior chaplain and he would rather not work for a Black. The truth was he had been tapped for a force chaplain's job that had just become available.

The chapel had clear windows, common in colonial style buildings. It seemed to me that it would be distracting to watch the flowers and shrubbery outside of the chapel or passing traffic from the other side. I decided to mount a campaign for stained glass windows. When the cartoons of the windows had been prepared, I took them over to the XO, CDR John Wunderlich who objected to my favorite one, saying, "That one looks too much like John Glenn." I had heard that Grace Episcopal Cathedral in San Francisco had installed such a window. I thought it quite appropriate for a Naval Station, although I admit it was not the usual subject type for a chapel.

As it turned out, the window project was scrapped by my relief, Dave Simmons, who called to tell me after I had gone to Washington. He concluded his conversation by saying, "And anything else I goof up that you started I will let you know." It was Dave's idea that such windows would spoil the colonial architecture. He also may have felt that his beard and the fact that he preached from the middle of the chancel attracted more attention than the view out the windows.

Nowhere else in my experience was there a finer Sunday school program. It was run by Norma Dollar, Ernie's wife. She recruited a staff of excellent teachers, conducted a training program for them and demonstrated a lot of skill in communicating. Some of the teachers attended the golfer's service, a welcome sight that time of the morning. Physical facilities were very adequate; there was no problem with supplies because of the fatness of the chapel fund. The youth program was vibrant also, largely due to the senior enlisted assistant, Bob Motley from Danville, VA, the last capitol of the Confederacy. He proudly wore his Confederate cap on picnics and other outings, but nobody seemed to be offended. I thought he looked good in it.

From Quonset we drove conveniently to the World's Fair at Montreal. I enjoyed hearing French spoken. but most of all we enjoyed the apartment we rented for $35 per night through a AAA reservation. The children were old enough to enjoy the international exhibits at the pavilions. I liked the ride on the boat that supported itself on a cushion of air.

We often made trips to Boston; we made the historical freedom trail walk and recommended it to visitors. The Chief of Chaplains of Norway, Borge Orsted, visited Quonset and preached at the chapel, wearing the pie-shaped pleated collar used by Lutherans in Europe. We took the Orsteds to Boston. They were interested in the statue of Bishop Phillips Brooks, author of "*O Little Town of Bethlehem*." A picture of the figure of Jesus standing behind the Bishop with a hand on his shoulder was taken by Mrs. Orsted for Mrs. Brooks. We also went up the Cape and saw what was left of Plymouth Rock and the replica of the Mayflower.

We made many trips to Newport, some recreational. A chaplain's wife, Helen Ray, was teaching in a private school there that had Groucho Marx's daughter as a student. Our Durham celebrity, Doris Duke, was there although we never saw her. The synagogue, which was one of the nation's oldest, had a letter from George Washington. One night I was trying to keep up with the service in Hebrew when a young fellow in a madras yarmulke came in late and asked me,

"Man, where are they now?" I had to admit that I didn't know. Our Hebrew teacher at Pittsburgh had warned us that he spoke the language with an Austrian accent, somewhat different from what one heard in the average synagogue.

The shortest route from Quonset to Newport was by automobile ferry. One of life's frustrations was to have to wait for another ferry when the first one filled up or pulled off just as you got to the pier. A group of employees at Quonset owned a large boat with which they commuted from Newport. They rented the boat and crew to party-goers on the weekends.

It was from Quonset that I went to my Dad's funeral. He was 72, the same age at which his father died, which may mean that I have three more years. At the time, I felt that the remarks of Rev. Cannon at the funeral were a little cold as he echoed the statement from Ecclesiastes that there is a time to die, and he had reached it, since he was retired and the children were grown. Years later, I used the same theme for an 80-year-old paralytic.

Just as had been the case in all previous duty assignments except Chaplain School, I had no desire to leave Quonset. When the Chief of Chaplains, Jim Kelly, called and offered me a new position in Washington or a tour in Vietnam, my impulse was to reply, "None of the above." But under the rule that a senior's slightest wish is to be interpreted as a command, I knew my days at Quonset were ending. Thinking that no special talent was needed for a Vietnam tour and that I felt eminently qualified for the Washington assignment, I opted for the position in Washington. The job was a new double-hated one, combining the old JA position as the Chief's Assistant for Plans with a new designation as the Chief of Naval Personnel's Assistant for Human Relations. I had not met Vice Admiral Benedict Joseph Semmes but had heard of him because of his admiration for an old boss of mine, Ed Slattery.

My opinion was that I had been uniquely trained for the human relations position, beginning with a graduate course in race relations, the year at the Menninger's Clinic, duty assignments in Asia, pre-and-post integration experiences in the Navy, membership in an integrated denomination and being former pastor of an integrated church. I was neither Black enough to be beautiful nor White enough to be right. Jim Kelly also told me to buy a house and forget about leaving Washington. Although we had to leave Washington in five years, we still have the house, now worth ten times its purchase price.

Bureau of Naval Personnel, Washington DC

Because one of our children was sick, I went to Washington alone house hunting and found a four bedroom, two baths, with an assumable 5½% mortgage the second day. I was tired of placing toilet tissue in four bathrooms at Quarters J anyhow. It was in the Hollin Hills development between Alexandria and Mt. Vernon, only 8 miles from the Navy Annex. The sellers, the Richmonds, had a son born the same day as Davey, who told the kids in school that David Richmond was his twin brother. The other Black family that lived in Hollin Hills was Dr. Johnson, who taught surgery at Howard Medical School, and his wife, the former Audrey Ingram.

When neighbors told Audrey a Black family was moving in, her response was, "Don't be telling me about it," until they told her "He said he had not seen you for 35 years." She came over to welcome us. The neighbor who sold me on the house was Joan Brackett, a graduate of the University of North Carolina who was married by Rev. Charles Jones. Rev. Charles Jones had been suggested as pastor of our Covenant Presbyterian Church in Durham when Rev. Cannon left because of his integrationist posture. I was led to Joan by Carolyn Holland, at whose wedding I was best man in Youngstown. Carolyn was teaching; her brother Simeon still runs the Washington office of Jet and Ebony. Her father was Executive Secretary of the West Federal Street YMCA in Youngstown and a founder of Alpha Phi Alpha Fraternity.

An Affirmation of Faith

Hollin Hills residents were mostly workers in the State Department, although our three closest neighbors were not. Mrs. Wells, out back, was a Christian Science Practitioner; Carl Mose, to our right, was just completing the statue of Stan Musial in his studio for the St. Louis stadium, and Jay Holmes to our left, was working at NASA. His wife, Bea, was an attorney at the Department of Agriculture.

Carl Mose had also done the eagle for the Air Force Academy. When Martin Luther King died, he came over with a small full-length plaster of him that he wanted to get a commission to execute. I contacted my friends at Tuskegee and my classmate E.G. Spaulding, head of personal accountants for the Rockefellers. I hoped a Rockefeller might give such a statue to Spellman or Morehouse. When I reported my failures to Carl, he assumed that his race was against him, so he said, "You can tell them my name is Mose." When Carl moved to Mexico City he sold me a plaster of St. Mark that a church commissioned but had not called for. I loaned it to Ruth, his wife, to use in shows of his work after he died.

Audrey moved from the neighborhood when her husband died. Roberta Flack moved into the only house on our circle with a swimming pool, thereby keeping us from becoming the sole surviving Black family. Jay Holmes was jogging around the circle twice, making a mile, hoping to lose enough weight to go into space. I followed suit because I was used to the exercise. One morning a dog from Roberta's yard surprised me by biting me on the elbow. I thought he was playing. After calling the health department, Marion and I went to see Roberta to tell her that the dog should be kept close for 30 days in case he had rabies. We admired her house and the two grand pianos, leaving with the promise that she would cooperate.

One of my failings is that, unlike God, I am a respecter of persons. Just the idea of working for the Chief of Chaplains was exciting to me and to be working for the Chief of Naval Personnel had me in orbit. I was at last one of the boys in the bureau. Jim had to be patient with me one day as I left for my weekly conference with Admiral Semmes. I asked him if there was anything that he wanted me to tell Admiral Semmes for him. He said, since you asked me, "No." This was a very shrewd answer because he could not tell how

An Affirmation of Faith

I would report anything from him. Then he asked, "What could you tell him that I could not tell him as Chief of Chaplains?" If Jim has been less magnanimous I would have been wrung out and hung up to dry. Months later one of the secretaries told me that I caused a lot of hate and discontent by my "Admiral Semmes and I" posturing.

Admiral Semmes was the soul of congeniality. As we began our conference he would say, "Let me tell you what you don't know." Then he would ask, "What have you got?" And I would move with great relish into a situation report, immanent plans, etc. After the first such conference, he concluded with "Have you got yourself a job?" "I have a job," I replied as I floated out.

I was also invited to the Chief of Naval Personnel's "Coffee Conference" on Monday mornings for the chiefs of the various divisions, mostly Captains, now practically all Admirals, some of them in separate commands as education and training. Captain Zimmerman was head of recruiting then and was first to report. On this day, he said he had not met his goal. The Admiral asked him what he was going to do. His reply was "Pray," and he could have said, "What else?" In any event, the quota was met by the next Monday.

When I had anything to add, I tried to be sure that it was pertinent and if possible humorous. On occasion, I felt that I had really scored, especially if the humor was of the sympathy gag type. In those days, the only service in which there was not a member of the Kappa Alpha Psi Fraternity of flag rank was the Navy. In fact, the Navy had no Black Admiral. *The Kappa Alpha Psi Journal* was supposed to feature me one month, but some wires got crossed and my picture was on the inside and Chappie James, Air Force General, was on the cover. The coffee conference really cracked up over this one.

Space was at a premium at the Annex as well as the Pentagon. A makeshift office was cut out of the passageway leading outside with a little cut off the last office in the suite. This gave room for three desks for Withers Moore, a secretary and for me.

For the first time in my life, I hired a secretary, Sandy Claggett, the first one I interviewed. She wanted a job for two years because she had gone to school to be an airline flight attendant, but was only 19 and could not legally sell alcohol. She was friendly, pretty, blond and very industrious. While she chewed gum and sat on her foot she could type for hours. I had a portable belt type Dictaphone that I carried home with me as well as on trips. Soon she was able to answer routine correspondences without my help and sign documents for me when I was away. I soon began to hope she would forget the airlines.

One of my jobs was the "Items of Interest," a newsletter from the Chief to all of the chaplains. I seized upon this right away as a vehicle for the human relations approach to the social problems we, and the whole nation, faced. I looked on the whole Chaplain Corps as a human relations task force led by the Chief of Chaplains. He had the policy of standing behind anything he signed, regardless of who wrote it. In civilian churches there was much controversy between those who felt that individual conversion was the path to social change and others who wanted change to come through social action programs. I believed the chaplains were uniquely fitted to work both sides of the street simultaneously.

One of the human relations crusades was for open housing within the vicinity of military installations. Chaplains were instrumental in persuading landlords to go for open housing when they had previously refused to do so. As I remember it, one chaplain got 75% of the refusals in his area to reconsider.

I considered it significant that chaplains had always been on the cutting edge of improved human relations. Chaplains were associated with the elimination of flogging in the pre-Civil War Navy. Religious services were integrated long before mess hall, wardrooms and berthing areas were. White clergymen served as pastors of Black churches and still do; to a lesser extent, the reverse is true, even though the most segregated hour in America is 11:00 a.m. Sunday mornings. At 3 p.m. or 7 p.m. there is more interchange as choirs visit in other neighborhoods and guest preachers go into other pulpits.

Opportunities for chaplains to do a lot of mixing were limited only by their imaginations. I felt they could do all kinds of bridge building between the subcultures and the dominant culture. They could learn the language of the ghetto, become familiar with its sights and sounds, bring church parties to ghetto churches, working parties to ghetto community service institutions and participate in fund raising for community uplift. Many of them did these things, so I passed the word around.

One of the main thrusts of the human relations effort was the Minority Officer in Recruiting Effort (MORE). To support this I made myself available to Black colleges and seminaries without cost to the institutions. Thus began my annual trek to Tuskegee to preach in that beautiful chapel. The recruiting districts were eager to book me for several days of TV and radio interviews, banquets scheduled for clergypersons, business executives, school administrators and other mostly Black community leaders. I had the double appeal of being the Navy's senior Black and a clergyperson, the natural leader of the ghetto.

The Navy went all out on the MORE program. Black Officers who participated in it received a letter for their service jackets from CNO to the affect that it was understood that the duty was not career enhancing, but the project was of such high priority to the Navy that they should be commended rather than penalized for the time taken from the usual career pattern. Off hand, I can remember three Black officers who were working full time for MORE in those days who later made Rear Admiral, Norm Johnson, Ben Hacker and Bob Toney.

Bob Toney invited me to accompany him to pay a call on Carl Rowan (the news columnist who recently shot an intruder). He featured Bob in his syndicated column as a person who deserved a lot more credit than he was getting for his efforts in recruiting Black officers. He told how he was an officer of the deck at the age of 17 and what tremendous responsibility it involved. Sam Gravely, the first Black Admiral, had been a personal friend since his days as a LT at sea in Sasebo. He had been promoted to CAPT the year after I was promoted, and I thought it best for him to be the first Admiral for several reasons. In the first place, I had been passed over for CDR. I honestly could not say that I was the best candidate the Chaplain Corps had at that time. In fact, from the time I became eligible until I became too old, no chaplain was picked who was not superior to me in many ways, in my opinion. Although it would have been a good public relations gesture and helpful for recruiting minorities to pick me, Sam was a better choice because Blacks were caught up with power in those days. I was many times asked if I commanded a ship.

Then there was the likelihood that if I had been picked, there would be a long time before another Black would have a chance. Carroll Chambliss, who was not too many years junior to me, had been promoted in due course as had Sam. Carroll was in a Black denomination, African Methodist Episcopal, the church of our first Navy Black chaplain, J. Russell Brown, and had a son, Chris, playing first base for the Yankees. Carroll was quite disappointed in not being selected for flag rank, but it left intact the history of all the services in having never selected a Black chaplain past the 0-6 level. If times had been different, I believe the Army would have selected John Deveaux in World War II. I am completely at a loss to explain why the Air Force did not select Simon Scott, who served with distinction in all four of the major commands, which would have been comparable to a Navy Chaplain holding the Atlantic and Pacific Fleet, Chief of Naval Training and Senior Marine Corps billets, a feat I cannot remember any chaplain doing.

One day Chaplain Dennis Kinlaw, of the Chief's staff, said to me, "Dave, the way things are going the Navy is going to have to pick a Black Admiral soon. You had better get yourself an operational job." I agreed with his analysis of the climate of public opinion but explained my preference for Sam. He accepted this. A facet of my personality also was incongruent with flag rank. Another Chief of Chaplains, Frank Garrett, was asked if he intended to have the senior chaplain in each Naval district act as district chaplain. He answered, "By no means, there are some senior chaplains who have an indifferent attitude toward leadership." I was present when he said this and assumed he was talking about me. I have the Jeffersonian attitude that the government governs best that governs least, so I think it logical that the supervisor supervises best who supervises least. It is an illogical position really, because I am quite gratified when someone under my supervision assumes the leadership role.

One of the hottest items in the MORE program was the establishment of Naval Reserve Officers Training Corps at a predominantly Black college, to be followed by possibly four additional ones. Spearheading the effort was CDR Rives R. (Rip) Taylor who so captivated President Thomas of Prairie View that this school pulled out all the stops to get the first unit, including a pilgrimage to Washington. Prairie View did get the first unit and Rip went to be professor of Naval Science. Prairie View already had an Army unit that was doing very well and which cooperated with the Navy enthusiastically. President Thomas was as pleased as punch, delighting to have the Navy march in parades and appear at community functions.

At the same time, I was anxious to have a unit at my alma mater, North Carolina Central University. My nephew, C.G. Kearns, was president of the student body, so the students voted in favor of it. Dr. Albert Whiting, the chancellor, had come from Morgan, where my cousin's wife ran the student union. Dr. Whiting also had his Ph.D. in sociology from American University. Norfolk State was trying for the unit also. One of the apparent problems with Norfolk State, we thought, was its location in a Navy town. NCCU got the nod and Sam Gravely made the commissioning speech.

NCCU proved to be a disappointment. Neither of my nephews would affiliate because the student loan paid the same amount without the drills. They were more affluent than some students because their father was a deceased Presbyterian Minister, entitling them to funds from the Presbyterian Board of Pensions and Social Security. After some unsteady years, the unit was disestablished. Norfolk State got an Army unit, which grew so that I was told that the only institution with more cadets in training was West Point.

Since then it has been hard to motivate me to contribute to scholarship funds at NCCU, when I think of the many thousands of dollars that would have been available through NROTC. I have also wondered if a Navy unit at Norfolk State would have had the spectacular growth the Army unit experienced, not having Col Howard Williams and Col George Lampkin.

There was one stormy episode at Prairie View. Rip was relieved by CAPT Francis Xavier Brady who had come from the Harvard Unit. He related unusually well with Blacks. I was at a party at Prairie View one night when someone started to tell a Black joke. A visitor tried to interrupt the joke by pointing at CAPT Brady, whereupon the locals reassured him that CAPT Brady was one of the guys. He and President Thomas had disagreements.

Dr. Thomas was a no nonsense type in spite of the era of protests and student violence. He told me of two student delegations that came to him and his responses to them. The first group came to ask for Black studies in the curriculum. His answer was that the curriculum was full of engineering courses but the Black Studies could be added. He asked for their preference as to whether they would go in the 1st, 2nd, 3rd, 4th, or 5th year, since the four engineering years would need to remain intact. The second group had just heard that Howard University had made ROTC optional; they wanted it optional at Prairie View. The president agreed that there would be two options, either take ROTC or go to some other college.

This kind of approach seemed to CAPT Brady to be inviting trouble, so Dr. Thomas told me when there was a protest and a fire was set. Dr. Thomas sent a message to Washington asking for the removal of the professor of Naval science. CDR Jerry Thomas, a Harvard graduate and the senior Harvard alumnus in the Navy, was moved up from the XO position. The storm blew over. Jerry was later promoted to CAPT and then Admiral, after picking up a Ph.D. at Yale. He is now American Ambassador to Kenya, although he majored in Russian at Harvard and is a qualified interpreter.

Very helpful in the minority recruiting campaign was the National Naval Officers Association. LT Kenneth H. Johnson, USN, in 1970, while serving as Advisor for Minority Affairs at the U. S. Naval Academy, sought methods to improve minority interest and find qualified candidates. CAPT Emerson Emory, CAPT Claude Williams, CDR Emanuel Jenkins, CWO James Harris and LT Johnson began discussing an organization. In 1972, NNOA was founded in Annapolis. I attended the organizational meeting in Annapolis and was happy about the new vehicle to assist in the recruiting and in the professional success of Black officers. The Organization is still vital today, officially recognized as valid by the Department of Department, as is the Navy League, and supported by Black Captains and Admirals as well as the recruiting command.

One stable and continuing influence behind the whole movement was Ms. Esther Boone, recently deceased. She knew everybody, kept up with everything, offered encouragement to the young officers and camaraderie and sage advice to the elders. She told me years ago that if any of the young officers made Admiral, Ben Hatcher would.

The pivotal figure in the whole structure was LCDR William S. Norman, a native of Norfolk and graduate of Norfolk State. Bill had breakfast with Admiral Zumwalt, Chief of Naval Operations every Thursday morning. He told me that he had never made any proposal to CNO that he had not replied, "Fine, let's do it." Knowing this would be the response made him do his homework extremely well. Bill was one of the most, if not the most, impressive persons I ever met. His diction was flawless, his presence commanding, his wife unusually beautiful and his El Dorado unexpected.

Some of the Zumwalts policies did not go down well with some elements in the Navy. Some commanding officers felt that their prerogatives were being pre-empted when a non-rated sailor could call the Chief of Naval Operations on the telephone and supposedly put his commanding officer on report. Permission was granted to use CNO's picture on a T-shirt. In general, the Blacks were in agreement that the Big Z was the best thing that ever happened to the Navy.

When I met him, I was glad that I was not in contention for Admiral because I felt so inferior to him. He asked me how I was doing on my Ph.D. program. I said that I was having a hard time. He said, "Really." I got the notion that what he was asking was how anybody could have a hard time in school. Certainly he never did. One of my memorable experiences in Vietnam was having a Sunday Service on his front porch in Saigon. The other is the night Bill Norman woke me up to read his message to the Admiral's selection board, which asked the board to take a good look at minorities and specialists like communicators. Sam Gravely was the only Black and a communicator. Bill said CNO told him the only thing further he could have done would have been to put Sam's name on it.

There were stories going around of COs being relieved of command for not getting with the equal opportunity program. Bill was offered a promotion to CDR if he would soften the thrust. At one high level meeting, when Bill was detained elsewhere momentarily, CNO told the waiting brass that he did not want to start the meeting until LCDR Norman arrived. Bill soon realized that he had better head for the hills when CNO left the Navy, which he did.

An Affirmation of Faith

Although I have heard much talk of the good old Zumwalt era, I have seen nothing in print about a Zumwalt backlash. Yet bell-bottoms have come back, CNO is not on T-shirts, and stories of COs being relieved for negative attitudes about equal opportunity are no longer going the rounds. Instead, one hears of minority junior officers being thrown off ships, minority officers receiving lower fitness reports, being passed over for promotion and then released. In frustration over my inability to help them I can only say, "I used to know the powers that be, but they went," and remind myself that the souls of the righteous are still in the hands of God, where no evil can befall them. The backlash does ruin lives and careers but not souls.

Before coming East, I had met a warrant officer in the Marine Corps, James E. "Johnny" Johnson, in California. He was superintendent of Bob Warren's Sunday school at El Toro. He retired, sold insurance in the millions, then raised money for Ronald Reagan's campaign for governor. Richard Nixon brought him to Washington in the number two slot in Civil Service. Bill called me one day for my opinion of him, which was the greatest. He became deputy Assistant Secretary of the Navy for Manpower, with a four star flag on his sedan. To go from Marine Corps steward to Four Stars just blew my mind.

Johnny was unusually friendly. During the lunch hour at the Pentagon he used to roam the corridors looking for strangers. When he found one, he would extend his hand and say, "I am Johnny Johnson; I want to be your friend." He eagerly participated in a Pentagon Bible class and accepted invitations to speak at religious conventions. His son joined the Marine Corps but never finished basic training at Quantico, dying at Bethesda Naval Hospital of throat cancer. He had led 17 of his buddies to Christ before his death. Bob Warren and I were at his funeral. He had been sworn in by the Commandant, USMC, at which time Johnny said, "It isn't every day that someone gets sworn in by the Commandant." The Commandant replied, "It isn't every day that a son of a deputy assistant Secretary of the Navy joins the Marine Corps."

Later on TV, likely Shakarian's Full Gospel program, Johnny told how someone tried to bug his wife, Juanita, by asking, "Where was your God when your son was dying at Bethesda?" Juanita answered, "The same place He was when His Son was dying on that cross for you and me." Johnny told me he got 3600 letters of appreciation for relating that incident.

Although we maintained our mutual admiration society, Johnny and I did each disappoint the other on one occasion. He called one day, wondering if there could be a way of having Bob Warren assigned to his staff. I told him "no way," that President Lyndon Johnson had tried the same maneuver but hadn't gotten to first base. When we heard that the Judge Advocate Corps reorganization plan had billets for four flag officers, we wanted the same allowance so that the two fleet chaplains could be Admirals, as their counterparts were. I went high-tailing it to Johnny Johnson to get his help. He said we could try if we wanted to, but he could not see it happening because the billets would have to come at the expense of line officer billets in the allowance. He said, "You might get one but don't hold your breath." As it happened the lawyers did not get theirs either, and we actually lost one of the two we had when we shifted one flag to Hawaii, then his relief to Norfolk. Admiral Zumwalt said that made it appear we didn't need the billet if it did not make any difference where it was located. We had to pull every string we had to get the billet back. Actually, others in the Chief's office and I suspected that if we got the two extras, we stood a good a chance of getting picked. I could have convinced myself that I was the fourth best chaplain since I was holding the number 3 job.

Since there were no Sunday responsibilities attached to my Washington work, I was at liberty to preach at local chapels and churches. There were two churches at which I was almost a fixture, the Garden Memorial Presbyterian Church in Southwest Washington, White, and the Tabor Presbyterian Church in northwest Washington, Black. The legal officer in the Navy Annex, CDR Perkins, was an elder in the Garden Memorial Church and engaged me for an extended period until a new pastor was found. I served the Tabor Church until a pastor was found in Rochester, NY, then again after he dropped dead at a graveside ceremony. The Rochester Church was Trinity Presbyterian, where R. Nathaniel Dett, and later Cab Calloway's mother, played the organ.

My brother-in-law, Charles Kearns, was pastor there when Marion and I married. Rev. Salmon's widow, Joan, entered the ministry, married again and was elected Moderator of the Presbyterian General Assembly.

St. Luke's Episcopal Church, in the Wellington area, was not far from our house. The rector had been a Seabee and still wore a crew cut. He invited me to preach for him and said I could play any role in the church that I cared to. Our daughter Evangeline was confirmation age, and since there was no current class at National Presbyterian, we enrolled her at St. Luke's, where she was confirmed by Bishop Smith. When Mae reached confirmation age, there was a current class at National so we enrolled her. The Episcopal ceremony was meaningful to me as I remembered Bishop Penick of North Carolina doing confirmation in St. Titus Church in Durham. I think I was there when Marion was confirmed. I remember sitting with Mae in National Church watching her caress the long stemmed red rose that she held, a precious memory.

The Senior Minister at National invited me to come on his staff as an assistant. He had cleared it with his Session. Although I did feel honored, since it was the highest position in the church I had been offered, I had serious misgivings. In the first place, I was not retirement eligible for full pension. Then I had been given authorization to go for my Ph.D. at American University at the Navy's expense, and so fulfill a nearly lifelong ambition, which I could hardly do if I left the Navy. Then, although Dr. Elson did not say so, I suspected the Session believed that I would attract a large number of Blacks to National. I really did not want this kind of obligation hanging over my head. What if it didn't work out, what would I do, where would I go? So I forewent the opportunity to work for Dr. Edward L.R. Elson, baptizer of President Eisenhower, a remarkable preacher and a warm person. National did not hire a Black assistant. My assumption was maybe unwarranted.

Perhaps my real problem with National was that in recruiting for the Navy, I had so brainwashed myself that no other life would do. I had made a complete turnaround from the World War II days when I put USNR behind my name with the "R" twice as large as the "USN." In attitude I had become a lifer in the sense of MacArthur, with his 50 years active duty, and the eternal Rickover, with his congressional promotions after his retirement, to have him remain on active duty.

Having been elected to the board of corporators of the Presbyterian Ministers Fund, the oldest insurance company in America and perhaps the whole world, and being the only military person on the board, I was invited to make the speech at the annual banquet. I decided to cast the speech in the form of an annual report to the stockholders on the Navy's stewardship of the taxpayers' resources and to begin it with a sea story told by Stan Salisbury about John Paul Jones, who replied "I have just begun to fight" when asked by the British CO to surrender. As Stan told it, there was a grizzled Marine down in the hold, who had been cut every way but loose, who heard Jones' statement and marshaled the strength to comment, "Some Navy birds never get the word."

Using as a title, "Stand By to Repel Boarders," I pictured the Navy doing this in the face of the threats from foreign attacks and the threats from internal attacks on morality and religion. After the speech, Dr. Helferich of Ursinus College said he would give me an honorary Doctor of Divinity Degree if I would give that same speech at the Ursinus baccalaureate in June. I said, "Sold."

So we went to Collegville, PA where the red carpet was rolled out daily. Davey was the first member of the family to have his shoes shined by a college President. When I found that the commencement speaker was to be William F. Buckley, I ventured the comment that maybe the school was a little conservative. Dr. Helferich said, "Wait until I tell you who it was last year, Al Capp, and at the request of the students too." Al Capp used to call Buckley "William Fast Buckley" in his "Lil Abner" comic strip. I found him to be very fast on his feet, sitting entranced as he spoke. Since I was sitting on the platform behind him, I could see him rise on his toes as he was swept up in his own propositions. I was left thinking that he could think circles around the average person.

Because Bob Warren had recently sold an article to *Naval Institute Proceedings*, I sent a copy of "Stand by to Repel Boarders," after having it copyrighted. They told me to cut it in half, which

An Affirmation of Faith

I did, and received a check for $200. Since then I have used that speech many times.

The usual pitch while on the recruiting circuit was the assertion that everything Blacks wanted out of life could be found in the Navy: job security, guaranteed upward mobility, housing, health care, education, financial independence, social status and opportunity for religious expression. I challenged them to come up with any need that the Navy did not supply on an equal opportunity basis, regardless of race, creed, or color. After holding forth on this theme in a luncheon in Philly, I received a letter from an attendee saying how it pained him to hear me stand up and lie like a rug. I asked him to name one, but never got an answer. I supplied this speech to Sam Gravely, who used it in Columbus.

Before religious audiences, I would picture the Navy as the nearest approximation I knew to the Kingdom of God, using the VALLEY FORGE as an example, with about 2,000 men living elbow to elbow, sleeping inches apart, eating, playing, working and worshipping together within a space of 800 feet. At a seminar in Washington when Clifford Alexander, Black Secretary of the Army, was bemoaning the disparity between what America was like for Blacks and what it should be, I piped up that his ideal picture sounded just like life in the Navy. He fired back, "How many Black Admirals have you got?" My easy reply was that I was the senior CAPT and was not even in the zone yet. He wasn't convinced either. I think I made things sound too good.

My recruiting tours did result in some hostility. On a Pittsburgh talk and call in show, there were no calls from the listening audience. At the church in Chicago where Jesse Jackson was speaking, I was refused admittance because of my uniform. The usher at the door said, "Brother, you have kinda got on the wrong clothes to come in here." I have no evidence that this was Jesse's policy. In Minneapolis a fellow said, "At least I am glad you are making all that bread."

In California's Bay Area I got even more attention. In a press conference at the 12th Naval District office a reporter from the *San Francisco Chronicle* asked me what I thought of the Black Panthers. I said that I admired their discipline, military structure and felt that they could be quite useful in Vietnam. The paper ran a two-column header on the first page of the second section, carrying my picture and reading, "NAVY CAPTAIN SAYS LET THE PANTHERS FIGHT THE KONG." The Marine officer then accompanying me was ordered not to be seen with me. The Marines had been trying to project a human relations picture of aid to orphanages and schools, etc. The Navy PIO thought the incident was serendipitous with the kind of coverage we could not pay for and so informed Jim Kelly in Washington. The local press was assured that I was not in the area recruiting Panthers, who were not qualified for Naval Service, but I was looking for anybody who qualified.

I was sure to put the chain on my hotel room at night. A radio talk show called and lamented over the air that I as a clergymen was taking a belligerent position; a supposed Panther on the air with him said, "It's a damn shame." Edwina Thomas, a now deceased friend in Milwaukee wrote, "I hope you are not in trouble." In any event, it was comfortable not to be in the running for flag rank.

It seems that I have a penchant to be intrigued by the spectacular abilities of those whose ministries are in such striking contrast to mine. One of those persons, Harold Menges, held the training job in the Chaplain Division at the time. I had first heard of him when he was sent to Key West because the Navy wanted a good preacher at the chapel since Harry Truman often went to church there. In 1957, I met him when he was at the Amphibious Base, Coronado, CA and I was chaplain with PHIBRON-1. He took a chapel with an average attendance of 17 and increased participation to over 400. He told me that at the Submarine Base in Pearl Harbor he had to have three Christmas Eve services to accommodate everyone and that five Southern Baptist Churches had been built in Honolulu to accommodate the overflow from his chapel program. I thought he should be sent to Chaplain School and that a monograph should be done on his ministry. He was called the Billy Graham of the Pacific.

Most of the people I talked to about him said the important thing was his transparent sincerity and commitment to his work. He would not participate in any collateral duties, a position that did not set well with some COs. In fact, the CO of PBIBBASE wrote a bad fitness report for him and showed it to the District Chaplain,

Eddie Harp, former Chief of Chaplains. Eddie said it was the first bad report he had seen based on a chaplain doing his work. I do not know what happened to that report, but Harold was picked up for CAPT that year, two years early.

Harold gave me a briefing on salient features of his ministry. In the first place, he preached 45-minute sermons, without apology. He did preach with conviction and was able to hold interest that long. His church bulletins were tastefully printed instead of being duplicated. He used the highest-ranking ushers he could get. His Coke bill for Sunday was more that the operating budgets of many chapels. Another chaplain told me that he kept a card file of everyone who had participated in one of his chapels. On arriving at a new duty station, he informed all of his following in the local area. My commodore had been in one of his previous chapels, so he went to the PHIBBASE chapel instead of the flagship service.

Since the training assignment included the Chaplain School, I thought Harold would make the Menges plan a part of the curriculum, with appropriate textbook, the rest of us could share. It never happened. Later I thought the Menges Plan would make a good subject for a Doctor of Ministry dissertation, but never did anything about it. So I am partially to blame that this technique is lost, as was the technique of Paganini.

Harold did create some hate and discontent, however. He was president of a selection board for Captains, which selected two persons less than the number authorized. It was rumored that two chaplains were to be deep selected, Withers Moore and John O'Connor. It appeared then that Harold was definitely opposed to such a maneuver and was saying that he could not find any others above, in or below the zone fully qualified. These two were promoted in due course and both made flag as well, so they were terrific chaplains. I heard Jim Kelly was furious. He asked me how I liked the board results. I replied that there was something missing.

The first Chief of Naval Personnel with which I had a disagreement was VADML Charles Duncan, and the difference of opinion came over the NROTC units at predominantly Black colleges. He held the logical position that graduates of such collages could not compete successfully in the Navy with graduates of Harvard, Yale,

Princeton, Chicago and Stanford. I did not have the presence of mind to say that they would not need to because we got so few officers from such institutions. My argument was based on my personal experience of finishing an 11th grade high school, an unaccredited college and a small seminary at which I finished at the top of my class because I worked harder, as God gave me strength.

In fact, in the seminary three years, I had finished four years work, earning two degrees, S.T.B. and S.T.M. at the same time, writing two theses. I was told this had been done at one other time in the history of the school. My feeling was that any Black officer would know that he would have to try harder to make it anyhow, regardless of his college, because his cultural background deficiencies would be additional handicaps. Furthermore, according to the racist myth, only the super Black succeeds anyhow in a competitive situation. The Black who does not make an "A" flunks.

Although I cannot say Admiral Duncan bought my argument, I can say that we did set up the five planned units at the predominantly Black colleges. At Savannah State, a White student joined the unit and wrote a letter of appreciation for the opportunity, which he could not have found elsewhere. He was likely a local person who could not afford to attend a distant college, possibly even a marginal student who would not have been accepted elsewhere. In any event, we in Washington were happy to hear his story.

Admiral Duncan pleasantly surprised me with his request that I not say anything in my speeches around the country about the BOOST program. We sent marginal Blacks to this specialized training at Bainbridge and San Diego to improve their communication and math skills. He was afraid that Appalachian Whites would agitate to be included if they heard about it. This did happen, but not until the Blacks had been given a running start.

The CNP who really blew my mind however, was Admiral Watkins, who later became CNO. At a seminar for Black chaplains in Washington he informed us that he had a Black brother-in-law, a musician. This was certainly against the "code of the hills," and even then a matter not mentioned. I had visions of his having ruined his career by such a disclosure, but also the very warm feeling that we had a friend in court. I still hold him in highest admiration.

An Affirmation of Faith

It may be that I was not abreast of the times, because I was quite surprised when Admiral Charles Rauch White married the divorced wife of CDR Gordon Fisher. Both Gordon and Ester are Black. Then I heard of a Black CO, who, just after his change of command, exchanged marriage vows with the divorced wife of one of his White LTs. I also heard that COL Ken Berthoud, USMC, married a White four-striper nurse at Quantico after his divorce. And so, when some years later a White Navy veteran asked for my daughter's hand, I gave him both of them.

In addition to the recruiting, which took me away from the office much of the time, I was invited to join the CNO's drug abuse team, a kind of Paul Revere operation to warn the whole Navy of the danger of drug abuse. CAPT George Sult, an aviator, was CO of the unit; Ron Ruesch, a civilian, of NIS, and CDR Joe Ruesch, psychiatrist, were the other team members. We played before all-hands audiences in theatres throughout CONUS, WESTPAC and Europe. With his Hungarian accent and store of adult stories and jokes, Joe was easily the star of the show.

He was in the clean-up position, so the men left the theatres in stitches, hopefully having gotten the point that drugs were dangerous in addition to being illegal. At the time we were discharging thousands each year for drug abuse, so I had a sense of being involved in an important mission. Nevertheless, the earthy atmosphere of the presentation did not set well with some chaplains. It caused the second strike against me with Frank Garrett (the first being my "indifferent attitude toward leadership"). I told complaining chaplains that the effort was to communicate in terms the men understood that Joe was married to a Lutheran minister's daughter. It was Joe who convinced CAPT Sult that he should stop giving me credit for one ribald joke I had passed on to him from another chaplain. The joke was about a young Priest who was making extensive innovations in his parish to the displeasure of his Bishop. When he saw that the Bishop was unhappy with him he said the Bishop could crap in his hat. It seemed that the Priest's father was a heavy contributor to diocesan causes, so the Bishop said, "I can always get another hat."

CAPT Sult used to say he was happy to have a chaplain on the team because he knew some good jokes. This one he appreciated

An Affirmation of Faith

because he was Catholic. Then he would tell the joke, which embarrassed me because I did not in my own conversation use the expression "crap." The team members assured me "crap" was not a dirty word. Knowing he was Catholic, I was floored when CAPT Sult used the joke.

When I left the drug abuse team a chaplain replacement was not ordered. I was of course disappointed but not surprised. I remember best Joe's rejoinder to those who had tried to discount his advice because he had not used drugs himself. He said he had yet to find someone who refused a penicillin shot for syphilis because Joe had not had syphilis.

When Jim Kelly told me about my orders to Washington he had said, "Buy yourself a house because you can forget about leaving Washington." When I asked permission of Admiral Duncan to work on a Ph.D., he said only if I studied in Washington and if I signed an agreement to remain on active duty an additional five years beyond my obligated service. He said he did not like to send CDR's to school, much less CAPT's. I signed the agreement happily because I wanted to stay in the Navy until I dropped.

The tour in the Chaplain Division was three years; the postgraduate tour for the doctorate was ordinarily two years, so I had a new lease on life. One of my last important tasks was to try to persuade Admiral Duncan to give Jim Kelly the Distinguished Service Medal. Withers Moore told me that he wanted it. It did come through for him.

Marion had made a bookplate for Dr. J. Saunders Redding, head of the American Studies Department of George Washington University, when he was teaching at Howard University. Therefore, I applied at George Washington only to be told that Dr. Redding would be out of residence so no new students would be admitted. Then I applied in sociology at American University because my human relations work seemed to be closest to that field. I was admitted reluctantly because my transcripts showed only one course in sociology, a graduate course in rural sociology. Fortunately for me, the head of the admissions committee, Dr. Vaderslice, had been the dissertation advisor for Dr. Albert Whiting, then president of my alma mater.

Providentially, I was detached from the Chaplain Division in June, so I could begin classes in summer school when stress is lighter, students older and competition for "A's" not as keen. So I had a stack of A's when fall arrived. I had the advantage of not having to unlearn anything because my knowledge of sociology was abysmal.

We had just remodeled our house, adding a third bath, family room, bedroom, laundry and an office I intended to use for marriage counseling after my retirement. The latter became my study, on the opposite side of the house from the other bedrooms where my typing at 4 a.m. or use of the nearby bathroom would not disturb the sleeping members of the family. I reverted to my collage and seminary schedule of studying from 4 a.m. - 8 a.m. daily, except Sunday, and going to bed at 8 p.m.

Marion had received a station wagon for her birthday present so we were a two-car family again. There would be no car pool to American University as there had been to the Navy Annex. The wagon replaced a Renault Caravelle convertible for which I had paid $300. Marion disliked it because it blew her hair, but the kids delighted in it. They liked the Chrysler wagon also, which was fortunate since we kept it 14 years.

Although I had no military duties while in school and did not wear the uniform, I did attend seminars, funerals, dedications, dinners and filled speaking engagements as requested. I tried to "keep my hand in" as far as the Navy was concerned. My first priority, however, was to continue to get A's.

Providentially, my nemesis at Chicago, the German language, had just been removed from the requirements at AU. Since I had passed French on the Masters level at NCCU and the doctoral level at Chicago I registered for the AU cram course with optimism. The subject matter would be different this time. For sociology, there was a statistics requirement. Having never studied it, I enrolled at AU and at Howard University at the same time, assuming the two classes would reinforce each other, which they did. Then I enrolled in a social theory course at George Washington University for mutual reinforcement with a similar AU course, which helped further. To again help the cause, I got new glasses and took an Evelyn Wood

An Affirmation of Faith

rapid reading course in downtown Washington, in which I used my sociology texts as the reading material.

When I entered the cram class for the statistics exam, the teacher, Dr. John Smith, announced that the report that he had flunked ten of the sixteen who had taken it the previous year was erroneous; he had flunked twelve. I piped up, "Dr. Smith, I always thought that a teacher who flunks a student is like a doctor who kills a patient." Dr. Smith said, "I never thought of that."

Five of my classmates and I hired a tutor who had never lost a student in the statistics exam. She began by assuring us that we had nothing to fear. If we got into a problem with class work she would call Dr. Smith for clarification She met with us on Sunday afternoons, my first experience in breaking the Sabbath, which I justified by the ox in the ditch principle. I missed only one Sunday session, when I preached in the chapel at Tuskegee. There I tried to get some help from the head of the math department but Dr. Smith's problem for that week was too much for him.

The examination was the strangest I ever took. Dr. Smith said we could bring to the exam anything except a tutor. I got copies of the exams for the last four years, indexed them in a notebook according to the type of problem and felt I was ready for bear. I examined each problem that had a counterpart in the notebook to be sure a process was not reversed or different wording used before writing any answer. Dr. Smith sat at his desk and perused each paper passed in as the student waited for his grade. I floated out of there with my "A," hardly needing the car to get home, praising the Lord all the way.

Social research proved difficult for me, partially because of the use of statistics, and partially because it was beginning to appear that it would be difficult to find some area to investigate that would be somewhat new and interesting, that would yield the expected results with some statistical significance. I found Dr. Karen Paterson an avid teacher of research methodology, but she considered ten years as the normal amount of time to get a Ph.D. When I finally got the nerve to take my comprehensive in social research, I failed it primarily on my treatment of multiple regressions. Dr. Muriel Cantor told me that

I used the right words in explaining it, but it was apparent that I did not know what I was talking about, which was so true.

Another comprehensive I failed was sociology of religion, which I took orally. The straw that broke the camel's back was my assertion that Patrick Henry was a Presbyterian because I had read that his ideas came from a Presbyterian preacher that he heard regularly. Dr. Howard Vollmer, head of the department at the time, corrected me loudly, "He was an Episcopalian."

The real reason I failed that comprehensive was that Dr. David Ruth, whose class I had taken on the subject, declined to be one of the examiners. I had enjoyed his class from the moment he said, "Unless there is some objection everyone will get A's. We went to see "Jesus Christ Superstar" as a class, had a picnic at his house, read far out works of Normen O. Brown and listened fascinated to his accounts of his experiences. One day I was trying to console a classmate who had flunked some kind of examination. I remembered Dr. Ruth had told us he did not know anyone who read those examinations, so I told him about her. The next day when I asked her not to quote me, he said it was too late and that the exam would be repeated. I assumed, I then went on Dr. Ruth's list. One would think I would have known better than to tell an "out of school" tale, so I paid for it in six more months of preparation for another comprehensive.

Dr. Jill Gollin, who had done her dissertation on the Moravians, saw that I did not understand Dr. Vollmar's conceptualization, so she gave me some coaching and a list of questions and topics for study. I also got into a course in sociology of religion at Wesley Seminary, next door to AU. So the next time the comprehensive was more manageable.

My dissertation was a problem also. My intention was to do something involving Navy recruiting. Unfortunately, there was a feeling against any kind of military or governmental subject. The Camelot fiasco had soured tastes against such a project. It seems that the Camelot project was some sort of a study of a South American country, in which AU was prominent, and significant funds would be available. Somehow Congress got in on the act and charged that the project involved an attempt to change the governmental structure of the country being studied and that somebody at AU was cognizant of this. It was an embarrassing episode.

During my trips to Durham, I spent much time in visiting with Dr. Ray Thompson, a teacher at NCCU then stricken with multiple sclerosis. One day in discussing my dissertation problem Ray said, "I'll tell you what you should write on, anything they will accept." Somehow, I hit on the study of occupational aspirations of high school seniors possibly because of similar studies reported in dissertation abstracts. Dr. Cantor decided that such a subject was more in the field of social psychology and that I should switch from her as an advisor to Dr. Annabelle Motz, which I did.

Dr. Motz guided me through the process of writing an acceptable proposal. Then I could understand how Dr. Carol Wise had rejected me as a Ph.D. candidate at Northwestern University because he already had enough students to advise. My ignorance of the process of dissertation writing amazed me, as well as the amount of time Dr. Motz needed to spend with me. I have tried since then, to go all out for students I have advised in writing D.Min. dissertations, to in some measure compensate for the help I received.

Even with the new dissertation subject I was able to include military service as one of the vocational options. Of the two publications that came out of the dissertation, one of them was in a magazine of the Chief of Naval Education and Training, the other was in one of the Saga publications.

The boys in the Bureau were quite excited about my graduation and had a Navy photographer on hand. Relatives came from New York as well as Durham. My brother-in-law, Dr. Charles Proctor, then teaching at Meharry Medical College in Nashville, told me that I was the seventh member of the family to earn a doctorate. I am sure I was the oldest at graduation.

Jim Kelly was relieved as Chief of Chaplains by Frank Garrett. I was relieved by Ross Trower, who later became Chief. I asked to go to the Washington Navy Yard, but Frank wanted to send Bill Noce there to provide Episcopal coverage for Arlington National Cemetery. Bill had asked for Norfolk. Frank reached for the phone to tell Bill of his new duty while I was standing before his desk with what I considered a logical request, since an Episcopalian was stationed at the Bethesda Hospital at the time. I did not raise this issue and I did not know that an Army chaplain was doing the Episcopal funerals at Arlington, which I would not have mentioned if I had known it. Frank said I had been in Washington long enough, five years, so I needed to get out. Then I could return. I had heard John Vincer was thinking of retiring. It would have seemed logical to me for the Navy to have its own Episcopal chaplain available for Arlington in addition to the Army coverage. Bainbridge was only 80 miles away, so we did not feel uprooted.

Bainbridge, MD

The move was possibly the easiest we ever had. Quarters awaited us, so we leased our home through a realtor who lived in the neighborhood. Again, as in Quonset, we lived on the golf course; the road was called "Whiskey Gulch" because of the quantity of bottles in trashcans on Monday mornings. Again, the chapel was within easy walking distance of the house, which again had a base telephone with a government long distance leased line. There was a small hospital that had been much larger when recruits of both sexes were on board. Until recently, WAVES were in training but the males had been missing for some time. All over the station there were temporary barracks in various stages of decay. One fellow, who came to find where his berthing had been, said a tree had grown where his bunk had been. Bainbridge still had radio and nuclear power schools, but efforts were being made to move them also and close the station.

The problem with Bainbridge was that Maryland had lost its political clout in Congress by the loss of all the senior congressmen. States with more senior congressmen were clamoring for military activities within their borders. One day I saw Congressman Mills, the only moderately senior representative left, and asked about our chances. He said, "We are hanging on by our finger nails." We invited Congressman Bauman to speak to our Men of the Chapel breakfast. He accepted our invitation and delighted us with his speech, but he was serving his first term.

When I met the CO, CAPT Edwards, I jokingly remarked that he lived in the quarters that should have been mine, Quarters J, since J

An Affirmation of Faith

stands for Jesus and I lived in "J" at Quonset. He said that if I could get him Quarters "A" I could have J. "A" was a 17-bedroom house that had belonged to the headmaster of the Tome School, which had relocated. The Naval Academy Preparatory School was housed in the former Tome campus, now a part of the station. In the master plan for closing Bainbridge, the prep school would go to Newport, nuclear school to Orlando and the radio students to San Diego.

Meanwhile our teenage daughters and all other female teenagers on the station were happy to have the prep school students aboard, for whiskey gulchers was just across the street. The chaplains, too, were glad they were so near. I had two picked out for sons-in-law. Both found wives elsewhere.

The Bainbridge community was the most stimulating intellectually than anywhere else I was stationed in all my 37 years. The course at nuclear power school was only six months long but was said to be the equivalent of two years of college. The students were in most cases brilliant; some were geniuses. The same was true of the faculty. One of the officer students had majored in Chinese at the Naval Academy. It was my feeling that anyone who could learn Chinese could learn anything.

Again, as in Quonset, we had two choirs with a more rapid turnover, since the nuclear students were on board for six months and prep students just one year. A party for the choirs that I sponsored caused my tax return to be audited and the deduction of the cost of the party disallowed. In addition to choir members and families, I also invited all the station officers. The party was catered at our new home, Quarters J, by the officers club at a cost of $400. The IRS ruled that if the Navy required me to have a choir, an allowance for it would have been supplied. My argument was that a sociological survey revealed that the primary reason most people attended church was to hear the music, so I had to have the choir to sustain attendance. Chapel attendance was one measure of my effectiveness as a chaplain. So that was my last choir party featuring an open bar and steamboat round of beef. Thereafter, the fare was chicken and soft drinks.

Even though I did not get Quarters A for CAPT Edwards, he did let me have Quarters J. The Navy decided that senior officers who were drawing flight pay, whether they were in jobs requiring flying or not, could no longer enjoy this privilege. To get flight pay, their orders had to specify that flying was required. CAPT Edwards said, "So they want my flight pay, they can have it all." He retired to Pennsylvania. Since his relief, CAPT "Tad" Wilson, was already in the quarters of the CO of radio school and did not want to move. I was allowed to get into my rightful place.

One of the choir members, Jeanne McGuigan, wanted her two sons instructed for baptism. When George and Bruce had completed their classes, I told Jeanna I would arrange for them to be baptized at a local Baptist church since she wanted immersion as the form of baptism. Her reply surprised me: "Do you mean to say that the United States Navy has to borrow a baptistery, cannot afford one of its own?" In weeks, I was able to get a mail order baptistery installed in St. Pauls's Chapel and to have Jim Kelly come to Bainbridge for its dedication. I suspect that I have done more baptisms by immersion than any other Presbyterian chaplain. Only one unusual circumstance occurred with the use of the baptistery. The candidates wore white robes. I had not given any instructions on what to wear under the robes until one Sunday, as the wife of a sailor climbed out of the baptistery with red lingerie very plainly visible through the wet robe.

We never had it so good. At Great Lakes we had lived in a trailer 8 X 33 feet. Two rooms in Quarters J were 10 X 40, the living room and the master bedroom just above it, both with fireplaces. There were 8 bedrooms and 4 baths in the three floors of the house, a 2-bedroom apartment behind the garage. There was a circular driveway in front and out back. We played host to as many out of town relatives and friends as we could entice. Some made return visits.

Now that all the children were in school Marion returned to art teaching. With my brand new Ph.D., I began teaching sociology at Harford Community College. We did not realize it until later, but the Bainbridge years were our most affluent because the needs of the children were minimal and the on station provisions for support were economical. We had apple and pear trees in our yard. Chestnut trees grew on both sides of the main road. Walnut trees were in a new abandoned area. Fees at the riding stable, golf course, bowling alley were minimal. Sunday brunch at the club cost a penny for each pound a patron weighed, in my case $1.55. Extensive medical care was available at Philadelphia Naval Hospital. The free dental care included orthodontic care for dependents.

The atmosphere at Bainbridge would be more expected at an overseas station rather than one stateside. There was a feeling that we were all isolated from the rest of the world and thrown together for mutual support. Cecil County, in which Bainbridge was located, was a poor county with marginal schools, small towns and very active Ku Klux Klan. We sent the girls to the Tome School and then the West Nottingham Academy, a very old Presbyterian high school, dating back to the 1740s. One famous graduate was Dr. Benjamin Rush, who did surgery on Alexander Hamilton. Another who did not graduate was John Wilkes Booth. Even then dropouts were dangerous. For the protection of the girls, we installed CB radios in both cars and a base station at the quarters.

Providentially, we were not involved in a single incident. When the Klan was having some kind of meeting on a farm, belonging to the brother of one of the civilian workers on the station, a black sailor got a load of white sheets on his truck and parked it on the shoulder of the highway. He had a sign reading, "Sheets for Sale." The police came and persuaded him to leave because he had no vendor's license. I saw pictures one sailor had of a Klan parade. We felt like we were walking on eggs when we went outside the gate. The only pool Blacks could use for swimming was the Navy pool, as guests under certain conditions. The civilian pool belonged to a fraternal organization that prohibited Blacks from membership.

At Bainbridge, we had our first experience with a theatre group. Marion made sets and painted scenery. We supported it in other ways. Three of the stars were very prominent in the ministry at St. Paul's Chapel: Warrant Officer Larry Wild, who with his wife, Bainie, were mainstays of the Sunday School, LTJG Claudia Bailey, who taught at the prep school and sang in the choir, LT Frederic Laurence Uhlemayer, personnel officer for the station, member of the choir, and leader with Claudia of the youth.

Fred had assisted Catholic Chaplain John Patrick Fay in Providence as Protestant Lay Leader. I had met Jack Fay in 1952 at Great Lakes, where his moral guidance lectures were so popular with the recruits that they yelled for more when it appeared he was ending his presentation. He used to say Bishop Sheen copied him. Fred, too, was a very talented speaker. His dialog sermon with an Army Captain in our chapel was the best I had heard. Since he was planning to leave active duty, I suggested that he enroll at Pittsburgh Seminary where I was on the Board of Directors. I knew there were student apartments in which he and his mother, Mrs. Toni Yett, would be comfortable.

Fred preferred to attend the Episcopal Seminary at Cambridge, but when he wrote his bishop in Florida about it the bishop said he would not ordain him if he went there. So he did go to Pittsburgh, and afterwards returned to active duty as a chaplain.

The chaplains at Bainbridge were an unusually fine selection. Bill Vast, next senior to me, was the traditional American success story. His wife was a Marion also; they had married at age 17. When he was called to the ministry he had four children and was teaching school. He asked an old deacon if he should take the financial risk of becoming a student again. The deacon replied, "What the Lord orders he pays for." When I called Bill from Atlanta to tell him he had been selected for Captain he said "That's the best news I have had since I got saved." Bill's son and namesake became a Captain in the JAG corps.

Don Wilson, next senior to Bill, was an old friend from my days in Japan where he was a Lutheran missionary at the time. He came to the conclusion that he was not cost effective for the Lutheran Church, which could employ several Japanese clergy for what he cost. So he applied for the Navy while in Japan. He had quite a bit of artistic talent, a fine speaking voice, and was fluent in Chinese, Japanese and Vietnamese. He inaugurated the 0800 hour Lutheran Communion, which I continued after he retired by changing its listing from Lutheran Communion to Holy Communion, Lutheran Liturgy. I became so enamored of the Lutheran Communion number 4 in the contemporary liturgy publication that I also used it when I transferred to Naval Hospital, Portsmouth. Don was the only chaplain from Bainbridge who appeared at my retirement, having driven to Norfolk from Pennsylvania.

The Senior Catholic Chaplain was John Morley of New York, a veritable "Mr. Congeniality." He bought Bill Vest's Oldsmobile 98 as a gift for his sister. John had a serious heart problem, which we thought had caused him to miss promotion to commander. He was selected the next year, however, and soon afterward died a very happy chaplain. I went to New York for his funeral Mass, and was given the thumbs up sign by John O'Connor. Next to the coffin on a small table was John Morley's new hat with the scrambled eggs on the visor. John's sister wanted to know if I was Bill Vest, since she heard so much of him from her brother.

Our other Catholic Chaplain was Al Weir, formerly a high school principal in Massachusetts. After watching him do a moral guidance lecture using the blackboard, I dubbed him "the fastest chalk in the east." He also made par for 18 holes on the golf course. Every Saturday he was part of a foursome, which included the CO of the station, the CO of the Reserve Center and the CO of our computer unit.

When I arrived, the secretary at the chapel was Ruth Knaus, who soon retired and was relieved by Erma Fretz, who commuted from Oxford, PA. Bill called her the "Mother Hen." When we cautioned her about her chain smoking she always replied, "Only the good die young." Brenda Wilson was secretary in the annex to the chapel, which also housed Red Cross and Navy Relief, in addition to the Sunday school.

My "Man Friday" at the chapel was Lloyd Smith Crawford PN1, who commuted from Cochranville, PA. For us he was a one man decommissioning detail. He inventoried all of our property and equipment, published a list to be sent to all stations having chaplains, received requests for gear and arranged for it to be picked up, or shipped. He even found a home for the baptistery. He stood the last watch on the main gate the last day Bainbridge was open.

As at Quonset, I was vice president of Navy Relief. Mrs. Skaggs was the executive secretary when I arrived, but when her main volunteer left she soon followed, finding employment at Havre de Grace Hospital. Her replacement was Norman Duffy, the first male and the only one I have ever seen in that role. Not being married, he had a good bit of free time, some of which he used to help with the typing for my dissertation. He related to the chaplains so well that he was considered to be a member of the team. Chaplains had the prerogative of writing checks on Navy Relief for emergencies after the close of the working day. Since we all operated on the same wavelength, it was not necessary to tell sailors to come back after hours to pick up a check.

Norm's secretary was Jeanne Thompson, wife of CDR Thompson, superintendent of the Sunday school. CDR Thompson was very grateful to God for his military career, which began as a seaman apprentice, and for his physical survival. At sea as a bugler, he was directed to move his berthing spot to another compartment. Before he got around to it there was an explosion in that compartment that ripped up the spot where he would have been sleeping. Jeanne spent much time with the neurosurgeons at Philadelphia Naval Hospital. She had gone in to request a hearing aid only to find that she had a brain tumor. After surgery she was still saying, "All I wanted was a hearing aid."

St. Paul's Chapel had one blessing not available to many chapels, CAPT Bob Stankowski, CO of the Reserve Center. He came from a family of florists. By buying flowers wholesale and arranging them himself, he made the chapel a show place. At Christmas, poinsettias covered the chancel steps and much of the chancel. A cross-fashioned of white poinsettias was in the center of a blanket of reds. This arrangement lasted until Easter because Smitty (PN1 Crawford) considered himself a sort of understudy to CAPT Stankowski and faithfully saw to it that the poinsettias were watered properly and kept at the right temperature.

It boggles my mind to try to imagine how the station CO, Ted Wilson, and his wife, Betsy, could have been more helpful. They were behind everything that went on at the chapel. Ted and I jogged a mile before work five days a week. Betsy went with me to call on new arrivals in their quarters. I never tired of watching her sweep into the living room flashing a smile and saying, "I am Betsy Wilson and I came to welcome you to Bainbridge. I hope while you are here you will be coming to our chapel." Due to our rapid turnover, it took every Wednesday afternoon to keep up. Ted took me, and

An Affirmation of Faith

often Pierre LaBrun, president of the local bank, to the Boy Scout Executive meetings in various locations in Delaware and Maryland.

One day Ted called me to his office for a surprise. He handed me my fitness report and smiled. It was a masterpiece with the primary thrust that I should be selected for flag rank. He in effect said that I could walk on water and not get my feet wet. I said how grateful I was for his thoughtfulness and generosity, but he would not get his wish because John O'Connor was in the zone and would indubitably be selected. I told him of the saying to which I subscribed, "There are two kinds of chaplains in the Navy; there is John O'Connor and then there is everybody else." Whether a similar saying is going around about Catholic Cardinals, I do not know; but if I heard it, I would believe it.

Ted was disappointed, and asked, "So such things are determined beforehand?" My reply was, "In this case, yes." Then I mentioned how John was the architect of the character guidance program when he was a LT, how his CO's screamed bloody murder when he got change of duty orders, how his book on Vietnam had been sold out and how he went through the Ph.D. program at Georgetown like a dose of salts. Furthermore, the Navy was considered to be long overdue in promoting a Catholic Chaplain to flag rank.

The XO, CDR Gunnar Moors, and his wife, Judy, were neighbors when we lived on the Gulch. They helped us move to Quarters' J when it became available. Gunnar got me one day after department heads meeting by asking if he had permission to go to sleep in church since I had gone to sleep in the meeting. I told him anybody had permission to sleep in church; I was in favor of it. By doing so, a person was refreshed physically and spiritually too.

Their son, Carl, served with Davey as an acolyte in the chapel. In advent season we had an advent wreath fitted with candles suspended over the center of the chancel out of reach of their candle lighters. Smitty lowered it by pulley to a level at which they still had to stretch to reach the top of the candles. Usually they would brush the wreath itself, causing it to spin around slowly. Then they would circle with the wreath, attempting to light the candles. I was told that people came to church early to watch this merry go round. Davey and Carl became such fast friends that Davey was permitted to go to the public school with Carl the next year rather than the Tome School.

Judy was a nurse. She was quite valuable in the Navy Relief program because we did not have the two nurses with sedans as at Bainbridge. Much of the time of Navy Relief volunteers went toward preparing kits for newborns. There was some feeling against providing the kits for unwed mothers. Because all of the items were put into plastic buckets, they were at times referred to as "bastard buckets." Our position was that the kits were for the babies who were innocent and possible victims also. It was from Betsy that I learned to use the term, "Fat Pills," for cookies.

When I had been at Bainbridge only two years, I got a call from Frank Garrett, offering the Fleet Marine Forces Atlantic (FMF) position in Norfolk. He sounded excited about it, likely because that position made me what the Corps called a Major Claimant, a supervisor of a considerable group of chaplains dispersed over a relatively large area. He said I would be relieved by Bill Vest, which would mean the loss of a chaplain at Bainbridge...not to my liking. The FMF job had no chapel involved, so I called the incumbent Dave Humphries and asked him a foolish question, "What do you do?" He gave me a foolish answer that corresponded with what my question implied, "In the morning I read the morning paper, in the afternoon I read the afternoon paper."

I decided he wasn't pulling my leg completely because he was past the age for flag, as was I, so it was strange that the offer was not made to someone still in the running. To forestall any misunderstanding, I wrote a letter to Frank explaining that Marion had already signed her teaching contract for the next year. The children were in excellent schools and the ministry was an incomparable challenge. Therefore, we wanted to stay longer. I took the letter to Washington on Saturday and placed it in the middle of his desk. I did not mention his promise that I could come back to Washington after leaving Bainbridge. Frank sent Ed Richardson to FMF; Ed was older than I was.

Another challenge to the ministry at Bainbridge was the Boost program, the same one that Admiral Duncan had asked me to omit from my speeches during my recruiting tours, in that it was designed to help the Blacks prepare for eventual commissioning as officers, and he was afraid the White Appalachians would clamor for equal time. Ministry was needed for the students who had no idea how rigorous the training would be even though they had been told. It was also needed by the staff, who lived with frustration daily. We were convinced that Bainbridge offered the ideal setting for all the training activities we had because of the lack of distractions in such a rural area.

Bainbridge was alive with Rickover stories; it was rumored that he personally interviewed all officer candidates for nuclear power school. One story was that he sat the candidate in a chair with a short leg to see how he handled the discomfort. It was reported that he would ask the candidate what time it was and note if he looked at his watch. In the days when some cars had six and others twelve-volt systems, he is said to have asked which system the candidate had. A chaplain told me that he confronted him with the question, "You are not going to pray for our enemies, are you?" The reason we build these submarines is to scare the Hell out of them. The chaplain replied, "I am going to pray for all men of good will." The event was the commissioning of a nuclear submarine. Only once was I invited to give a commissioning prayer for a submarine, the George Washington Carver, but Rickover was not on hand.

CDR Barr, CO of the nuclear school, told me he had to call Rickover three times a week, write him once a week, and the prevailing feeling was that Rickover would stand for no inefficiency or nonsense and wanted to keep everybody on his or her toes. I was told that when he came in the zone for Rear Admiral the board left him off the list. The Senate returned the list unsigned, with the statement that no list would be acceptable without his name.

I never saw him until I came to Norfolk for the commissioning of the AMERICA. I felt complimented to receive an invitation until I arrived in town and called a friend to see if he was going. He told me 15,000 invitations had been sent, so I was tempted to go back home. Nevertheless, I am glad I went to the ship for the chance of seeing President Ford land as the 1MC announced, "United States Arriving" and to get a good long look at Admiral Rickover. I hoped to use him and General MacArthur as precedents in my desire for extended active duty.

We at Bainbridge were with all of the equal opportunity programs that were the hallmark of the Zumwalt era. In addition to the seminars, the task forces and the equal opportunity officers, there was a desire in Washington that stations have some kind of public recognition day with special music, a distinguished speaker, etc. Bainbridge inherited from recruit training days a theatre that would seat about three thousand and an amphitheatre that would hold a thousand. I had checked on the capacity of the theatre because a local pastor had asked if we had any space that would seat 3,000 because Jimmie Swaggart said he would come if that size facility was available. At the time I had never heard of Jimmie, but I did report my findings. Jimmie never got around to us.

We decided to use the amphitheatre for our extravaganza. Getting a band from Washington was no problem. My job was to engage a speaker. While I was engaged in the process of calling and getting excuses, Ted said one morning, "Tell me you found us a speaker." I knew I had better get moving, so I went to the top of the equal opportunity heap, Rear Admiral Charles Rauch, whom I considered to be really my relief in Washington, although his job was larger in scope than mine had been. He saved the day for us, and he saved me as well. The weather was mild and the attendance good. It was because of the favorable weather that I resolved when I left Bainbridge that I would never bother the Lord about weather again. St. Paul's Chapel was somewhat removed from the junior officer and enlisted quarters; therefore rain cut into the Sunday attendance considerably. I prayed for fair weather each Saturday and got an affirmative answer except for ten Sundays out of more than three years. On six of those ten Sundays, I had Baptist chaplains preaching.

When Bill Vest was transferred and Don Wilson retired, I established a practice of inviting a Baptist chaplain to assist me with Communion on the first Sundays. I felt the need for a White face around the chancel, maybe because of the complaint of a Navy Captain to the Chaplain Division that I was going to be the only chaplain on board when I carried out my orders to sea. I tempered this feeling with the memory of the Jewish sailor in Sasebo, who replied, when I said I would speak to the Jewish chaplain who was to visit us the following week, "If you can't take care of my problem yourself, then you are not a chaplain." My favorite visiting chaplain was Andy Jensen who had been court martialed for adultery but had been adjudged not guilty.

While he was under suspicion he failed selection to Captain. After his acquittal, the next board was authorized to pick an additional person to the original quota and was instructed to regard Andy as not having failed selection the previous year. Therefore, he was selected for promotion. A book was published on his experience and a TV documentary was made. He told me he had paid $15,000 for his defense, which he had not recovered. The money had come from savings for the education of his children. Providentially, the first son got an appointment to the Naval Academy. A congressman in California sponsored a bill to have the government repay his legal expenses. To say that Andy was interesting as a preacher is to put it mildly. To me, and I am sure to others, any preacher who has endured some great tragedy or some great sorrow knows whereof he or she speaks when telling of the fulfillment of the promise of Jesus to be with us always, even to the end of the world. Many Navy chaplains speak with this kind of authority, including chaplains Berg, who was healed of blindness when in seminary, Earl Greenlaw, who was stricken with polio, along with four members of his family, Matt Curry, who was horribly burned by a shipboard fire caused by a kamikaze pilot, whose rolling head he picked up and discarded, Glyn Jones, who was shot five times by a Japanese sniper in a tree while he was conducting a funeral service.

The chapel was never closed; the piano was never locked. It was a grand piano, kept in tune and extensively used by the students, particularly after class hours. It got so I could identify the pianists by their repertoires. I was told that some of them felt that they would not have graduated had not the piano been there.

One night I heard a magnificent baritone voice with no accompaniment. The voice belonged to a student, Kirk Jones, who was standing in the center of the chancel, filling the whole chapel with glorious sound. I sat enthralled until he finished. Then he came down and told me his story. He had been engaged and a date for the wedding had been set. His grandmother was having her teeth pulled, so she would not be able to get to the wedding. Kirk started for his grandmother's home with his fiancée so his grandmother could see her. The fiancée went to sleep on his shoulder. He became sleepy too, so he rolled down the window. This was the last thing he remembered until he regained consciousness. His car hit a tree; his fiancée died.

Kirk said her family treated him like a son. He found that if he could sing for a half hour in the evenings he could cope with the rest of the hours of darkness and the next day. If somebody happened to be at the piano when he arrived at the chapel he would wait his turn.

There were many weddings in St. Paul's Chapel. Maryland laws on marriage were not as stringent as some other states. One couple came from New York because of the imminent departure date of the bridegroom's ship. The reenlistment bonus for nuclear power personnel was $15,000, which made marriage financially feasible. One unfortunate incident occurred during a wedding. One of the attendants had the flu and vomited on a bridesmaid gown. A nearby bathroom and towels on hand for baptisms helped to repair some of the damage. Providentially, neither the bride nor the groom or the chaplain was splattered. My most embarrassing moment came at Bainbridge because of a wedding. One Saturday afternoon I was reading in the office when a couple came in wearing Levis. I introduced myself and asked if I might be helpful in anyway. With a mixture of hurt and disgust, they told me that I had married them in the chapel the previous year and they had driven up from Norfolk to see the chapel again. I had the feeling I had ruined the whole trip for them.

Before we came to Bainbridge we had never been bowling. In Durham Blacks were not allowed in bowling alleys except as pin boys. Mr. G.P. Holloway, who owned a barbershop on Pettigrew St., opened a bowling alley, which soon closed. At Bainbridge the CO, XO and other chaplains were in the bowling league, so we joined, had balls fitted and did fairly well. One night during the tournament, Marion was bowling way over her head, causing us to defeat the Stankowski team, which likely would have won the tournament otherwise. It was in an early round and Marion returned to her normal level as we lost the next match. I felt so badly about it that I wrote a note of apology to Bob Stankowski. He spent more time on Saturday at the chapel than I did, arranging flowers for Sunday.

The best individual bowler was Elizabeth Beamon, chapel organist. She had another interest, which was new to us, barbershop harmony. She booked barbershop quartets (female) for Sunday services. The two families we got to know best were not bowlers but were in the choir, the Funks and the McGuigans. Dan Funk, a nuclear officer student, and his mother, Helen, both sang in the adult choir. He had finished the NROTC program at Georgia Tech and was an excellent swimmer. Helen had done a lot with art and graphics and did portraits of me and Mae during their brief stay.

Jeanne McGuigan, who led me to install the baptistery, was a Seabees wife. Her husband, Lloyd, ran the CPO Club until he retired. She also was into art, especially painting. We have several of her works hanging in our home, including a portrait of me nearly life size. Years later we entertained Bruce McGuigan in our home when he was stationed in Norfolk, and saw much of the Funks when he was ordered to NIMITZ, home ported in Norfolk.

During this period, Helen designed and constructed a set of banners for Messiah that are incomparable. In the recent celebration of the uniting of the Presbyteries of Virginia, each church in this area was asked to bring a banner to be carried in the procession. The Messiah banner was in a class by itself. Helen also produced several dramas at Messiah, using members of the congregation.

Because golf was taken so seriously at Bainbridge I decided I should return to the game. Ted gave me a set of clubs. I bought another set from Erma Fretz's husband Herbie. I did get enough confidence to play in a Scotch foursome but came up with the low score. Davey however took to the game. He would hit the ball, then take off running after it with a couple of clubs in his hand. When we moved to Portsmouth, the coach at Norcom High School said he was his only player who made a higher score every time he played. I think my problem with the game remained the relative lack of exercise as compared to running. It also bothered me to lose a ball in a water hazard.

Bainbridge gave me my only experience of a station shutting down around me. Ted and Betsy, Gunnar and Judy, the other chaplains, residents of senior officers housing, left. The schools moved; the chapel closed for services. Smitty remained to dispose of the last of the equipment. On a visit to Washington, Frank had told me I would be going to Portsmouth Naval Hospital, which he hoped would be all right. I told him it would be great because I had wanted hospital duty since the Menninger days in 1955-56; I had at one time requested assignment to Bethesda. I did not mention his promise that I could come back to Washington after Bainbridge because it appeared that he had decided where he wanted me, Norfolk area.

Portsmouth, VA

I had visited Dr. Glen Tippin in Portsmouth Hospital and was quite impressed with it. I knew Harold McNeil, who gave me the complete rundown on Quonset, had served there. I knew Wayne Detick from San Diego and Governor's Island and looked forward to relieving him. I went to Norfolk to check the housing situation and found that the most suitable ones were in Virginia Beach at prices I considered inflated. The best buy was a four bedroom for $56,000, which I suspected, cost $30,000 a few years previously. I should have snapped it up; it is worth over $100,000 now. I decided to move into quarters because it would be easier getting to the hospital for emergencies without having to fight the Portsmouth tunnel, which was often blocked by accidents or floods.

Harold McNeil was the only chaplain who had lived on the hospital compound in a set of quarters that made been converted from some other use, I applied for on base housing confident that I would be senior to any other applicant. There was only one set of quarters available ½ block from the main building. The housing officer decided to assign it to a pediatrician LCDR, who had either five or six children, I couldn't compete there; God had said, "Be fruitful and multiply." I had only added. I also agreed with the housing officer that it would be convenient for the other families living aboard to have a pediatrician nearby. So my dream of getting rid of one car and walking to work flew out the window.

The next closest available set of quarters was in the Norfolk Naval Shipyard at the other end of Effingham Street in Portsmouth. It was an ancient duplex, but it had nine bedrooms and five and a half baths. It was across the street from the shipyard chapel. As in Bainbridge, the air conditioners were the window types. There was some government furniture. I opted for Quarters D without hesitation.

We moved to Portsmouth the weekend of July 4, 1976, when everybody was celebrating America's 200th birthday. Much of our gear was left on the sidewalk in the rain until the 5th, but there was no loss or minimum damage.

We were just as anxious to have the holiday off as the movers. Marion and I had been invited to New York for the weekend to watch the parade of tall ships from the FORRESTAL. We were delighted to be on the same ship with the President and other notables. We took the children to be with my brother-in-law, Dr. J.W.V. Cordice Jr. His family watched the parade from the office of our classmate, E.G. Spaulding Jr., Head Bookkeeper for the Rockefeller family. The weather was dreary and without sufficient wind for sails to be used, but the parade was still impressive

The apartment was designed with servants' quarters on the ground floor. I suspected that the original servants were slaves with Navy stewards coming later. We used this floor for a family room, the bathroom for a dark room and the bedrooms for storage.

By climbing 17 steps, one arrived at the enclosed porch that was the length of the apartments, supported by metal columns, and said to be ancient canon barrels. Navy dining room furniture was on the porch. From the porch, one entered a small sitting room leading to the hallway, stairs and living room with fireplace. The kitchen and dining room and a bath completed this floor. Bedrooms, closets and baths were on the next two floors.

I had been much impressed by Jim Kelly's "Chicken Every Sunday" for midshipmen in his quarters at Annapolis. I started a "Chicken Every First Sunday" for the chapel family at Quarters D. One of these occasions happened to coincide with Ross Trower's birthday when he visited Norfolk as Chief of Chaplains. We had a birthday cake, an expanded guest list and a power failure due to excessive rain. A neighbor, CAPT Jobe, brought in hurricane lamps from the club. Some guests thought this was an intentional gimmick for atmosphere. Because Marion was teaching, we did not try to

An Affirmation of Faith

duplicate Frances Kelly's feat of preparing the chicken. We brought the whole meal in from Giant Open Air Market.

It was a pleasure tinged with sadness to relieve Wayne. He had held the billet for six years, so I hoped to do the same. He asked for an additional two years to take him to the mandatory retirement age of 62 but his request was denied. It appeared I would have less chance of getting eight years, which would be two years past my mandatory retirement age. On the other hand, I knew a doctor and a dentist who continued on active duty a year at a time. The dentist said he planned to stay on active duty until he died.

Wayne had two concerns of importance to him. First, he had designated his ministry and that of his chaplains as a pastoral care service rather than a chaplain department. I liked the concept and continued it at Messiah Presbyterian Church. The other concern was whether I would be willing to stand duty watches. Often Captains do not stand the duty; sometimes commanders do not either. I assured him that I would stand the duty and that I would take every Sunday since my children were older than those of the other chaplains.

The difference between a pastoral care service and a chaplain department is whether the work chaplains do is considered clinical or administrative. We felt that the chaplain is a clinical specialist much like the psychiatrists and psychologist. In our view the chaplain would therefore have access to patient's charts, could make entries in them when appropriate and would be considered a clinical colleague by other clinicians. Wayne had sponsored annual medical religious symposia for the entire hospital staff, a practice I continued. Our best-known speaker was Dr. Raymond Moody of the University of Virginia Medical School who had just written *Life after Life*. A review of the book appeared in *Readers Digest* after we had booked him, or perhaps we would not have been able to afford him.

This also was the situation with Ruth Carter Stapleton after her brother became President. She wanted two first class tickets from Texas, plus her honorarium. One ticket was for her secretary. When I met the Stapleton's some years later at Duke University Medical Center I found that Dr. Stapleton, a veterinarian, had cared for Trixie, my uncle's dog, in Fayetteville.

We also invited Dr. C. Everett Koop. I think he really wanted to come down because it was two months before he determined that he could not make it. Somebody else, who did make it to Portsmouth, although not at my invitation, was Joe Pursch, My former buddy from the drug abuse team. He did the cause of religion and medicine a lot of good by his visit and by his frequent references to me in his presentation, picturing me as an esteemed colleague. I was delighted to see him again, and made it a point to sit on the front row.

One of the ways I made use of my doctorate was to become an adjunct professor at San Francisco Theological Seminary to work in the Doctor of Ministry program at the Armed Forces Staff College. In a sense, members of the clergy have historically felt somewhat disadvantaged that the entry degree in medicine is a doctorate. Then when the entry legal degree became a Doctor of Jurisprudence instead of a bachelor of laws the situation became more acute. Seminaries started giving a master of divinity instead of a bachelor of divinity or bachelor of sacred theology. The push toward an honorary Doctor of Divinity, usually given to prominent clergy by an alma mater or some other college or university, continued. I recommended that the Pittsburgh Seminary begin this practice but was rebuffed. Then I suggested that some older graduates who had bachelors in sacred theology could exchange them for masters of divinity, and those with masters in sacred theology should be able to exchange them for doctors of ministry. This Idea was also rejected because the former is a scholarly degree and the latter a practical one.

Not to be outdone I then suggested to the Pittsburgh Board of Trustees that the Seminary invite various boards and agencies of the church to become resident on the Seminary campus. I further suggested that Pittsburgh invite the Trinity Episcopal Seminary, then meeting in temporary quarters in Sewickly, a nearby affluent suburb, to move to the Pittsburgh campus in a collegial arrangement in which faculty and resources could be shared. One of the Presbyterian organizations that I particularly wanted in Pittsburgh was the Presbyterian Charismatic Communion. I thought of the seminary as the potential headquarters of most of what was going on in the church.

One of my fellow trustees, Dr. Clinton Marsh, also Black, and a former Moderator of the General Assembly, wrote a cogent reply to my proposals that voiced the sentiment of the other board members. He said that the seminary would actually lose its identity if it became the college I envisioned. I agreed that much parochialism would likely be lost, but after all my years in the ecumenical cooperation without compromise in the Navy, it seemed the most logical and cost effective thing to do. A later seminary president told me he wished the invitation had gone to the Episcopal Seminary. He nominated me as Alumnus of the Year and invited me to come to Pittsburgh to inaugurate a non-traditional course curriculum to hopefully involve Pittsburgh Black clergy.

It appeared that the Doctor of Ministry program would solve several problems. First, it would take the pressure off schools for the honorary D.D.'s. Then it would more easily satisfy the felt need for a doctorate without the extended work required for a Ph.D. It would also lead to fuller utilization of faculty and campus facilities since one of the four quarters in the curriculum would be taken on the seminary campus.

One of the main attractions of the D. Min. was that much of the work could be done not only off campus but even out of state. San Francisco had classes in Norfolk. The thrust of my course was sociology of religion, an attempt to determine the causal effect of religion on social structures. All of my students were chaplains and were able to utilize military educational funds for school expenses. In addition to teaching classes, I also acted as advisor to individual students on their dissertation projects, another exciting adventure.

The Naval Hospital permitted the staff to "moonlight" nine hours per week. Since the D. Min. classes were in session only four hours per week, I on occasion taught in the field of sociology at Tidewater Community College and Old Dominion University. These also were thrilling experiences for me as I watched the students broaden their outlooks through study, writing and discussions.

To compound my excitement over things educational, the office of the Chief of Chaplains asked if I would like to have the residency program for hospital chaplains at Portsmouth. Since its inception, the program had been at Naval Hospital, Oakland. I could not adequately express my enthusiasm for this venture for several reasons. First, it would give us three additional chaplains on board, thereby extending the ministry to the wards and to the staff. Then it would enhance the professionalism of the chaplains who went through the experience, particularly in counseling. Although I was told it would not be integrated into the Clinical Pastoral Education program, I still held out the hope that a resident would be able to get most of his or her work done on a D. Min. and get four quarters of CPE (Clinical Pastoral Education) at the same time.

The first academic director for the project was Dr. C. Roy Woodruff, who was certified as a supervisor in Clinical Pastoral Education and was a diplomat in the American Association of Pastoral Counselors. He also promoted, with his wife, the Bi-Polar technique of counseling. We welcomed the residents and found them to be a definite assist in pastoral care. Although completing CPE and the D.Min. were dreams of mine that did not come true, the value of the experiences to the residents was readily apparent. The current Chief of Chaplains, Ross Trower, and his coordinator for the project, Al Koeneman, had both finished the residency in Oakland. Today Al is the Chief of Chaplains.

Although I could not get CPE in the residency, I did find time to enroll myself at Tidewater Psychiatric Institute under Dr. Kim Nielsen, who now directs the Portsmouth residency.

During my tour at Portsmouth, I was able to complete four quarters of CPE, the usual qualification for civilian hospital chaplain. After completing the work, I was able to understand how my dream of the same qualification in one year for the residents was probably too ambitious.

In addition to the Board of Trustees of Pittsburgh Seminary, I continued on the Board of Cooperators of the Presbyterian Ministers Fund. When attending annual meetings, accompanied by Marion, I was steadily moving into the rank of senior citizen in this organization of mostly oldsters. To round out my Presbyterian involvement during this period, I was invited to preach often at the Community Presbyterian Church in Portsmouth. At the hospital, I had services at 0800 hours and 1000 hours. Therefore, I could not get to the 1100 hour service at Community on time, but always providentially in time for the sermon. The back door leading into the chancel was left open for me. I parked on the lawn very near the door, still in vestments from the hospital service. When it was suggested that I leave the Navy and become pastor of Community, I demurred but suggested instead that they consider my younger brother, Ward, who was then preaching in Camden, NJ. They looked at him, and then decided on another younger candidate.

Wayne had been on the board of the Crisis Center, and he passed this assignment to me when he left. Much of their attention was given to battered wives. At one of the training sessions I said that I had never seen a wife battered who had not "pulled the trigger." This caused some consternation because it appeared that I believed all battered wives had pulled the trigger. I explained that it was just that I had not seen any other type in my counseling. I told of the last one who had called me at 0200 hours. I asked her if she hit him first; she did admit to throwing a glass that smashed on the wall where his head had been. When I asked her why she threw the glass, she said she did not want to talk to me anymore and banged down the telephone. I was understandably not reelected to the board.

As at Bainbridge, the school situation at Portsmouth was ideal. Evangeline was accepted to my alma mater, NC Central. Mae took courses at Craddock High School and Old Dominion University and was admitted the next year to Smith College, Northampton, MA. Davey finished junior high, and then was admitted to I.C. Norcom High School, a most unique institution. Norcom was named for a former Black principal in the days of legally separate schools. After integration, Norcom was allowed by the school board to admit only students with "B" averages and to expel anyone who dropped below "C." Davey came home one day with some anxiety because a smoking room had been set up in another Portsmouth high school, so he and many of the students were afraid that the same would be done at Norcom. Their prime interest was in scholarship.

Davey did so well at Norcom that he came in second in his graduating class. He was accepted by the Naval Academy. He rejected an offer from MIT because he wanted to save us the expense of his college education. I was quite proud of him for being so thoughtful. It was a beautiful moment when I heard the awards being read and the announcement was made, "Thomas David Parham III, $100,000 scholarship at the US Naval Academy."

As far as possible, I tried to transfer activities from the Bainbridge Chapel to the Hospital Chapel. We were able to get a choir together that grew so large that when Darcy Clayton put out recruiting fliers in the passageways and on bulletin boards, the choir had to sit in the congregation. Darcy was a Black corpsman who introduced us to the music of Andre Crouch. I had played Andre's music from the steeple at Bainbridge but had not used it in chapel. Objections were raised over the fliers he posted, but by then the chair had been recruited. He also used to write "Jesus loves you" on the butterfly band-aids he affixed after drawing blood samples until someone objected to this practice also.

We had a guest book just inside the chapel door. I used to read the comments visitors made and often wrote notes to them, particularly if they asked for prayer. It became a kind of "pen pal" ministry. When the visitors were relatives of patients, it was often possible to meet them and on occasion to minister to or with them. One delightful mother who was also a pen pal said one day that she was disappointed I was not a Catholic. I apologized with the explanation that I was born this way; she accepted this graciously.

We copied the practice I found at Bethesda Naval Hospital of praying aloud for each person on the serious or critical list. We were gratified over the number of recoveries and rejoiced with the relatives who had joined in prayer with us. I considered it providential that the recovery rate in the cardiac care unit and in the intensive care unit was over 90%.

At the hospital, I put a lot of stock in what we called the "ministry of presences." Every ward had an assigned chaplain. The two Catholic Chaplains were able to see every Catholic patient. Ed Richardson, now at my recommendation, saw every Marine in the hospital every Thursday; John Rosenblatt came to see Jewish personnel. Paul Pyrah was on our staff, so the Orthodox were well cared for.

One of my most fulfilling activities was my visitations in the recovery room each morning before surgery patients were brought there to be prepped, and then returned there after surgery. I liked the idea of a patient seeing the chaplain around the last moment before going to the operating room and finding him there when surgery was over. There were many opportunities to comfort and console relatives all through the day as they sat outside watching for the patients to be wheeled to the operating room and return.

One morning an 11 year old piped up, "Well here is the chaplain. Who is going to die today?" I replied "Nobody! Nobody has ever died in here. This is the safest place in the whole hospital." I won that round. Nobody died that day, or any other day while I was stationed there.

Another day, one of the anesthesiologists came over and said of another 11-year-old male patient, "No way am I going to put that guy under as hyped up as he is; maybe you could calm him down for me." After much silent prayer and quiet conversation the little fellow did seem more relaxed and was wheeled away. On another occasion, when a patient was anxious about the anesthesia, I was able truthfully to say to her, "If I were having surgery myself, I would rather have these two anesthesiologists than anybody else I know."

I had the highest respect for anesthesiologists because I could remember when it used to be said that 50% of all surgical fatalities were due to anesthesia. In my time at Portsmouth there were no anesthesia fatalities. Dr. Richard Norton, the head of the department, invited me to do an invocation at the annual banquet closing his symposium for six consecutive years. In the first invocation, I pictured God as the first anesthesiologist, causing Adam to fall into a deep sleep before making Eve out of one of Adam's ribs.

Among the wards that I cared for personally were 12c officer's surgery, 9b neurosurgery and the intensive care unit 3b as well as 8b, cardiac care. This does not mean that the other chaplains did not visit these wards frequently. One day I came in 9b through the east door and another chaplain came through the west door. The nurse quipped, "Do you guys know something I don't?" Portsmouth did not do open heart surgery; therefore, I watched my cholesterol very carefully. I did not want to have surgery anywhere; also I needed to guard against needing a by-pass.

An Affirmation of Faith

On seven different occasions, I maintain that we had a miracle at Portsmouth. The two most spectacular miracles involved growths that disappeared. The first was a brain tumor in a soldier. He informed his doctor that he had prayed for God to remove it, which He had done; therefore, he needed more X-rays as proof. While the X-rays were being scheduled he made flight reservations for New York that afternoon to see a sick uncle. After the pictures had been taken he came down to the ward, put on his dress uniform, packed his bag and waited in the lounge for word to come that he could go, which it did. He had plenty of time to catch his flight.

The other was a situation of abdominal cancer, possibly, but at least there was a mass that indicated removal. This patient's father was hopeful for a healing but did not request another set of X-rays. When the surgeons opened him up the mass was gone, and they took his appendix so it would not be a completely dry run. The father said the Lord beat them to the mass and removed it Himself.

My own healing was not spectacular, but just as much appreciated. On 12c there was a retired CDR John Upshur, a descendant of the Secretary of State with the same surname who succeeded Daniel Webster. He lived in Upshur House in Maryland, an historical landmark. He worked with Rockefeller on behalf of Williamsburg in the Williamsburg restoration projects. Had time permitted I could have listened to him all day. He had a severe arthritic condition; his right arm and shoulder were in a cast and the pain was at times intense. We talked also about my arthritis in the lumbar region that made it difficult for me to walk or stand. One day I made my ward visits in a wheel chair.

One Thursday when I entered his room he greeted me with, "Where were you yesterday?" I told him I got bogged down with my work but I wondered what had happened with him. He said that the pain was so intense that he wanted us to pray with him. After I did not come, he got down on the deck and prayed, "O Lord please do something." The pain ceased and he had felt nothing since. Then I realized that my back was not hurting. I said, "Brother, am I glad you thought about me even though you were angry." The Lord healed us both at the same time. The last time I saw CDR Upshur he was swinging along with no cast and no pain. I am still without my pain.

Another memorable incident was attributed to luck by the surgeon. I got a call that a patient had been admitted with an aneurism in his aorta the size of a grapefruit, somebody said a football. In any event, when they had begun surgery I met his wife in the passageway near the elevator. She said, "Tell me my husband is going to be all right." I replied, "I cannot tell you that but we can ask Jesus." I took her hand and we knelt on the deck as I implored the Lord for mercy. While we were waiting I called the OOD to inform him that the patient had been placed on the critical list, as I had promised the doctor in the emergency room. When I told the OOD what was going on he said, "That's all for him." I then phoned a nurse, with whom I had an appointment, to explain why I wasn't there. She said she was surprised that he was still alive.

Soon the glorious news arrived. The aneurism had ruptured, but the team was able to repair the damage so quickly that there was no damage to his lungs from the lack of blood supply. The surgeon came out to speak to the wife. I remember his saying, "I would rather be lucky than good."

The most unforgettable person I ever met at Portsmouth was a double amputee named Orrick Toliver. The first time I saw him he was riding on a gurney on his stomach, propped up on his elbows, smiling. I assumed he was a Vietnam veteran. Then I learned that he was a victim of spina bifida, a birth defect in which the spinal cord is outside the spinal column in the lower back. His mother was told he had two months to live. He was then 27 but had spent most of every year of his life at Portsmouth Hospital. At 17 his legs were amputated for lack of circulation, he had never walked. He did not have enough of his legs left to get fitted with prostheses, nor even to balance when sitting. Without fail when anybody would ask him how he was, he would smile and say "OK." He was quite adept in handling his wheelchair and hanging on one as he entered or left a car. With almost no legs and of slight build, he did not weigh much. He told me he had lost count of the operations and that his records filled two boxes.

Orrick was of invaluable help to me on two occasions. The first time involved a patient named Gilbert, who was admitted with a shotgun wound. Following surgery he became infected. When he

An Affirmation of Faith

was told he would need surgery again he panicked. I went for Orrick, who without legs was able to wheel himself almost into Gilbert's bed. Orrick grasped him on the shoulder and said, "Man, you be going to make it. All you need to do is to hang on to Jesus." Look at me. I have been dead four times. For the first time Gilbert smiled in response to Orrick's smile. And he kept smiling through surgery and out of the hospital in due time. Gilbert knew Orrick, a Black, was sincere; Gilbert was White.

The second blessing for me from Orrick was the giving of his testimony one Sunday morning in the chapel. He came in a gurney propped up on his elbows, a microphone in his hand. His testimony replaced my sermon. In introducing him, I told the Gilbert story. Then Orrick shared with us his faith in Christ, indomitable through all of his medical problems. Many of his relatives were on hand. They invited me to the Toliver's family reunion, at their church first, then a nearby park. There were 200 on hand. Orrick had more occasions to hang on to Jesus. His father died, followed in a year by his mother; both died of cancer. I was blessed to be with him. Now he lives in an apartment with a handicapped roommate. He is still doing OK.

Kathryn Kuhlman used to say, "The Greatest miracle is a changed life, the reception of Jesus as Lord and Savior," two such incidents I have relived many times. Both involved terminal patients, although we did not know it at the time. The first was a retired warrant carpenter we called "Chips." He had enjoyed his Navy career. He told me he paid a bar girl to sit on the lap of the ship's chaplain, for which the chaplain promptly docked him. Since the chaplain was retired in Norfolk, I arranged for him to visit Chips. I watched their faces as they gripped hands. From what I read in their faces, they could have embraced and wept tears of joy. It was one of those rare moments one never forgets.

Chips was philosophical about his throat cancer and the scheduled surgery. When he was told that he might lose his larynx he replied, "Then I will make signals." Chips requested baptism. When I was satisfied that he was sufficiently prepared, I scheduled it. He had been coached to respond "I do" to the four questions in the *Book of Common Worships:* "Do you believe in God the Father Almighty

An Affirmation of Faith

Maker of Heaven and earth; and in Jesus Christ His only Son our Lord; and in the Holy Spirit the Lord and Giver of life? Do you confess your need of the forgiveness of sins and with a humble and contrite heart put your whole trust in the mercy of God, which is in Christ Jesus our Lord? Do you promise to make diligent use of the means of grace, to continue in the peace and fellowship of the people of God, and with the aid of the Holy Spirit to be Christ's faithful disciple to your life's end? Do you desire to be baptized in this faith and to be received into membership in Christ's Church?" Instead of responding "I do" each time, Chips said "Yes sir, chaplain, I sure do."

They did have to take Chips larynx and he did make signs. His most used sign was the "thumbs up" gesture. As the weeks passed, however, the thumbs-up was followed by a horizontal movement and later by no response at all to my cheery "Chips, how are you doing today?" At his funeral, I told of his unusual responses to the baptism questions. I can imagine that as he approached the Pearly Gates St. Peter called out, "Chips, come on in here, I heard you when you said "Yes sir, chaplain, I sure do."

The second patient to receive Jesus in an unusual way was a Marine Colonel, also on 12c, who was fond of television. His set was on every time I visited him except for one Sunday night. He had told me that he thought he was an atheist until a Catholic chaplain told him that if he were an atheist he would have killed himself because he would have no reason to live. Thereafter the Colonel had labeled himself an agnostic.

On the visit on a Sunday night when his TV was off, I asked if there were something wrong. He quickly replied that nothing was wrong and turned on the set. Richard Roberts was preaching a very moving sermon, the best I have heard from him. As he closed, he appealed for everyone without Christ to receive Him, and to so indicate by reaching out to take the hand of somebody also in the room. Until this day I am eternally grateful I was there to take the Colonel's hands. He lived another two weeks. It blows my mind to imagine what the odds were that I would go to the hospital that night, then drop by his room, ask about the TV and catch the final minutes of the Roberts sermon. I am convinced God wanted it that way.

Of the four patients who told of seeing Jesus while fully alert, two had very unusual experiences. The first was a female patient who had been sitting near a TV set that exploded, burning her severely and extensively. She heard a doctor tell her husband that she would not last through the night. Possibly an hour later when the ward was quiet, Jesus came into her room and stood by her bed. He told her not to worry about her condition, that she would be fine. When he left, she called the nurses' station and asked if anybody had been seen at her end of the wards. She was told nobody had gone down that way nor had anyone been seen in the vicinity. She knew then she was awake. She interpreted Jesus' visit as a commission to her to have the necessary surgery to restore her appearance and to influence other burn victims to do likewise. She said Jesus was wearing blue and that He had red hair.

The other patient had been working on his roof when he fell to the ground. He suspected he had broken everything he had, and was waiting for the paramedics, hoping he would last that long. Then Jesus came to him assuring him that he would be fine. Again, Jesus was in blue and with red hair. Neither of these patients was a red head. Both of them did recover as they strengthened the faith of those who listened to them. I have no doubt they saw what they said they saw.

Of the three patients who told of having died and returned to life, one was not a typical *Life after Life* case. A nurse called from the cardiac care unit, asking my help in calming down a patient who was creating a disturbance on the ward. I grabbed my recorder and headed for the ward, but the patient was quiet when I arrived. He said that Jesus had told him to read the 25th chapter of Matthew to the other patients, and he would not be talked out of it, even if they threatened to kill him. He had finished the reading, and was back in bed. I asked for his permission to tape our conversation, which he readily gave.

The patient told me he had died but was hovering over his bed watching the doctors and nurses working to revive him. Then he found himself going down a pipe, at the end of which was light. There he found Jesus, from whom he asked permission to return and live 7 more years until his daughter reached the age of 18. His request was granted and the direction given to read Matthew 25 to the ward. When I raised a question as to the direction he was going in the pipe, he corrected himself and said he was moving horizontally. When I suggested that he had not used a very loud voice in reading Matthew he said that he had talked pretty loudly. He was excited about the tapes, hoping it would strengthen the faith of others. He also decided that he no longer needed any medication for his heart because he was guaranteed another seven years. I countered that he would still be eating, so he should still be taking his medication for his comfort at least. So he agreed to do this.

He was of particular interest to me because he had not read *Life after Life* or any other comparable literature. He often went to his wife's Methodist Church where I had been invited to preach. He was the only Black patient to tell of having died or of having seen Jesus. On the tape his speech is somewhat slurred, as is the case with some patients recovering from a stroke. I have used his tape with many kinds of groups.

Only at Quonset Point had I worked directly for Admirals MaGruder Tuttle and "Hy" Massey, but in an additional duty situation because my primary assignment was to the Air Station. At Portsmouth, as the head of a clinical service, I attended the department head weekly conferences that were often presided over by the Admiral. My first CO at Portsmouth was Admiral Jacoby who worked at establishing warm relationships. He was an ardent Catholic in a way that drew admiration. He took Catholic Chaplain John Maiorana to Navy Relief board meetings in his vehicle. He took me to Washington, with his wife, for me to conduct a funeral for one of our Admiral patients.

Admiral Jacoby was enthusiastic about plans to beautify the chapel. He was as interested in the new sky blue carpeting as if it were to go in his quarters. One day he dashed up the ladder to my office with a color photo of me in vestments that had just been delivered to him by the photo lab. He was as proud as punch of the lab's workmanship. He agreed to submit an improved fitness report on one of the chaplains that did not seem to us representative of that chaplains work.

Admiral Gorsuch and I had a strange relationship; it seemed that we agreed to disagree. I was so very thankful that I was not vulnerable, or the situation would have been stressful. Were I eligible for promotion, I would have wondered if he would ruin my chances, although I doubt he would. We disagreed on the marking of fitness reports, yet he sent the chaplain's reports in as I had written them. My position was that hospital work was unusually hard; therefore high fitness reports were a kind of compensation. He told me that to mark them all as high as I did was ridiculous and anybody who would do such was ridiculous.

He even took the issue up with the Chief of Chaplains. Chaplain Trower said Admiral Gorsuch asked him how chaplain selection boards could pick the best candidates for promotion if all of them had perfect fitness reports. His reply was, "We know." This likely made him even more frustrated, although he never mentioned the incident to me and I never altered my policy.

Although I believed I was senior to all the doctors, I had never been put in command of one of the units at inspection, even though I always attended. So Admiral Gorsuch gave me a unit and I blew it. When he got to us, we were at parade rest and I forgot to call the unit to attention until he had inspected the front rank. I asked the Master Chief Petty Officer if they should have been called to attention. He said they should have but it was now too late. Back at the office, I wrote a note of apology. At the next department head meeting the Admiral said we could have a good inspection if the chaplain would call his unit to attention, smiling as he said it. I never read one of Admiral Gorsuch's fitness reports on me.

Admiral Colley was a fascinating person. During a previous tour in Norfolk, he had played violin with the Norfolk Symphony. One Sunday afternoon he presented his daughter, a contralto, in recital in the auditorium. His wife did weaving. His other daughter was in the German Merchant Marine. He told me he had always wanted an assignment which allowed him to walk to work and to walk to church. He was a Presbyterian, had attended the First Presbyterian Church in Bel Air, CA, then the National Presbyterian Church in Washington, where Louis Evans was preaching. Usually there was a high-level conference on Sunday morning that conflicted with our

Service, so he changed the time and announced the reason for the change.

Annually we celebrated Martin Luther King's birthday on a Thursday afternoon nearest his actual birthday. The employees who worked in food service could most easily get off at that time. On his first such occasion, Admiral Cooley was sitting next to me listening to the speakers lambaste all responsible, in his opinion, for current racism. He turned to me and said quietly, "This is taking free speech too far." The speaker reminded me of preachers who castigate those who miss church but are not there to hear his invectives, which fall on the faithful on hand. When Ross came to my retirement, he said it was a smart thing for him to do. I considered Admiral Cooley to be as non-threatening as I considered myself.

Continuity in the religious programs at shore stations is often due to the presence, for some years, of civilian specialists. At Portsmouth, it was Peggy Buchannan, who was for 22 years secretary to the senior chaplain. She was a mother to the younger chaplains, a sister to the older, a confidant, adviser and support for the senior chaplain. She and her husband, "Buck," opened their waterfront home in Suffolk to all hands on numerous occasions. Also providing continuity was John Sammons, the organist and choir director for Catholic and Protestant worship. His family came to the Hospital chapels. I baptized their children, Johnny and Ruth. All chaplains remember the fresh strawberry homemade ice cream at the Sammons home.

In no other chapel had I found anyone comparable to Peyton "Pat" Price and his wife, Sue. Pat was an ex-Navy Chief Machinist Mate with a colorful career in the Far East and many subsequent interesting experiences on the inland waterway. Pat and Sue usually ate lunch with us after church in the mess. They arrived early on Sunday morning and made their rounds inviting people to church. Sue brought flowers in season from her gardens. Pat proudly wore a nametag reading "Deacon Price" that was made for him by Chaplain Ignatius Smith some years previously. Pat told me when I arrived that he had not missed two consecutive Sundays in eight years. I know of sailors, whom they promoted during enlisted tours at the hospital, who later earned commissions. Pat had angina, but a doctor

An Affirmation of Faith

friend had advised him never to have a by-pass. After several hospitalizations over the years, he finally worsened; oxygen and IVs did not reverse the trend. On my last visit before taking a trip, he held my hand and kissed it. When I returned he had gone. Sue misses him, particularly on Sundays,

"Smoky" Seiders, former Atlantic Fleet Chaplain, said hospital duty is second only to combat in requiring the best of a chaplain. It was my considered opinion that the performance of the hospital chaplains was second to none. Darrell Patton, Methodist, was next senior. I gave him full administrative responsibility and promptly forgot all about it. He acted for me in all my absences and carried a full load of wards as well. I was proud that his daughter had finished Harvard Divinity School, and that he and his wife, Claudine, were expert in the field of religious education.

"Jerry" Turner was our senior Catholic with the longest tenure. He was so conscientious about the needs of Catholic patients that he was not in favor of a unified watch bill, which would call for his and Bob Kinel to stand a watch once a week and be on emergency call half the rest of the week as in other Naval Hospitals. He preferred that one of them be on watch every night. Jerry volunteered to serve as a police chaplain in Portsmouth, rotating with civilian clergy in driving the police car with "Chaplain" in large letters on the sides. In his car and at his home he had powerful ham radios that he used to communicate with other hams all over the world.

Gail "Buck" Buckley was ordered to us at the request of the head of the alcohol rehabilitation units. Since he was in excess of our allowance, I was glad to have his office on the unit and happy to have a chaplain in fulltime clinical work. He actually ran the unit from time to time. He became my supervisor on location for my CPE work. He was, therefore, in my estimation, somewhat of a celebrity, an attitude not shared by the rest of the chaplains, who thought he should stand as many duty watches as the rest of us. My feeling was that anything he did for us was gravy.

Saying that he had come to join me in my last hurrah, Dennis Casey, Catholic was both a workhorse and a morale builder for the chaplains and their families. His sense of humor was delightful and hilarious. He did most of the legwork for my retirement, so was great comfort to Marion. Gene Olson used to say that his grandfather changed his name when he came to America from the original Olesonovitch. He had seen enlisted service and was no stranger to Norfolk. He had accepted Christ at Tabernacle Church.

LCDR John Maiorana, Catholic, was the soul of consideration. We had a very senior patient addicted to tobacco. He had already lost one lung, the other was failing. In a year his hair had turned completely white. His wife said she had prayed, fussed, pleaded, and cried, all to no avail. The patient continued to smoke. One night, when it appeared that he would not make it, John sat up all night with her in the waiting room, she told me, holding her hand and comforting her. Within a week the patient was dead, within a year the wife was dead of a broken heart, in my opinion.

A younger Catholic chaplain, Bob Kinel, had learned in a few years what it takes many chaplains years to learn about relating to people of all sorts and stations. With remarkable surges of energy and a winning smile, he gladdened the hearts of all whom he touched. In addition, he had the appearance of a movie star. He was the type to be voted most likely to succeed by a college class. He reminded me of a comparable chaplain who checked in at MCRD in 1962, brunette instead of blond, as Bob was, of whom Marion asked, "Is that guy for real?"

Murray Ethridge and Bill Flanagan seemed to be a pair. They had both been at Bethesda and had done some CPE. With their encouragement, we began to have group meeting, at which verbatims were presented. Murray was working in Building 1 where the neuro-psychiatric unit was located. He was quite helpful to the psychiatrists in providing therapy for patients. He was a practitioner in transactional analysis and interested us in the process. I took a training weekend in Chapel Hill, and so did others from the hospital staff at Murray's urging. I remembered two chaplains who had become millionaires by setting up transactional institutes and acting as consultants to industry.

Bill was built like a football player but talked softly. Anyone who needed a shoulder to cry on turned to Bill. Patients attached themselves to him without hesitations. I was standing nearby when a man whose sub-compact had been hit by a limousine and whose daughter had been on the critical list for two days came to Bill and announced that his daughter had just expired. Bill reached out that big right hand and gripped the grieving dad on his shoulder, looking him squarely in the face with his big eyes while his mouth quivered. As Bill held him, I was reminded of how a picture is worth a thousand words and decided that the expression on Bill's face was worth ten thousand. Murray said Bill was the best he had ever seen in a one-on-one relationship.

The chaplains in the residency program were kept quite busy with their hours of study and their ministry to patients as a part of the training program. They were not permitted to be on the hospital watch bill but could occasionally offer a Catholic Mass or preach at a Protestant Service in the hospital chapel. They were also welcome at the social events, where we learned to really appreciate them and their families when on board. Two chaplains, Glenn MaCrania and Ray Fullilove, did tours as staff chaplain and as residents.

Ray was a triplet; one brother had died in infancy. One day at an air station in Vietnam, an army chaplain came over and said, "I know why you are looking at me so hard, I have a twin brother who is a chaplain in the Navy." I could hardly believe my eyes. They were identical, even to the receding hairline at the temples and the bald "running lights" at the back of their head. I liked to read Ray's poetry. He would often dash out a poem for the relative of someone just deceased and present her or him with a typed copy. To do this he had to spend some time with the patient and relative before the death.

Glenn gave us a new twist on what some chapels call the "ritual of friendship" and others call "passing the peace." He borrowed the telephone commercial, "reach out and touch someone," which became more natural and spontaneous than a ritualistic greeting unfamiliar to many patients. He began a D. Min. dissertation, under my supervision, on the ministry to the families of deployed personnel.

For the first time in my Navy experience I was blessed by volunteers in the office, Dorothy White and Duva Hanna. Dorothy had graduated from Berea College in Kentucky and had been infused with its evangelical zeal and pietistic approach to life. She had read extensively in religious literature and was fond of writing devotional materials. The Senior Catholic Chaplain at the time, Ted Gryga, introduced her to the staff and announced her desire to assist us. It was a serendipitous event in my opinion, re-enforced when I learned that she typed 90 words per minute. Dorothy's husband, Tom, accompanied her to the religious activities at the hospitals. They soon opened their home to stranded dependents. Orrick Toliver called Dorothy "Mom." She had the ability to mother many people, dependents and patients. When the workload of typing got out of hand, she took some of it home to do.

Dorothy recruited another volunteer, Duva Hanna, who made quite an efficient receptionist with very little orientation. Her Will was born, to Paul's delight, while she was still with us.

When I arrived at Portsmouth I felt deprived in that Jim Rittenhouse, of First Baptist Church, Virginia Beach, and Stan Beach would not be on hand. Jim had already been detached; Stan's departure was imminent. There had been a chapel at the hospital, a detached building with an adequate social hall they called the "Living Room." Stan had organized a Bible class that became very popular with the nurses, called the "Living Room." This grew to 40 odd persons and was so tightly knit that there were marriages among the members as well as serious Bible study and Christian fellowship.

Providentially, another Regular Baptist was ordered in as Stan left, Bob Mitchell, who had become converted while listening to the "Morning Cheer" program over a radio station in Pennsylvania. I had visited the conference center where the program originates and listened to a sermon by Tony Campolo, after which I applied for a position at Eastern Seminary where Tony was teaching. Applicants promised to inform the school if they ever abandoned their non-smoking stance.

Bob was the only chaplain who lost a wife, Marilyn, during my tenure. I offered him the option of a transfer, but he refused it. He felt that he had a deeper ministry to offer because of his experience. In time, he and Gloria, a Red Cross volunteer whose husband had also died of cancer, became attracted to each other and married.

Our first female chaplain at the hospital became quite a conversation piece. The detailer, when he called to see if she would be acceptable, told me she was Black, her husband White and civilian. Chaplain Carolyn Cecil Wiggins wore her hair in Afro styles. Her husband, Timothy Persons, wore a short beard. She was a Norfolk native and had finished Maury High School. She met Timothy when he returned from a Peace Corps assignment in Chad to his home in Rochester, NY. She was in seminary at Colgate Rochester. "Ceci" found a berth on the female basketball team and participated in community long distance runs including marathons. Timothy kept himself busy commuting to University of Richmond Law School, but took time out to be sworn into the Naval Reserve by Ceci. Her experience convinced me that hospital duty was ideal for female chaplains. I said so to the Chief's office. Hospitals were already accustomed to female nurses, doctors, therapists and technicians, so a chaplain would be a natural progression.

Two chaplains stood out for their senses of humor. Norvelle Knight, a Baptist resident, had the capability of keeping me in stitches much of the time. He specialized in such riddles as, "Who was the shortest man in the Bible?" The answer was Bildad the Shuhite. Jack Kemper, Catholic, had an endless stave of anecdotes and sea stories that he told with such gusto that one began to smile as soon as he began.

We were ably assisted by the enlisted personnel assigned. Marti Shuflin, a Southern Baptist Charismatic, seemed to me more of a colleague than a subordinate, though she did not use our relationship to throw her weight around. She saw in it a green light for her own ministry to the poor. She organized and directed a Sunday afternoon Charismatic Service in the hospital chapel. Jim Rios was the other assistant with a strong religious commitment. He had not gone to a college, but had pre-enrolled at Harvard Divinity School. He assisted me at the 0800 hours Service.

Retirement

For years I had heard of officers "putting in their papers" for retirement. I never did this. A letter came from Washington informing me that since I would be 62 on 21 March 1982, I would retire 1 April. I tried to forestall this letter. I wrote to Coach Burghardt, who was a friend of President Nixon, asking him to lobby for me to be retained. Unfortunately, the coach died. I talked to Congressman Whitehurst, who said, "We've got to do something about that." Carroll Chambliss was beating the bushes for me saying, "The Navy kept Rickover for nuclear power; they can keep Parham for Black power." My heart sunk when Ross decided not to keep Ed Richardson in the face of an acute Catholic shortage. There is a sense in which a White Southern Baptist chaplain would be a more acceptable replacement for a Black chaplain than any kind of Protestant would be for a Catholic." Nevertheless, I did appeal to Ross. The next time he came to Norfolk he invited me for lunch and explained that he had given it much thought, but the answer was negative. I heard through the grapevine that one chaplain was being retained by request of higher authority for one year.

I was amazed at the difference ten years can make. When I asked the Chief of Naval Personnel, Admiral Duncan, if I could go to graduate school he said he would permit it if I did not leave Washington and he thought I should sign an agreement to remain on active duty an extra five years, which I did. Now I was asking for one year and could not get it.

In my anxiety to prove that I was not ready for the bone yard yet, I made applications for all kinds of positions: college and seminary teaching, civil service employment in human relations, and Baptist and Presbyterian churches. Finally, I was accepted at the Duke University Medical Center as a Supervisor in Training in Clinical Pastoral Education. This cleared up a lot of stress and anxiety, but the old feeling of being cast off persisted.

Marion and Dennis Casey really staged a great retirement. Family and friends were invited to a banquet the evening before at the hospital club. Invitations went to the Christmas list, plus all of our neighbors in Norfolk. We had moved from the shipyard in December. At the retirement ceremony, having words to say, were Ross Trower, Dave Chambers of the Presbyterian Department of Chaplains and Admiral Cooley, with a surprise Legion of Merit. Admiral Sam Gravely came down from Haymarket and Chaplain Don Wilson from upper Pennsylvania.

Six Captains in the Chaplain Corps were side boys. My son, Davey, was there in his midshipman's uniform, and the Norview High Band, in which he played, provided the music. TV cameras were on hand.

In my best passive-aggressive style, I dwelt on how fortunate I felt to be able to attend my own funeral while very much alive. I called my six side boys my pallbearers, the speeches and eulogies I was able to hear. Peggy told me that my anger was quite transparent, although I was smiling. It was frustrating in that I had helped in the fight against race and sex discrimination but was powerless against age discrimination. At the time, the Russian Chief of Naval Operations was in his 70s. Still, I had been marvelously blessed by many people, some of them in the audience. Therefore, I left them with a sense of gratitude and a very deep feeling of love for all of them.

It was God's will that I become a minister of the gospel and serve as a chaplain. It was pre-ordained. I was born for the service. My life was enriched because I listened to the still small voice and did God's will.

Breinigsville, PA USA
13 December 2010
251239BV00003B/2/P